❀ SEASONAL ❀
CONTAINER GARDENING

with Creative Recipes for Conservatory, Edible and Historical Plantings

Also by Kathleen Brown
CREATIVE CONTAINER GARDENING (with Effie Romain)

SEASONAL CONTAINER GARDENING

with Creative Recipes for Conservatory, Edible and Historical Plantings

KATHLEEN BROWN

MICHAEL JOSEPH
London

MICHAEL JOSEPH LTD

Published by the Penguin Group
27 Wrights Lane, London W8 5TZ, England
Viking Penguin, a division of Penguin Books USA Inc.,
375 Hudson Street, New York, New York 10014, USA
Penguin Books Australia Ltd, Ringwood, Victoria, Australia
Penguin Books Canada Ltd, 2801 John Street, Markham, Ontario, Canada L3R 1B4
Penguin Books (NZ) Ltd, 182–190 Wairau Road, Auckland 10, New Zealand

Penguin Books Ltd, Registered Offices: Harmondsworth, Middlesex, England

First published 1991

Typeset in 11/12 pt Linotron 202 Goudy Old Style by Wilmaset, Birkenhead, Wirral
Colour origination by Anglia Graphics, Bedford
Printed and bound in Singapore by Kyodo Printing Co Pte Ltd

A CIP catalogue record for this book is available from the British Library

ISBN 0 7181 3249 1

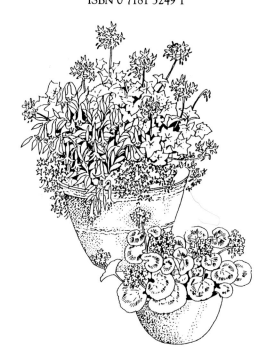

Contents

Acknowledgements   vii

List of Recipes   viii

GENERAL INTRODUCTION   1

LONGTERM SCHEMES   9

INTRODUCTION TO THE LONGTERM RECIPES   9

Barrels and Pots mainly for Winter and Spring   13
Spring Miscellaneous   20
Pots, Troughs and Barrels for Summer and Autumn   26
Hanging Baskets   40
All Year Round   46

WINTER AND SPRING SCHEMES   49

INTRODUCTION TO THE WINTER AND
SPRING RECIPES   49

Window Boxes   53
Chimney Pots and Wallpots   56
Hanging Baskets   61
Wicker Baskets   66
Pots   69

SUMMER AND AUTUMN SCHEMES   83

INTRODUCTION TO THE SUMMER AND
AUTUMN RECIPES   83

Hanging Baskets   87
Window Boxes   102
Wallpots, Wicker Baskets, Troughs and Pots   106

CONSERVATORY SCHEMES   119

INTRODUCTION TO THE CONSERVATORY
RECIPES   119

Spring Miscellaneous   122
Summer Pots   131
Late Summer to Early Spring   141

KITCHEN GARDEN SCHEMES   147

INTRODUCTION TO THE KITCHEN
GARDEN RECIPES   147
Window Boxes   150
Hanging Baskets   157
Pots and Tubs   163

VICTORIAN AND EDWARDIAN SCHEMES   175

INTRODUCTION TO THE VICTORIAN AND
EDWARDIAN RECIPES   175
Window Boxes for Winter and Spring   185
Hanging Baskets for Winter and Spring   191
Urns and Pots for Winter and Spring   195
Window Boxes for Summer   201
Hanging Baskets for Summer   208
Tubs, Urns and Pots for Summer   214

STRUCTURED GROUPS OF CONTAINERS   220

Specialist Suppliers of Plants   225

Specialist Suppliers of Containers   226

Index to Introductions   227

Plant Index   228

ACKNOWLEDGEMENTS

I would like to thank Jim Keeling for lending me so many wonderful pots from his range at Whichford Pottery, Whichford, Shipston-on-Stour, Warwickshire; Renaissance Casting Company Ltd, of Coventry for lending me the two beautiful lead containers; Haddonstone Ltd, East Haddon, Northampton for the loan of several large reconstituted stone pots and urns; and Erin Ltd for the gift of some large planters. It is thanks to them that I have been able to widen the range of the containers used.

I am very grateful to John Taylor of O. A. Taylor and Sons Bulbs Ltd of Holbeach, Lincolnshire for all his practical help; Adrian Bloom of Bressingham Gardens, Diss, Norfolk; Peter Harkness of R. Harkness and Company Ltd, Hitchin, Hertfordshire; and John Mattock of Mattocks Roses, Nuneham Courtney, Oxford for their advice on parts of the script. I also wish to thank Dr Brent Elliot and his staff at the Royal Horticultural Society Library in Vincent Square where I researched the background to the Victorian and Edwardian container planting schemes, and Peter Barnes of the Royal Horticultural Society, Wisley who read the text with reference to the botanical names.

I would also like to say a sincere thank you to Tim Woodcock who has once again taken so many excellent photographs.

My grateful thanks go also to Ernest Russell of E. D. Russell Ltd, Hannah Nurseries, Chingford; Hazel Key and her daughter Ursula of Fibrex Nurseries Ltd, Pebworth, Nr Stratford-on-Avon; and Mr Wrench of Box End Nursery near Bedford. Thanks also to The Garden Centre at Alexandra Palace; Frosts Garden Centre; Willington Garden Centre; Milton Ernest Garden Centre and Poddington Garden Centre.

Special thanks go to Jane and John O'Connor. Jane painted the tiles for one of the window boxes, and John constructed the 11-foot window box. Both items appear in the historical section. Thanks also go to Rosamond Brown and Evelyn Wain for the gift of containers and plants, and to Audrey Baker, Ruth Butler, Jean Edwards, Kath Francis, Betty Hillier, Barbara Humphriss, Alma Mayes, Anne McNab, Elaine Mustoe, Margaret Pryn, Rosemary Stanbridge and Sarah Tusting for providing sites for photographs and in some cases carefully looking after the plants for the season. Particular thanks must go to Diana and Helen Bates, Cynthia Eames, Stella Ebsworth, Sian Rosser, Rebecca Stammers, Kim Wills and Carol Woods for providing help in so many other ways.

Lastly, a very big thank you to my husband Simon and children Jonathan and Suzanna for their patience and loving support during the making of this book.

LIST OF RECIPES

LONGTERM SCHEMES
BARRELS AND POTS MAINLY FOR WINTER AND SPRING
1 Winter Crocuses and Summer Lilies 13
2 A Holly Pot 14
3 My Favourite Scents 16
4 Mid Winter Pleasures 17
5 A Pot of Silver 18
6 A Conifer Barrel for Spring 19

SPRING MISCELLANEOUS
7 A Winter and Spring Window Box 20
8 A Flaming Chimney Pot 22
9 An Unusual Pot of Scented Bulbs 24
10 A White Dicentra Pot 25

POTS, TROUGHS AND BARRELS FOR SUMMER AND AUTUMN
11 Heady Scents, Shady Delights 26
12 Creamy and Fragrant 27
13 Foxy Haunts among Ferns and Hostas 29
14 Rich Greens in an Acer Pot 30
15 The Splendour of Roses 31
16 A Summer Pot of Soft Pinks and Greys 32
17 White Agapanthus 33
18 An Alpine Pot 34
19 An Alpine Trough 36
20 The Longdon Green Pot 38

HANGING BASKETS
21 Snow in a Summer Basket 40
22 Second Time Round 43
23 A Longterm Winter Basket 44

ALL YEAR ROUND
24 Four-in-One Pot 46
25 An Ali Baba Pot 47

WINTER AND SPRING SCHEMES
WINDOW BOXES
26 Peeping Tom 53
27 Bright and Cheerful 54
28 Spring Salmon 55

CHIMNEY POTS AND WALLPOTS
29 Spring in a Chimney Pot 56
30 A Golden Wallpot 57
31 Minnows in a Wallpot for Mid Spring 58
32 Peach Blossom in a Chimney Pot 59

HANGING BASKETS
33 A Cheery Basket from Autumn through to Spring 61
34 A Basket of Golden Crocuses 62
35 Hyacinths in a Hanging Basket 63
36 An Upside-Down Basket 64

WICKER BASKETS
37 The Wishing-Well Basket 66
38 A Basket of Dainty Daffodils 68

POTS
39 Mauves, Lilacs and Purples in a Strawberry Pot 69
40 Apricot Beauty 70
41 One for the Connoisseur 72
42 The Orange Emperor 73
43 Ten Salmon Parrots 74
44 Scarlet Tulips and Primulas 75
45 Anyone at Home? 77
46 The Lovely Angelique 78
47 A Traditional Barrel of Tulips and Wallflowers 79
48 Red, White and Blue 80
49 The Gaudy Professor 81
50 A Cherub Pot 82

SUMMER AND AUTUMN SCHEMES

HANGING BASKETS

51	A Symphony of Yellow and White	87
52	Traditional Reds and Blues	89
53	An Orange Ball	91
54	A Pink and Blue Ball	93
55	Four in a Row	94
56	A Colour Match	97
57	Bright and Cheerful	98
58	A Wedding or Christening Arrangement	100

WINDOW BOXES

59	Salmon in High Summer	102
60	Subtle Shades for Autumn	103
61	A Rich Tapestry of Colours	105

WALLPOTS, WICKER BASKETS, TROUGHS AND POTS

62	A Bridal Wallpot	106
63	Golden Orf in Summer	107
64	Summer Bedding in a Stone Trough	108
65	A Donkey Cart	109
66	Thrifty Salmon	111
67	A Begonia Pot	112
68	A Web of Lime-Green	114
69	Grandma's Pot of Pink and Mauve	115
70	Bronze and Apricot	116
71	A Barrel of Dahlias	117
72	A Pot of Chrysanthemums	118

CONSERVATORY SCHEMES

SPRING MISCELLANEOUS

73	A Rustic Spring Basket	122
74	A Period Piece	124
75	A Terrarium	126
76	Early Herbs	127
77	A Simple Basket of Daisies and Pansies	128
78	A Cascading Green Wallpot	130

SUMMER POTS

79	Spotty Foliage	131
80	Exotic Canna Lilies	132
81	Lilies and Scented Mignonette	134
82	A Stately Regal Pelargonium	136
83	Heaven Scent	138
84	Fragrant Pink and Baby Blue	139
85	Sweet Mimosa	140

LATE SUMMER TO EARLY SPRING

86	Cool and Green Like a Woodland Scene	141
87	A Nest of Ferns and Flowers	142
88	Conservatory Bells	144
89	Christmas Cheer	145

KITCHEN GARDEN SCHEMES

WINDOW BOXES

90 A Companion Planting for Tomatoes 150
91 A Late Spring Window Box of Herbs and
    Edible Flowers 152
92 Violas and Parsley 153
93 A Mixed Green Salad 154
94 An Early Spring Window Box of Herbs and
    Edible Flowers 155

HANGING BASKETS

95 Tomatoes in a Hanging Basket 157
96 Mainly Mint 159
97 A Strawberry Basket 160

POTS AND TUBS

98 A Green Pepper Pot 163
99 Scarlet Runners and Nasturtiums 164
100 Sweet Peas and Runner Beans 166
101 Dark Secrets 168
102 Yellow Courgettes 169
103 Herbs for Fish 170
104 Plentiful Herbs 171
105 A Galaxy of Greens 172
106 Herbs in a Strawberry Pot 174

VICTORIAN AND EDWARDIAN SCHEMES

WINDOW BOXES FOR WINTER AND SPRING

107 Early Tulips Followed by Hyacinths 185
108 Sweet Violets, Hepaticas and Primroses 186
109 Brimming Over with Colour 188
110 A Cottage Window Box for Winter and
     Spring 190

HANGING BASKETS FOR WINTER AND SPRING

111 A Cottage Hanging Basket for Winter and
     Spring 191
112 A Victorian Hanging Basket 193

URNS AND POTS FOR WINTER AND SPRING

113 The Warwick Vase 195
114 Design with Colour 197
115 Edwardian Spring 198
116 Old-Fashioned Favourites 200

WINDOW BOXES FOR SUMMER

117 Mullion Windows in Summer Raiment 203
118 Unruly but Colourful 204
119 Ferns for Shady Places 205
120 A Cottage Window Box for Summer 206

HANGING BASKETS FOR SUMMER

121 A Cottage Hanging Basket for Summer 208
122 A Ball of White 210
123 Pink Frills 212

TUBS, URNS AND POTS FOR SUMMER

124 The Agave 214
125 The Tulip Urn 215
126 The Czar 216
127 Mrs Pollock 218
128 Pink and White Delights 219

GENERAL INTRODUCTION

Planting in containers has become a popular form of gardening in the last decade. On a grander scale it has been practised for centuries in the great gardens of this country where large pots have been displayed in formal settings on the terrace, flanking steps, or used to create an imposing feature on a wall. On a more modest scale, container gardening has been regarded as a town phenomenon, bringing colour to balconies, basements and roof gardens. Nowadays, it is seen everywhere: sunny patios with their pots and tubs to the rear of a house, and hanging baskets and pots at the front, whether the location is in the city or the country. The garden centre phenomenon has greatly increased the sales of both the containers themselves and the plants to put in them. Patio gardening has become an everyday phrase and closely allied to it is this great and burgeoning interest in containers.

The aim of this book is to set out in detail how to plant up 128 different containers. Each one is laid out in an attractive and simple format so that the reader should feel able to follow the text, and feel confident enough to make up some of the displays in their own containers. The art of container gardening is to grow the plants so successfully together that they become a focal point in the garden or on the patio, and look like living flower arrangements, that will last not just for days but for weeks or months, or in some cases even years. Emphasis is given to colour, shape, site, scent etc so that something of great beauty is created. Each planting scheme is illustrated by its own colour photograph, taken to show the container at its best, as proof of each scheme's success. They have all been planted and grown especially for this book, and all tried and tested throughout the autumn and winter of 1988–89, and the spring and summer of 1989. In

addition, some of the longterm schemes had been planted in 1987.

The planting schemes are called 'recipes'. Each one provides a full list of 'ingredients' which are the plants used in each container, followed by a detailed 'method' of planting with depths given for drainage material, bulbs etc, and then lastly some helpful hints on aftercare so that you know how to look after the plants both during the growing season and, where relevant, during the winter which follows. In every case the size of the container used is given so that the reader has some idea of how to copy or adapt the given recipe.

The list of ingredients in each recipe is complete and includes all the plant names. The common ones are referred to wherever possible but in each case the Latin name is given in italics so that the reader is positively able to identify each plant. Common names vary throughout the country, and one name may actually refer to different plants depending on where you live. But each plant has only one Latin name and this is the one to refer to when you use any mail order service or visit the garden centres.

In some cases you will find the recipes easy to copy because the plants are widely available. At other times you might have to resort to the mail order suppliers listed at the back of the book. If you do ask them to send you plants through the post be sure and order early so that they will have them available and you can get on with your planting at the right time of year. There will be times when you may not want the bother of the mail order system and your local garden centre simply does not have the exact plants which you want to use. Do not worry. There are plenty of substitutes available. Try others and experiment for yourself. I would be the first to admit that one particular coloured pansy or lobelia or petunia could be substituted by another and still be used to good effect. Very often it is a matter of personal taste anyway, and others might not share my own. Some will love bright pinks and purples and mauves. Others will prefer the softer, subtle shades of apricots, primrose yellow and salmon pink. Be flexible. Where you have difficulty with finding particular plants, treat the list of ingredients merely as a starting point from which to create your own displays.

The recipes which follow cover the full range of longterm and seasonal gardening, as well as sections on plantings for the conservatory, kitchen garden and Victorian and Edwardian containers. As such they involve a wide range of topics and plant materials.

LONGTERM

The first section in the book is devoted to longterm planting schemes where the plants are allowed to mature over a period of years. The pots with evergreen shrubs like the holly and mahonia, the evergreen ferns and creepers, provide all-year-round interest each with their own special ingredients to give added highlights at various times. Others with deciduous trees and ferns offer the delight of new growth as the buds swell and fresh leaves appear. Then in the autumn we get the colourful tints, as the leaves turn to russet and then fall. There are perennials and bulbs to provide other displays, each with its own season of glory. Chosen carefully, just a few of these placed together can provide an entire container garden display; on the other hand they can provide the backbone to other more temporary combinations.

SEASONAL

The second section concentrates on seasonal recipes. First there are the recipes relating to winter bedding and spring bulbs where the planting is done the previous autumn. These recipes span a six- or seven-month period; sadly, this is often a period of neglect when containers lie idle, or even worse still are seen sporting the remnants of the previous summer's displays. There is no excuse! A wonderful range of spring bulbs, golden daffodils, scented hyacinths, delightful crocuses and tulips can be used to fill the containers so that they are brimming with colour when spring comes at last. Add a carpet of winter bedding and the season can be extended for weeks if not months especially now that winter-flowering pansies are so freely available.

Then there follow the recipes for the summer months, not forgetting a few for autumn as well. These are the most rewarding for they grow so quickly and you can soon see the fruits of your labour. There is so much plant material available to use that it is difficult ever to tire of the exercise. There are always new colour combinations to try, other plants to use, perhaps different combinations of containers to group together. Regular attention to the containers is of course essential, but then when they are planted with care, and looked after with love, the job becomes a pleasure not a chore.

CONSERVATORY

Conservatories are a popular addition to the home, and are often used these days as an extended living area rather than an isolated plant room. The conservatory attached to my previous house in London had a beautiful backdrop of plants but it was also a children's play area and a place to sow and grow seeds; in early spring it was full of lovely spring bulbs and in late autumn it was a haven for summer containers, where they could grow on for another few weeks. In high summer it was extremely hot, even with blinds and automatic vents. Many of the plants moved outside, and so did we! Shading is extremely important, especially over the roof area. If you can establish it with blinds or creepers then the battle is half won. There are lots of books written about conservatories with lists of suitable plants, but few dwell on planting combinations themselves. I offer just a small number, limited by my own experience. I should add that several of them could adapt quite well to a light indoor situation, while if it gets too hot in summer several of them could be placed, quite happily, outdoors. Many of them involve well-known plants and bulbs, easily available and straightforward to look after. Others may be slightly more unusual but worth a try.

EDIBLE

Containers can be used to grow a wide range of fruit and vegetables, herbs and edible flowers. Indeed, it is quite possible to have an entire range of pots and baskets planted up with edible crops so that you can create a kitchen garden at your back door. Moreover, they can be designed to look very attractive. Mix scarlet runner beans with yellow nasturtiums, or white flowering beans with old-fashioned sweet peas. Plant yellow courgettes with dark blue lobelia (the lobelia is poisonous so don't try and eat it), or strawberries in a hanging basket surrounded by honey-scented alyssums. Plant tomatoes, French marigolds and basil together and enjoy all the pungent aromas as well as the brilliant colourings. There are lots of ideas for winter and spring plantings too. The hardy herbs look attractive throughout the year and are an important source of flavouring when cooking in the winter months, while in early spring they can be joined by such delectable partners as sweet violets, primroses, violas and cowslips. All these flowers can be used to scatter on top of salads, to decorate pâtés, to display on cakes and pavlovas and many other excellent dishes. Try them out and delight your friends!

HISTORICAL

Container gardening has been practised for centuries, but in the Victorian and Edwardian eras it became even more popular as new plants were introduced from far-off places. Fashions in gardening changed and the bedding-out system, both for summer and winter, became one of the hallmarks of the period, reflected in the gardens themselves and in the many containers. Contemporary gardening journals and books were often referring to ways of planting conservatory hanging baskets, winter vases, window boxes etc. Plans were shown of great displays of pots and urns, not just two or three but fifteen or twenty at a time. Descriptions are given in July 1900 of detailed planting schemes in window boxes at the Oxford colleges; 125 were filled at Christ Church, and 63 in the garden quad at Trinity, 9 at Lincoln, 20 at Exeter, and many more besides. One book, *The New Practical Window Gardener*, was devoted to container gardening, both on the balcony and window-sill outside and in the home. It was published in 1879 and written by John Mollison. It provides a wonderful source of information on the subject just over a hundred years ago and means that we can learn a great deal about earlier techniques and ways of displaying plants. Many old favourites such as auriculas, double primroses, hepaticas, violets, mignonette and heliotrope have long been unfashionable. Some of them are making a revival so it is much easier to copy several of these old recipes. As there is now a great interest in restoring interiors to match the original features, why not, if you live in a Victorian or Edwardian house, plant up your window boxes and pots in the old style?

CONTAINERS

The containers which are used in the book are made of many different materials and aim to reflect many styles and shapes. But inevitably they are restricted to the ones I have had access to. You might notice that some have been planted twice for displays at different

times of year. Many I actually own and have planted up for several seasons, but some are borrowed from kind friends. In addition many have been specially lent to me by the manufacturers thereof, for which I am very grateful. Many of the delightful handthrown pots seen in the recipes which follow come from Whichford Pottery Ltd of Whichford near Shipston-on-Stour in Warwickshire. They all carry a ten-year guarantee against lamination in the frost and can be purchased from a wide range of garden centres or from the factory itself. The stone reproduction pots are borrowed from Haddonstone Ltd of East Haddon in Northamptonshire. These, too, are sold throughout a wide range of garden centre outlets and also from the factory itself. The two lead containers are borrowed from Renaissance Casting Company Ltd which is based in Coventry. All these three firms make traditional as well as modern designs, which is useful where Victorian, Georgian or Tudor style containers are wanted for historic planting schemes. They all exhibit at the Chelsea Flower Show so you can order them direct.

However not all pots, boxes, tubs etc have to conform to normal standards. The donkey cart seen in the photograph on page 4 certainly makes a more unusual container. When we moved out of London, we found we were gaining not just a house but a donkey called Melissa as well! We purchased her old donkey cart and then discovered she had not pulled it for seventeen years. It was already gaily painted so I seized on the opportunity to turn it into a garden container. A large enamel bowl with holes drilled in the base served as the inner lining, and soon Melissa's cart was bedecked with plants, some very tasty ones. To take this photograph she had to be offered a juicy carrot otherwise the nasturtium flowers would have disappeared! The exercise just goes to show that almost anything can be used to display plants: wheelbarrows or old tyres. I've even seen old boats used in Brittany.

An inner liner of plastic sheeting or a pot can be used with wooden barrels where you want to preserve the wood and cast iron urns where you want to prevent rust forming. It is also relevant to wicker baskets where you want to prevent the cane work rotting and the soil escaping. This idea is no different from the principle of using moss in a hanging basket, but it means that with little expense and just three coats of yacht varnish you can transform an old wicker basket, even one with holes in it, into an item of great beauty. Indeed, they have become one of my favourite containers over the years.

The important factor is that the main plant

container itself should have adequate drainage with plenty of holes in the bottom, and that it should be empty and clean before you begin. Don't bring last year's diseases and pests into this year's planting schemes.

Even a donkey cart can be adapted as a container

HANGING BASKETS

Hanging baskets are an important feature of container work and over the past ten years they have grown tremendously in their popularity. There are many different types on the market: ones with wooden sides, solid plastic baskets, wire baskets, some made of compressed peat. But the one I favour most is the plastic-coated wire one with quite wide gaps – about 4cm (1.5″) – between each circle of wire. Choose a type where the wires are sturdy but not so strong that they are inflexible. This is because it sometimes helps to be able to prise them apart, pass a plant through the opening and then close it up again back to its normal position. If the wires crisscross or are too strong to move, this becomes impossible.

I also think it helps if the basket has a flat, not rounded, bottom. This makes planting much easier. It is far more stable resting on a bench or table and takes away the necessity of sitting it in a bucket. It also allows for a greater planting area as the sides only gently converge at the base. With the round-bottomed ones, the planting area is more restricted in the bottom half of the basket.

Size is most significant. I strongly favour the 35cm (14″) diameter basket which has a depth of 15cm (6″). All too often very small baskets are used. They restrict the number of plants that can be grown in them and allow for only a small amount of compost which tends to dry out even more quickly than in the larger baskets. By all means, however, buy a 40cm (16″) basket if you can find one. It will hold even more plants and make a far better display.

There are various lining materials on the market ranging from foam, compressed peat and moss. Black bin-liners are sometimes used too. But nothing compares with moss, particularly for the first six to eight weeks of the basket's life. It looks so fresh and natural and feels so soft to work with. It is far more flexible than the other kinds and forms a snug wall around the sides of the basket. You will find moss sold in small packs in the garden centres, but if you go to a good florist you can buy it loose and cheaper. If you have three or four to make up, you could buy half a sack or so and if necessary share it with a friend. I don't advise you to use lawn moss for summer plantings unless you can see there are no grass seeds or roots in it. However, good tufts of it are fine for winter or early spring baskets when the grass will not be a threat to the overall planting.

Solid plastic baskets should not be overlooked. They have different advantages. They are easier to plant because no moss lining is necessary. They are also easier to water because the water cannot escape through the sides and can only percolate downwards through the soil. The drip tray at the base means that a small reservoir is created after each watering, which is helpful in very hot weather. It also means that the basket does not continue to drip after watering like the moss-lined ones. Where the basket is in a passageway or in a conservatory this can be quite advantageous. But the one great disadvantage is that they are fairly small, usually with a maximum diameter of 27.5cm (11″) and a depth of only 10cm (4″). They have only a third of the planting space compared with the 35cm (14″) diameter basket described above (I don't know why they can't be made bigger?). Secondly, although they are easier to plant, you cannot create a two- or even three-tier planting out of them, which means plants cannot cascade out of their sides – they can only trail from the top. That being said, I have seen some wonderful displays growing out of them.

Always buy sturdy brackets or hooks. The weight of a fully planted hanging basket is considerable. Ten litres of wet soil can be extremely heavy. The brackets can be fixed in brick, stone or wood but make sure you use the right equipment and if the fixing is in brick don't choose the easy way out and put the screws/nails into the mortar between the bricks where it is easier to drill. You must drill into the brickwork itself; otherwise you may wake up one morning to find the basket and plants in ruins on the floor. For a 35cm (14″) basket, use a 27.5cm (11″) bracket. For a 27.5cm (11″) solid basket, use a

22.5cm (9″) bracket. Consider each size of basket individually. If the bracket is too short the plants at the sides and back will be squashed against the wall and be damaged as they rub against it. If it is too long then the basket will catch the wind and swing around so that some of the larger special plants at the front might get damaged. Hooks allow greater flexibility in some cases.

Siting is of paramount importance. Extremes of full sun or dense shade are the most difficult to tolerate. Full sun is wonderful for some planting schemes but the majority enjoy a little relief from endless sunshine. If possible, place the bracket where the basket will have sunlight for at least half the day. In summer there are many plants which will tolerate shade, but again, most prefer light shade. It is also important to consider whether the site is a windy one. Avoid exposed positions, especially on corners where plants will get damaged by continual buffeting and the baskets will dry out all the quicker.

Don't make the mistake of fixing the bracket so high up that you can only see the basket's bare bottom. In time the plants may disguise it, but it would be much better if you could see the contents of the top and sides. Position the basket at eye level and you will derive the maximum pleasure; there you will be able to see the plants growing day by day. They will be so much easier to water and look after generally, and if they are scented you will be able to enjoy them without having to stand on tiptoe. If some of the plants trail too low you can always snip them off to keep the basket tidy. On the other hand you must be wary of putting the basket where it will create an obstruction. Plan ahead and then there won't be any disasters.

Hanging baskets are labour intensive. They may only take you twenty minutes or half an hour to make up, but after that they will require hours of your time. In hot weather you must be prepared to water them daily. This does not mean that you give them a quick spray with a hose and then walk on. It means that you must do the job properly. Soak the basket until the soil is wet throughout and the moss is moist to the touch. It is best to water the basket gently to begin with, let the water soak in, then water again. You may even have to repeat the process once more. While you are waiting, deadhead the flowers or check for greenfly etc. Be sure to keep them neat and pest-free at all times. Baskets with large leaves like tuberous begonias and geraniums can act like umbrellas and prevent the water reaching the soil. In these circumstances it is best to water at soil level. This will avoid another problem which is that some

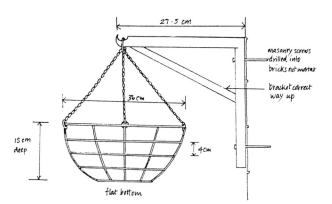

flowers are spoilt by rain. Petunias have tissue paper-like petals and these soon get damaged by being wet.

If you water the baskets in the daytime when the sun is shining on them, you will find unsightly marks on the leaves of the plants known as scorch. For this reason it is always best to water the baskets in the evening or early morning, then this problem will not arise.

Feed regularly. Great demands are being made of a very small soil capacity so food is vital to the success of the scheme. Constant leaching of the nutrients makes matters worse and I think it is essential to apply a liquid feed. I use Phostrogen or Tomorite. Tomorite is slightly easier to use because it mixes in better, but I find both of them most satisfactory. However, I am sure there are many other good brands available.

There are twenty-two hanging basket recipes contained in this book. Some are made to last more than one year; these you will find in the Longterm section (see Recipes 21–23). Some include spring baskets and will be found in the Winter and Spring section (see Recipes 33–36). Some include herbs and fruits such as tomatoes and basil, lemon balm and mints, strawberries and marjoram. These will be discovered in the Kitchen Garden section (see Recipes 95–97). Some reflect Victorian patterns of planting using ivy as a green covering to the basket and can be seen in the Historical (Victorian and Edwardian) section (see Recipes 111, 112 and 121).

The majority, however, are straightforward summer baskets (see the recipes in the Summer and Autumn section), some planted very traditionally, with geraniums, fuchsias, petunias etc. Others have been planted with an eye to colour schemes: yellow and white, all-white for a wedding, salmon pinks, rich pinks and blues. Two have been made using strips of bedding plants only (see the pink and blue ball of little begonias and lobelia, and the orange French marigold and coleus basket) in a deliberate attempt to keep the cost low. There are lots of unusual schemes for both summer, winter and spring work. Look through the different sections and try out some new ideas. Feel free to adapt the recipes and experiment for yourself.

DRAINAGE

The first thing that goes into the container when you begin a recipe is the drainage material. Traditionally this would have been broken clay crocks. With the plastic revolution – which means that all today's plants come in little plastic pots or polystyrene strips – most of us don't have many clay pots, broken or otherwise. If you have they can certainly be used for this purpose. You can buy drainage material from garden centres in the form of Hortag or horticultural grit, but the latter is so small that it would shoot straight out of many drainage holes. The best material I have found is polystyrene, the sort that so much packaging comes in these days whether it is electrical goods or plant trays. Broken up into reasonably small pieces it becomes a valuable drainage material. Its temperature barely fluctuates, so in wintertime the plant roots benefit. It does not absorb water so it always remains light and easy to work with, a factor which makes it eminently suitable for containers where weight might be a problem, on a roof terrace, for example. Nor does it seem to disintegrate, so it is fine for longterm planting schemes as well.

SOIL

My advice is the same as it would have been one hundred years ago: never dig up the garden soil and use it in your containers. It is alive with worms, bugs and weeds and all sorts of other undesirables. Be prepared to use sterile soil which for most people means buying it ready prepared. This will have the advantage of containing the correct balance of food nutrients, loam and grit. There are many different ones to choose from, but I generally recommend John Innes No 2 or 3 depending on which plants are used. John Innes is not a trademark; it is a formula for making a compost. It is actually sold by various companies whose output will vary slightly according to which district they draw their loam from. The alternative is to use a peat-based compost which is lighter and kinder to the hands. It is particularly suitable for hanging baskets and roof terrace work. However, it does seem to dry out quicker and, once dry, is more difficult to water properly. Where ericaceous soil is needed for acid-loving plants, then be sure to ask for a special mix which contains no lime. It is easily available from all garden centres.

At least 5cm (2″) of soil is generally placed over the drainage material before any plants or bulbs are put into the containers. At the top of the container it is practical to leave a 2.5cm (1″) gap between the soil level and the rim of the container. This allows for watering. If the level was brought any higher, the soil would be washed out and wasted, and the sides of the container made dirty each time.

The amount of soil needed for each recipe will vary according to the size of the container. Sometimes it is worth taking note of the inside measurement as it can be very different from the outside one, particularly with stone and reconstituted stone troughs etc. It will also vary with the amount of soil already included around the rootball of all the plants to be used. Where bulbs are to be planted this will be negligible, but where young trees and shrubs are involved, this might be considerable. As a general rule, however, an accurate method is to take metric calculations and convert the volume required to litre measurements.

If you have an oblong trough or window box, then measure the length, width and depth in centimetres and multiply these figures to arrive at the required volume of soil.

For example:
Large window box or trough
87.5cm (35″) long, 20cm (8″) deep, 12.5cm (5″) wide
would need
87.5×20×12.5=21875=21.9 litres

If you have a tub or round container, then measure the radius (ie half the diameter) and depth. The formula is 3.14×radius squared×depth.

For example:
Large wooden half barrel
60cm (24″) diameter, 37.5cm (15″) deep
The radius=0.5×60cm=30cm
would need
3.14×30×30×37.5=105975=106 litres

Use the calculation as a guide only. This figure will always be on the generous side allowing for 5cm (2″) drainage and 2.5cm (1″) space at the top of the container, and also taking into account the soil that might come with the roots. However, it is always better to have too much soil than to be left short; there is nothing more frustrating. The surplus soil will always come in useful on another occasion, especially if you clip or fold over the top of the soil bag to stop rain water getting inside.

WATERING
Very few pots will get the required amount of water from natural rainfall although in a wet winter and early spring they may survive quite well. At other times, when growth is rapid and plants are thirsty, additional watering will be essential, particularly where the containers are placed in the shadow of the house, under a wall, or on a window-sill. In high summer you must be prepared to water daily, even twice a day on occasions. Be patient with the task. It is not a job to rush. You should water generously,

allow it to soak in, and then water it again, and so on until the basket is very moist throughout.

Timing is important. The main problem to avoid is scorch. That happens when the sun shines on wet leaves or flowers and they are left with burn marks. This will be most noticeable for containers placed outside as the sun's strength grows from early summer onwards. For conservatory plants, however, it is a factor to remember at all times. Try to make a habit of watering only in the morning or evening; then the problem will not be encountered. It can be very satisfying to water on a summer's evening when the heat of the day has passed. The containers will soak up their drink quickly and have the cool of the night to revive.

Some plants cannot cope with water on their leaves or flowers. In the conservatory it is best to water African violets at soil level or else the leaves will spoil. Try to avoid wetting petunia flowers or else they, too, will be damaged. Many of the occupants of summer containers have large leaves, in particular tuberous begonias and large-leaved geraniums, where the leaves act like umbrellas; no amount of watering will penetrate below, unless you take care to water under the leaves at soil level.

FEEDING
In most cases the containers are thickly planted and great things are expected of very small planting spaces. All the plants will therefore need additional food at some stage. Even the longterm recipes – planted with John Innes No 3 soil which already contains the most nutrients – will need replenishing from time to time. A general slow-release fertilizer may be used in the early spring and again in the autumn. For the seasonal recipes a liquid feed is more appropriate. Generally, where John Innes No 2 soil is used there is an adequate food supply mixed in to last six weeks; adjust this to four weeks for soil-less composts. Liquid feeds would then be given after that period. I sometimes think that with so much watering the nutrients must be quickly washed out, so I only use this as an approximate rule. In high summer when the containers are in full bloom it is useful to feed each week. Take a tip from a couple of very busy, keen young gardeners in Islington who produced the best hanging baskets I've ever seen. They gave their plants a liquid feed every Saturday morning. That way, they made it into a habit which they never forgot, and the results were apparent for all to see.

PEST CONTROL
Greenfly, whitefly and blackfly are enemies of the

first order, sapping the strength of the plants so that they wither and die. They must be controlled before they cause too much damage. Fuchsias, petunias, tobacco plants, tulips, pansies, nasturtiums and canary creeper seem particularly susceptible. Spray with insecticide to kill them immediately, and then again and again as they reinfest. Nowadays there are several different preparations available for different kinds of plants. Where edible fruits and leaves are concerned you should use one that is described as being 'safe'. In fact I use this type of spray on nearly all my containers. It seems to work well and I know that I am not injuring precious insects like bees and ladybirds which are so important to us. It also means that I can crop the fruit, leaves and flowers safely. Apart from the ones mentioned in the edible section, this includes the rose petals in the longterm section and the scented geranium leaves and flowers in the Conservatory section, which can also be used in the kitchen.

Companion planting is another means of pest control which I have appeared to have had great success with, especially in the enclosed atmosphere of the greenhouse and conservatory, where I have grown masses of French marigolds and basil. They are reputed to be a deterrent to whitefly on tomatoes. But in fact, I was free from any kind of aphid on my indoor tomatoes, peppers, aubergines and fuchsias.

Having moved from London to the country in 1988, it came as quite a shock to discover the ravages caused by the little black rape beetle. It attacks yellow flowers in particular, and I know of nothing to counteract it. It may be wiser not to plant certain yellow flowers at all. The canary creeper was destroyed, and for a few weeks the courgette flowers were a seething mass, quite inedible! The beetle loved to squirm inside sweet pea flowers, too, but thankfully seemed to avoid the darker ones which I could then pick.

In the conservatory, aphids may be controlled by insecticide sprays as described above or by special smoke cones. Be sure to plug any keyholes which might allow the fumes into the house and to put a mat at the interior door. Alternatively, you could buy predatory insects although these are probably more appropriate to the greenhouse. As far as greenfly is concerned, it may be cheaper and easier to find plenty of ladybirds to gobble the greenfly up. Gather them on a sunny day as you see them, and immediately take them for a finer feast indoors! It certainly seems to work.

CLIMATE

Recent experience has taught us that our climate is unpredictable. A severe winter in 1985–86 has been balanced by mild winters from 1988–90. Poor, wet summers have been contrasted by hot, dry ones. Very bad storms have wreaked much damage, leaving uprooted trees and shattered pots. Extremes of cold or heat, drought or rain mean that we have to be more attentive to our containers. In severe winter weather, they may well need protection. Bring them into a shed or barn, greenhouse or conservatory for as long as necessary, or cover with sacking. Keep watering down to a minimum. Even if the plants look bedraggled and almost dead, don't give up hope; they will probably revive when the temperatures warm up and they can rehydrate themselves once more. Pansies and wallflowers can look dreadful after a bad frost, but they are both quite hardy and will survive most wintry conditions.

Wind can be a serious problem. Not only does it cause physical damage by smashing pots and breaking plants, but in winter and early spring, it can have a chronic drying effect so that plants can die. Where possible keep containers in sheltered spots in the garden. The plants will much prefer it at any time of the year. If gales threaten, be prepared to move the pots out of the wind. Take care not to put them against a wall where the wind whips round in these conditions. You might think it safe but it could be worse than ever. You will soon know your garden in this respect, and find the safest place. When the summer is very hot you might consider moving some of your pots out of the glaring heat, particularly if you have too little time to water them properly each day. Some plants, of course, will bask in the warmest temperatures, but in extreme heat there are quite a few which would prefer a little shade at some time in the day.

LONGTERM
SCHEMES

INTRODUCTION TO THE LONGTERM RECIPES

A few longterm planting schemes in containers are always useful. There are the kind that add an all-year-round evergreen effect to the terrace or patio. These often act as a backdrop against which to put the more colourful seasonal pots; look at the ivy and virginia creeper in the Ali Baba pot. Then there are the kind that provide exotic inspiration to the garden and can only be achieved by leaving the plants undisturbed. The wonderful displays of agapanthus and nerines are two examples. There is also the sort that simply looks better after two or three years of growth rather than one season's planting. The mahonia and holly pots already have a certain maturity, and will improve still further over the next few years.

WHAT DOES LONGTERM MEAN?

Just because these recipes are described as longterm, it does not mean the plants will live for ever. They will still need dividing and cutting back and eventually replacing just as much, if not more so, than the plants in the border. But what it does mean is that if the plants are watered and well cared for, they will survive longer than one season in a pot. They will often become bigger specimens the following year, give a greater display and be generally more pleasing. As already mentioned this is certainly true of the nerines and agapanthus, and of the acer, holly and mahonia which all make a much more effective

display after two or three years of planting. The ivy has taken several seasons to clothe the Ali Baba pot, while it will take a few seasons more for the sempervivums to spill over the side of the four-in-one pot. Obviously there is a significant cost advantage in allowing these plants to remain, as large specimens are often very expensive in the garden centres.

DIFFERENT SCHEMES NEED DIFFERENT TREATMENT

Some of these longterm specimens are labour-saving. Hardly any special attention needs to be given to the sempervivums. Others merely need a late autumn face-lift. Clear away the debris of dead leaves and stalks and then carefully remove the top inch or two of soil. If you take up little crocus corms be sure to put them back safely. Now you can put fresh supplies of soil, generally John Innes No 3, in the top of the container bringing the level to within 2.5cm (1″) of the rim. You may use this opportunity to divide some of the herbaceous plants like the primroses under the mahonia and the sedums, periwinkles and pulmonarias under the holly. If the daffodils were showing signs of decline last spring then now is the time to replace them. If the ivy is getting too rampant, clip its roots back severely. It will still survive.

You will harm plants like the lily of the valley and the hostas if you remove the top layer of soil, as they both grow too near the surface. Probably the best

Late winter grouping showing scented mahonia in full flower, pink hellebores and spring snowflakes which peep from below the holly

help you can give them is a mere topping of fresh soil. This will help replace the shortfall which will have occurred at the top of the pot. The same is true of the smilacina, dicentra, agapanthus and nerines. Different plants will require different treatment and it is difficult to generalize.

FEEDING

Feeding is essential to these container plants. As a general rule an early spring application of a slow-release fertilizer will be of great benefit. There are many specimens which would enjoy a midterm feed at the time of flowering as well. At this stage a liquid application of Phostrogen or rose feed would be in order, depending on the subjects involved.

LIFESPAN

Some plants will outgrow their pots and after three years or so may need dividing, like the hostas and lily of the valley, the dicentra and sedums. This does not mean that you have to start again; on the contrary, you can probably make up two or three new pots if you wanted to, using the divisions as individual plants. Some, like the roses, might need replacing after the third year of flowering. So, too, will the longterm hanging baskets, although cuttings and divisions may be taken of some of the plants. Others, like agapanthus, are best left undisturbed for as long as possible, until the display starts to deteriorate. Then they need dividing and repotting, and after a period of recuperation the show will continue. No wonder they were always so popular!

Trees like the mahonia, holly and acer will live for years in the pots if they are well cared for, but there must come a time when they would prefer a larger

The same group in spring, now with a mass of wild primroses, golden daffodils and striking purple crocuses. The hellebores are still in flower

root space. It is difficult to judge. If you leave it until the plants are showing signs of deterioration it will be too late; if you do it too soon you might lose a very good container specimen for another year's display.

ADVANTAGES OF LONGTERM PLANTING SCHEMES

One of the advantages of planting some of these subjects in pots is that they can be moved without disturbing their roots. This means that the plants can be fully appreciated while at their best and then tucked away in the background again. This is particularly true of the scented pots. While the mahonia, yellow iris, lily of the valley and smilacina are in full flower they should be placed near your path or door so

that you can enjoy them to the utmost. Afterwards they can be moved further away. This also applies to the pots with spring bulbs in them. The bulbs look attractive as they are growing and, of course, when they are in flower, but afterwards they can look rather untidy and are best not seen in the front row.

Another feature of growing these plants in containers is that they can be shown off as individual specimens to be thoroughly appreciated in their own right. Some of the longterm subjects are exquisite and worth seeing closer to eye level, which is the case when they are put in containers. The white dicentra has far more impact grown in a pot than appearing amongst other spring flowers in the border, especially if it is raised up so that its arching stems can be enjoyed to the full. Similarly if you lift the hellebore and bergenia pot off the ground and put it on a bench or wall you can look into the hellebore flowers and see the wonderful markings. This is very different from seeing the tops of their heads against bare earth.

The white dicentra raises two other noteworthy points. It is one of those plants that responds to a warm spell in late winter and early spring and begins to grow before it is really safe to do so. Then if a cold spell comes with frost as well, the foliage can be damaged in a single night and that year's display will have been jeopardized. But if it is grown in a pot, the problem can be avoided. If frost threatens, move it to a greenhouse or put it in a sheltered spot by the house. It can soon be moved back to its old position when the weather changes again. The Victorians used pink dicentras for forcing in their conservatories. The practice is worth copying. As new growth appears bring the pot into the warmth of the conservatory, and watch the plant grow at an amazing rate. It makes a superb display which will give immense pleasure year after year.

COMPANION PLANTING

Some longterm specimen plants can be very much enhanced by the plants which grow around them. They are also easier to control here than in a whole border where other plants naturally enter into the picture as the eye wanders to what lies beyond or on either side. In a pot the companion plants are chosen with care and their numbers are limited. The acer looks marvellous with its bright green carpet of low-growing plants: a scene which remains in harmony for the whole of the summer. The rose pot looks glorious with its blue spires of the veronica rising up in the front and its yellow-green backcloth of *Alchemilla mollis*. In a garden environment it would still have been worthy of comment, but it would not have created the focal point which the pot version was able to present.

CONTINUITY OF FLOWERING

Continuity of flowering is an important consideration with all containers, but especially so where longterm plantings are envisaged. With careful planning, some of these schemes can provide a wide range of interest and colour for months on end. The winter and spring window box in Recipe 7 is a good example. Three photographs chart its course from January through to April. It starts off in January with the white heather just beginning to flower, while the gold on the tree heather complements the bright yellow dwarf iris which suddenly comes into bloom towards the end of the month. By February the white heather is a mass of bloom, the pale blue crocuses are out and the white periwinkle is in full array. In March and April the anemones are in flower – a wonderful sea of colour. They are joined by the pretty dwarf daffodils in the middle of April. Still the periwinkle is in flower, and still the white heather is in bloom although the best of its show is now over. By the end of spring the display has finished, apart from the flowering of the tree heather. The bulbs must be allowed to die down naturally. But when summer comes the dead leaves can be removed and a few summer annuals could be added.

SENSE OF AWAKENING

Evergreen plants can get quite dirty after a few years, especially if they are grown in a basement site near a busy road. It is always worth giving the leaves a good clean from time to time so that the grime is washed off and the plants can breathe again. Deciduous trees, shrubs and perennials naturally avoid this problem. They produce fresh green foliage in early summer which lasts the season and then dies away for the winter. Their new leaves can be so welcome. I love to see the fern fronds unfolding and the foxglove pushing up its spires. At the same time the hosta is unfurling its leaves – one of the summer's great pleasures. There is a great sense of awakening. Gardeners experience it with the spring bulbs as well, but with this type of plants you know it means the onset of summer.

PROBLEMS WITH SLUGS

Unfortunately, hosta leaves are as attractive to slugs as they are to us. Container-grown plants may have the advantage over border-grown hostas, however, in that the slugs first have to climb up the side of the pot or tub to reach the leaves. It is true they are capable of doing so but they are not quite so keen if there is a broad band of sharp grit at the base of the container. Moreover, if the hostas are growing out of a vase or urn placed on a pedestal, raised off the ground by two feet or more, the ascent becomes even harder and the damage consequently less. If you do see any slugs, pull them off at once and exterminate them! The leaves are much too precious to be given as slug fodder. If you want to use chemicals, put slug pellets down around the base of the containers and at soil level, or water in with an anti-slug solution. Slugs apart, hostas make excellent subjects for a wide range of containers. Bold outlines, a graceful overall shape and attractive markings and colourings to the leaves – to say nothing of the handsome lilac flowers – make them a prize plant. They tolerate shade and partial sun, though would scorch in too much sun. Gertrude Jekyll certainly favoured them in her pots at Munstead Wood at the turn of the century.

1 WINTER CROCUSES AND SUMMER LILIES

Simple to plant and look after, this pot has the advantage of looking lovely both in winter and summer. First come the pretty blues of the crocuses and pulmonarias, and then the soft pinks of the lilies and thyme.

Site
Shade or partial shade.

Container
Medium terracotta pot: 35cm (14″) in diameter, 25cm (10″) deep. The depth of this pot is important for the lilies.

Planting Time
October.

At its best
February to March; and June.

Ingredients
3 short lilies *Lilium* 'Sunray' (yellow) or 'Liberation' (pink) or you might prefer white *L. regale* but it would need staking. Choose lime-tolerant kinds; otherwise use ericaceous soil.
1 creeping thyme *Thymus serpyllum* to provide a pink (or white) and green carpet for the lilies in summer.
1 *Pulmonaria saccharata* 'Argentea'. The leaves have a spotted silver-white effect and the flowers are pink, changing to sky-blue as they age.
1 *Pulmonaria officinalis* known as the Jerusalem cowslip or sometimes as spotted dog! It bears white spots on its leaves and the flowers are purple-blue.
10 pale blue crocuses *Crocus chrysanthus* 'Blue Pearl'.
20 litres of John Innes No 3 soil.
Drainage material such as old crocks or pieces of polystyrene.

Method
1. Cover the base of the container with 5cm (2″) of drainage material and add 5cm (2″) of soil.
2. Space the three lily bulbs in the centre of the pot. Firm them gently into the soil and add 8cm (3″).
3. Plant the thyme in the centre-front of the pot, and the pulmonarias on either side. Plant the crocuses in the middle.
4. Fill in the gaps with more soil, bringing the level to within 2.5cm (1″) of the rim of the pot.
5. Water well. Firm in the plants and add more soil if necessary.

Aftercare
Maintain the soil moisture throughout the year (the pulmonarias and lilies both like to be kept moist). The pulmonarias are also apt to be attacked by greenfly so spray when necessary. The lilies may need staking depending on your choice of bulb and whether the site is sheltered.

Mulch annually in the autumn with leaf-mould or peat and apply a slow-release fertilizer in the spring. The lilies may need to be changed after two or three years. At the same time divide the pulmonaria and thyme and repot using new soil.

2   A HOLLY POT

Even in the depths of February, this pot was full of interest with the variegated leaves on the holly, periwinkle and ivy, shiny red berries on the gaultheria, and precious spring snowflakes to complete the scene. By the end of March it was ablaze with early daffodils, crocuses and pulmonarias. An excellent combination for longterm planting and colour.

Site
Any.

Container
Hand-thrown terracotta pot: 45cm (18") in diameter, 40cm (16") deep. The ornate design is valuable for a winter planting as it adds extra interest.

Planting Time
Autumn: early September onwards.

At its best
Very exciting in February when the spring snowflakes come into flower, and then in late March and early April when the daffodils, crocuses and pulmonaria flower. Then there are the alliums in summer and the red berries of the gaultheria in the autumn and winter.

Ingredients
1   variegated holly *Ilex aquifolium* 'Aureo-marginata' with gold-edged leaves. This is a female form, and should bear berry in time (needs a male partner in the vicinity). Choose a tall plant, at least the same depth as the pot. You could train it into a standard shape eventually.
  1   *Gaultheria procumbens* known as the partridge berry; a creeping evergreen which has pretty white flowers in summer and scarlet berries from autumn to spring.

1 *Pulmonaria rubra* 'Bowles Red' with unspotted leaves but beautiful pinkish-red flowers. Known commonly as lungwort.
 1 *Sedum reflexum* to trail over the edge.
 1 variegated periwinkle *Vinca minor* 'Aureo-variegata' with blue flowers.
12 early dwarf daffodils *Narcissus* 'February Gold'.
 6 *Leucojum vernum* known as spring snowflakes; they flower later than the snowdrops and have a larger head. They are rather expensive but unusual. (You can use ordinary snowdrops.)
 1 variegated ivy *Hedera helix* 'Heise'.
12 purple crocuses *Crocus vernus* 'Purpureus Grandiflorus'.
 6 *Allium ostrowskianum*; small pink alliums which flower in June.
65 litres of John Innes No 3 soil.
Drainage material such as large crocks or pieces of polystyrene.

Method
1. Cover the base of the container with 7.5cm (3″) of drainage material and then add 20cm (8″) of soil.
2. Plant the holly at the centre-back of the pot, adjusting the soil level beneath the rootball so that the top of it sits just under the rim of the pot.
3. Plant the daffodil bulbs at the base of the holly so that they form a group across the centre of the pot. Cover the bulbs with soil until just their tips show.
4. Plant the snowflakes in a well-spaced group to the right of the holly.
5. In a circle around the edge of the pot plant the ivy and gaultheria at centre-front, the pulmonaria, sedum and vinca to the sides.
6. Plant the crocuses and alliums in front of the daffodils and in between the perimeter plants.
7. Fill in the gaps with soil. Firm down all the plants. Water well and add more soil if necessary. The level should be to within 2.5cm (1″) of the rim.

Aftercare
Maintain the soil moisture throughout the year but particularly in spring and summer. Never water in frosty weather. Leave the bulbs to die down naturally and only then remove untidy leaves. The holly can remain untouched unless you want to train it into a standard. Keep an eye on the pulmonaria which is apt to attract greenfly in the spring. Spray as and when necessary.

Give a general slow-release fertilizer early every spring. Divide the pulmonaria, sedum and gaultheria every second autumn. At the same time cut back the roots of the ivy severely if it is growing too rampant and replace the bulbs, if they are showing signs of deterioration. Now is also the time to replenish the soil. Remove as much of the old soil as possible and replace with fresh John Innes No 3.

3 MY FAVOURITE SCENTS

The mahonia produces wafts of lily of the valley-type scents from January through to March. Wild primroses peep out from the bottom. What could be lovelier?

Site
Sun or shade, but a sheltered position is best as the wind can soon topple the pot. The branches of the mahonia seem to act like umbrellas and make the pot unstable. Place it near the front door from late winter to early spring so that you can enjoy the scent.

Container
Large pot: 30cm (12″) in diameter, 35cm (14″) deep.

Planting Time
September to October.

At its best
January through to April. The mahonia is the first to flower and continues to dominate for the next three or four months, then the early blue crocuses, followed by the primroses and white crocuses.

Ingredients
1 *Mahonia japonica*, evergreen shrub with yellow flowers, each like a tiny daffodil, tightly packed on drooping racemes. They smell like lily of the valley. Lovely to cut a few for indoors.
4 wild primroses *Primula vulgaris*; easily available from garden centres these days.
10 pale blue early crocuses *Crocus chrysanthus* 'Blue Pearl'.
10 white crocuses *Crocus vernus* 'Jeanne D'Arc'.
25 litres of John Innes No 3 soil.
Drainage material such as old crocks or pieces of polystyrene.

Method
1. Cover the base of the container with 7.5cm (3″) of drainage material and add 15cm (6″) of soil.
2. Plant the mahonia in the centre of the pot, adjusting the soil level so that the top of the rootball sits just beneath the rim of the pot.
3. Add more soil and plant the primroses around the front and sides of the pot.
4. Plant the crocuses in between the primroses.
5. Fill in the gaps with more soil. Water well. Firm down the plants and add more soil if necessary to bring the level to within 2.5cm (1″) of the rim.

Aftercare
Maintain the soil moisture throughout the year, particularly in late winter and early spring, but never water in frosty weather.

Remove the pot to a shady, sheltered site for the summer and autumn. Feed with a slow-release fertilizer in late winter.

Divide primroses every two years after flowering. At the same time replace the crocuses if they are not performing as well as they should. Take this opportunity to renew the top 5cm (2″) of soil.

4   MID WINTER PLEASURES

Delicate pink flowers emerge from the hellebores in late winter, surrounded by the purple bergenia foliage. Watch them closely. Their nodding heads can be tossed by the wind to reveal a striking picture within.

Site
Shade or partial shade.

Container
Medium terracotta pot: 30cm (12″) in diameter, 27.5cm (11″) deep.

Planting Time
October.

At its best
Late winter to mid spring. First the hellebores flower and then the bergenias.

Ingredients
- 2 *Helleborus orientalis* known as the lenten rose. The broad dark green leaves are often evergreen. The flowers can be crimson, pink, purple or white. They sometimes have spectacular markings inside. By buying when the plants are in flower you can choose which you like best. Keep in the container and plant in the autumn.
- 2 *Bergenia cordifolia* 'Purpurea'. If this particular bergenia is difficult to find choose a mid- to late-flowering one with a purple tinge to its leaves. By flowering in April or May it will be attractive when the hellebore flowers have faded.

15 litres of John Innes No 3 soil.
Drainage material such as old crocks or pieces of polystyrene.

Method
1. Cover the base of the container with 5cm (2″) of drainage material and add 7.5cm (3″) of soil so that when the hellebores and bergenias are planted the tops of their rootballs sit just below the rim of the pot.
2. Plant the bergenias at opposite sides of the pot with the hellebores in between, also near the edge.
3. Add more soil bringing the level to within 2.5cm (1″) of the rim.
4. Water well. Firm down all the plants and add more soil, if necessary, to bring the level back to within 2.5cm (1″) of the rim.

Aftercare
Maintain moist soil throughout the year (the hellebores in particular like a damp soil).

As the bergenias mature they will gradually form a mass of interesting dark foliage which glistens in sunlight. The round, fat leaves are said to be like elephant's ears, hence it is sometimes known by this name. The hellebore leaves are quite different. They are deeply incised and make a delightful contrast. New growth is made in the spring each year. If they get straggly by mid winter, cut them off so the pretty flowers won't be spoilt by untidy foliage.

Apart from keeping the leaves tidy and cutting the flower stems off the bergenia after flowering, there is little maintenance. Remove the top 2.5cm (1″) of soil each autumn and replace with more John Innes No 3. Apply a slow-release fertilizer in the early spring. Both plants are best left undisturbed for a number of years although eventually the bergenias will need dividing.

5   A POT OF SILVER

This is a pot for the whole year with its mass of grey evergreen foliage and the wonderful smell of thyme, crowned by snowdrops, crocuses, white achillea and hybrid pinks all in their season.

Site
Full sun.

Container
Medium pot: 37.5cm (15″) in diameter, 40cm (16″) deep. This one is called a 'pedestal urn' and is made by Whichford Pottery.

Planting Time
October (add snowdrops 'in the green' in March).

At its best
January to February; and June to July.

Ingredients
  1 *Achillea argentea*.
  1 silver lemon-scented thyme *Thymus × citriodorus* 'Silver Queen'.
10 common snowdrops *Galanthus nivalis*; these perform best if planted 'in the green' with their leaves still intact.
  2 hybrid pinks *Dianthus × allwoodii* 'Diane'.
10 *Crocus chrysanthus* 'Lady Killer' (or 'Prins Claus' or 'Whitewell Purple').
25 litres of John Innes No 2 soil.
Drainage material such as old crocks or pieces of polystyrene.

Method
1. Cover the base of the container with 5cm (2″) of drainage material and add sufficient soil to bring the level to within about 10cm (4″) of the rim of the pot.
2. Plant the achillea to the centre-right and the thyme to the centre-left of the pot near the edge.
3. Plant the snowdrops between the thyme and the achillea.
4. Plant one dianthus at the back of the pot, one at the front.
5. Plant the crocuses in the centre of the pot.
6. Fill in the gaps with soil. Water well. Firm in the plants and add more soil if necessary to bring the level to within 2.5cm (1″) of the rim.

Aftercare
Maintain soil moisture throughout the year. Never allow the pot to dry out and never water in frosty weather. Apply a general slow-release fertilizer in early spring and remove long growths on the pinks; deadhead them when they have flowered. Trim all flower heads off the thyme after it has finished flowering. The pinks will need replacing after the second flowering season is over. At the same time divide the achillea and thyme. Repot with new soil.

6 A CONIFER BARREL FOR SPRING

The little violas flower on and off all through the winter, then comes the outstanding display of late daffodils and iberis.

Site
Sun or partial shade.

Container
Wooden half barrel with an inner plastic liner raised on low supports to preserve the wood. The inner container is 40cm (16″) in diameter, 30cm (12″) deep.

Planting Time
September.

At its best
April/May although of interest from September onwards.

Ingredients
  1 slow-growing conifer such as *Chaemaecyparis lawsoniana* 'Ellwoodii'.
15 late daffodils *Narcissus poeticus* 'Actaea'.
  1 *Vinca minor* 'Aureo-variegata'.
  2 *Iberis sempervirens* 'Snowflake'.
  1 strip of purple violas *Viola tricolor* 'Prince Henry'.
40 litres of John Innes No 3 soil.
Drainage material such as old crocks or pieces of polystyrene.

Method
1. Raise the inner container off the floor of the barrel with some low supports and cover the base with 5cm (2″) of drainage material. Add 10cm (4″) of soil.
2. Plant the conifer in the centre of the container, so that the top of its rootball is about 2.5cm (1″) below the rim of the container.
3. Plant the daffodil bulbs around the conifer. Cover with soil so that just their tips show.
4. Plant the periwinkle at the centre-front so that it will trail over the front of the barrel.
5. Plant the iberis on either side of the periwinkle and close to the edge so that it can fall over the sides.
6. Fill in the gaps with soil.
7. Carefully divide the strip of violas and plant around the container.
8. Water well. Firm in the plants and add more soil if necessary to bring the level to within 2.5cm (1″) of the rim.

Aftercare
Maintain soil moisture throughout the year, particularly in early and mid spring. Never water in frosty weather. Allow the daffodils to die down naturally, only removing the unsightly leaves when they have yellowed in late June or July. Discard the violas. At this stage you might like to add a little summer colour using late bedding plants, or try a few chrysanthemums or cyclamen to take the container into the autumn. Deadhead the iberis after flowering and then trim back to encourage dense and tidy growth. If necessary cut back the periwinkle to reduce straggly ends and encourage bushy growth.

Feed the container with a general slow-release fertilizer in early spring. After the second summer replace the top 5cm (2″) of soil. Take care not to damage the bulbs. Replace any that have not flowered well in the second year.

7 A WINTER AND SPRING WINDOW BOX

As winter merges into spring the quiet beauty of the box is transformed into a blaze of colour. Just one planting in September can produce continuity of colour for three or four months. The photographs chart the changes.

Site
Any.

Container
Window box which looks like lead but is actually fibreglass (much cheaper and lighter): 90cm (36″) long, 17.5cm (7″) wide, 17.5cm (7″) deep.

Planting Time
September to October.

At its best
January: the white heather is just beginning to flower, and the lovely gold on the tree heather is complemented by the bright yellow irises. February: the crocuses, white heather and white vinca are in full array. March/April: the anemones, daffodils, periwinkle – and the white heather still – are in flower. Summer and autumn colour can be added through bedding plants.

Ingredients
1 tree heather *Erica arborea* 'Estrella Gold'; wonderful soft golden foliage; excellent for containers.
1 winter-flowering heather *Erica carnea* 'Springwood White'. Its white flowers last for several months from the depths of winter to mid spring.
2 lesser periwinkles: white *Vinca minor* 'Alba' and blue *Vinca minor* 'Aureo-variegata'.
10 yellow dwarf irises *Iris danfordiae*; one of the first bulbs to flower and scented too.
20 early crocuses *Crocus chrysanthus* 'Blue Pearl'.
10 *Anemone blanda* mixed blue and white.
10 *Narcissus tazetta* hybrid 'Minnow'; several creamy flowers on each stem so good value in a container.
5 *Narcissus jonquilla* 'Double Campernelle'.
25 litres of John Innes No 2 soil (both heathers are lime-tolerant).
Drainage material such as old crocks or pieces of polystyrene.

Method

1. Cover the base of the container with 2.5cm (1″) of drainage material and add 5cm (2″) of soil.
2. Plant the 'Minnow' in two groups of five at either end of the box. Plant the 'Double Campernelle' in the centre.
3. Raise the soil level so that just the tips of the bulbs are showing and then plant the irises in a group in the centre in between the daffodils.
4. Plant the two vincas at either end so that they trail over the sides.
5. Plant the golden tree heather to centre-left and 'Springwood White' to centre-right quite near the front so that it can tumble over the edge.
6. Plant the crocuses and anemones mixed right across the box.
7. Add more soil to bring the level to within 2cm (1″) of the rim. Water well. Firm in the plants and add more soil if necessary.

Aftercare

Maintain the soil moisture throughout the year, but particularly during the late winter and early spring when so much growth is taking place. Add a slow-release fertilizer in late autumn each year to achieve best results.

Trim back the heathers after flowering to allow them to regenerate and remain neat. Allow all the bulbs to die down naturally in the early summer and then remove the dead leaves. Remove the top inch of soil and replace with more John Innes No 2, bringing the level back to within 2.5cm (1″) of the rim. Now you can plant a few small summer bedding plants, or sow a few nasturtium seeds for late summer and autumn colour.

If the periwinkle trails get too straggly, just tuck them into the soil elsewhere in the box so that they will root and form new plants.

This box will mature well over the course of the next two or three years; after that time some subjects will need replacing. By then the heathers will have grown too large and would be better planted in a tub or pot. The vincas can be divided and used for other pots or hanging baskets.

8   A FLAMING CHIMNEY POT

An easy spring planting to brighten any front door or patio corner. It is easily transformed into a glorious summer arrangement by the simplest of changes (as can be seen in these two photographs).

Site
Sunny.

Container
Tall clay chimney pot fitted with an inner plastic container which in this case is 30cm (12″) in diameter, 22.5cm (9″) deep. This scheme can be adapted to almost any container.

Planting Time
October to November, and then May.

At its best
April; and June to September.

Ingredients
8 mid- to late-season tulips *Tulipa* 'Fidelio'; red with orange tips, a good colour against the clay chimney pot.
1 *Vinca minor* 'Alba', the lovely white lesser periwinkle. Choose quite a large plant so that it will look effective. New growth in late spring and early summer is a marvellous fresh green and looks wonderful against the dark red geranium. It continues to flower well into early summer.
1 red upright geranium *Pelargonium* 'Bruni' which was culture virus indexed with large, brightly-coloured flowers. Any good strong red geranium would be appropriate.
½ strip of mixed lobelia *Lobelia erinus* 'String of Pearls'; dark blue would be more dramatic.
10 litres of John Innes No 2 soil.
Drainage material such as old crocks or pieces of polystyrene.

Method
1. Rest the plastic pot inside the top of the chimney pot and cover the base with 5cm (2″) of drainage material. Add 10cm (4″) of soil.
2. Space the tulips in the centre and at the sides of the pot leaving the centre front free. Push them down firmly but gently into the soil so that they are completely hidden.
3. Plant the vinca at the front of the pot so that it trails over the side of the chimney pot.
4. Top up with soil bringing the level to within 2.5cm (1″) of the rim. Water well, firm in the vinca and add more soil if necessary.
5. Around June – when the tulips have gone and the foliage has turned yellow – the geranium should be planted in the centre of the pot and the lobelia around the sides, using extra soil as you do so.

Aftercare
Maintain soil moisture throughout the year, but never water in frosty weather. Allow the tulips to die down naturally and only when the foliage has turned yellow should it be removed in order to tidy up the pot. This will probably happen in June. Deadhead the geranium regularly to encourage new flowers and to keep the pot tidy. Give an occasional liquid feed during the summer months.

In the autumn pot up the geranium and save it for another year (see page 86). Discard the lobelia. After the second flowering season, the tulips may grow weaker and need replacing. Take the opportunity to divide the vinca and replace the soil.

9 AN UNUSUAL POT OF SCENTED BULBS

The white grape hyacinth and the more unusual yellow iris are scented. Together they make a delightful picture, rather different from other spring displays. Easy to plant and simple to look after.

Site
Sunny.

Container
Yellow Chinese pot: 27.5cm (11″) in diameter, 20cm (8″) deep.

Planting Time
September.

At its best
April to early May.

Ingredients
3 *Iris bucharica*, a bulbous iris from Turkestan, about 46cm (18″) high with a succession of cream and yellow flowers, all beautifully scented and lasting over a long period. Even the leaves look attractive as they catch the sunlight.
10 white grape hyacinths *Muscari botryoides* 'Album'. It was once known as the Pearls of Spain.
12 litres of John Innes No 2 soil.
Drainage material such as old crocks or pieces of polystyrene.

Method
1. Cover the base of the container with 5cm (2″) of drainage material and add sufficient soil to bring the level to within 2.5cm (1″) of the rim.
2. Plant the iris bulbs around the centre of the pot so that their tips are about 5 cm (2″) below the surface of the soil.

3. Plant the white grape hyacinth bulbs around the edge of the container so that the top of the bulb is about 5cm (2″) below the surface of the soil.
4. Water well.

Aftercare
Make sure the soil is kept just moist throughout the autumn and winter but never water in frosty weather. It is particularly important that during the flowering period and for several weeks afterwards the level of moisture is increased. But after the foliage dies down naturally in June withhold all watering until the autumn. The bulbs like to be dry for the summer so the pot can be left in a quiet, sunny spot and forgotten. No extra plants have been added for the summer months as this would spoil the drying-out process.

Top-dress with a little more soil early the following spring. Repot in early autumn after two or three years. Remove offshoots.

10 A WHITE DICENTRA POT

White dicentra makes a splendid subject for a pot. It looks delicate and graceful with its ferny foliage. Its flowers hang down in long racemes, each flower shaped like a heart.

Site
Sun or partial shade. Growth starts in late winter/early spring depending on the season and can be badly damaged by frost. So cover with sacking if frost threatens or move to a frost-free place – one of the advantages of growing it in a container. As growth matures shelter it from strong winds as the delicate stems may be broken. The Victorians often used to grow its pink relative known as the 'bleeding heart' in pots in the conservatory where it was easily forced. It makes an ideal specimen whether white or pink.

Container
Medium-sized terracotta pot: 30cm (12″) in diameter, 25cm (10″) deep.

Planting Time
October to March. An October planting will produce a bigger show the following spring.

At its best
April and May for the dicentra and then August and September for the sedum.

Ingredients
1 medium to large white dicentra *Dicentra spectabilis* 'Alba'. Should this be difficult to find, plant the better-known pink variety. It will look equally beautiful although less unusual.
3 *Sedum spectabile* 'Autumn Joy' with fleshy leaves and salmon-pink flowers. Others are rose-pink. If you find it in a five-litre pot, buy only one and divide before planting.
15 litres of John Innes No 3 soil.
Drainage material such as old crocks or pieces of polystyrene.

Method
1. Cover the base of the container with 5cm (2″) of drainage material and add sufficient soil to bring the level three-quarters of the way up the pot.
2. Plant the dicentra in the centre of the pot with the three sedums around the edge. Adjust the soil level as necessary to get the top of the rootball sitting about 2.5cm (1″) below the rim of the pot.
3. Fill in the gaps with soil. Water well. Firm in the plants and add more soil if necessary to bring level to within 2.5cm (1″) of the rim.

Aftercare
Maintain soil moisture throughout the year but particularly in the spring. Never water in frosty weather. If frost does threaten protect the pot so that the early shoots are not damaged. Similarly, protect the plant during spring storms when the stems might be damaged by strong winds.

The dicentra will die down completely during the summer. Remove untidy stems so that the sedum can be enjoyed. This will grow quickly in the summer months and by late summer/early autumn it will be a mass of colour. Again it needs shelter from strong winds as the stems are rather brittle. Butterflies love the flowers. Don't be tempted to remove the dead flower stems over the winter. Leave them until early spring, then take them away.

Top-dress with more John Innes No 3 in the late winter and add a general slow-release fertilizer in early spring. Apply a liquid feed in April and again in August. Leave undisturbed for three years and then divide and replant the entire pot using fresh soil.

11 HEADY SCENTS, SHADY DELIGHTS

I noticed this combination planted in a wide pot in a cottage garden and thought it delightful. The fragrance from the lilly of the valley is outstanding while the attractive leaves of the hosta provide a perfect back cloth.

Site
Shade or partial shade.

Container
Medium to large terracotta pot or wooden tub: 35cm (14″) in diameter, 30cm (12″) deep.

Planting Time
September or October.

At its best
May; the hostas will flower in July and August.

Ingredients
  6 plump lily of the valley crowns *Convallaria majalis*.
  3 hostas *Hosta* 'Thomas Hogg' or any medium-sized hosta eg *Hosta crispula* with white margins to echo the white lily of the valley flowers.
30 litres of John Innes No 3 soil.
Drainage material such as old crocks or pieces of polystyrene.

Method
1. Cover the base of the container with 5cm (2″) of drainage material and add sufficient soil to bring the level to within 2.5cm (1″) of the rim.
2. Plant the lily of the valley crowns in the centre of the pot about 7.5cm (3″) apart, with their pointed ends uppermost so that the tips are just below the surface of the soil.
3. Plant the hostas around the edge of the pot so that their tips are about 2.5cm (1″) below the rim.
4. Water well, firm in the hostas and add more soil if necessary.

Aftercare
Maintain the soil moisture throughout the year but particularly in spring and summer. Top-dress with more John Innes No 3, leaf-mould or peat each autumn when the leaves have died down.

Slugs are rather partial to hosta leaves so watch out for them. Destroy any seen climbing up the pot; you can also scatter slug pellets around the base of the pot and on the soil around the edge. Otherwise use a liquid anti-slug solution or place the pot in the middle of a circle of sharp grit which the slugs will hate.

After three years the plants can be divided and planted again using new soil. Grow the surplus plants in another container or in a shady spot in the garden.

12 CREAMY AND FRAGRANT

Smilacina is an unusual subject for a pot, but it is so delightfully fragrant that it should be enjoyed far more. Ideal for a shady nook on the terrace or in the basement garden.

Site
Shade or partial shade.

Container
Medium-sized terracotta 'Cherub' pot: 30cm (12″) in diameter, 25cm (10″) deep.

Planting Time
October to March, though you will get a better first-season display from an autumn planting.

At its best
May and June for the scent, June to August for the lime-green flowers (wonderful for flower arrangements) of *Alchemilla mollis*. Another pleasure is to see the alchemilla with water on its leaves after it has been raining. Tiny drops are held by the hairs of the leaves – most attractive.

Ingredients
1 *Smilacina racemosa*.
1 *Alchemilla mollis* also known as Lady's mantle.
12 litres of John Innes No 3 soil.
Drainage material such as old crocks or pieces of polystyrene.

Method
1. Cover the base of the container with 5cm (2″) drainage material and add sufficient soil to bring the level to within 2.5cm (1″) of the rim.
2. Plant the smilacina towards the centre-back of the pot.
3. Plant the alchemilla towards the centre-front.
4. Water well. Firm in the plants and add more soil if necessary to regain the former level.

Aftercare
Maintain soil moisture throughout the year but particularly during the early summer when the plants are in full growth. They both like to be kept moist. Move the pot to somewhere where it can be fully

appreciated whilst it is in flower; it can be tucked away out of sight later on. Cut the alchemilla flower stems to within an inch of the soil after flowering. They will both die down and lie dormant for the winter.

Top-dress with more soil, leaf mould or peat in the early spring. Apply a general slow-release fertilizer at the same time. The pot can be left undisturbed for several years. Eventually in the third or fourth October, empty the pot, divide the plants and replant using new soil. Find a shady, damp spot in the garden for the excess plants.

13   FOXY HAUNTS AMONG FERNS AND HOSTAS

Tall foxglove spires rise out of the carpet of hostas and ferns. Together they make a wonderful show in early summer.

Site
Shade or partial shade. Perfect beside a north-facing back door or in a shady basement.

Container
Wooden half barrel with an inner plastic liner 40cm (16″) in diameter, and 30cm (12″) deep to give extra protection to the wood. Raise it up slightly off the floor of the barrel.

Planting Time
The trilliums are best planted as soon as available in August or September. The rest of the plants can be planted either then or in early spring in which case leave the trilliums until the following autumn.

At its best
April to August. Once established, the trilliums will start to flower just as the hostas and ferns make their wonderful new growth in late April and May. The foxgloves will begin to flower in June starting at the bottom of their tall spikes, gradually rising to the top until just a few pink speckled flowers are left nodding on the end. Then the hostas will produce their blooms, smaller but still pretty.

Ingredients
1 wild foxglove *Digitalis purpurea*. Normally biennial but often perennial under ideal shady and moist conditions.

3 hardy ferns. *Athyrium filix – femina* is our native deciduous lady fern (in the photograph it is the one most visible). *Phyllitis (Asplenium) scolopendrium* is the common hart's tongue fern and *Phyllitis scolopendrium* 'Christatum' is another hart's tongue fern but its fronds are branched and crested at their tips. Both these are evergreen, which gives the barrel its interest throughout the winter months.

2 hostas *Hosta fortunei* with blue-green leaves and handsome lilac-blue flowers in July and August.

3 *Trillium grandiflorum* known sometimes as wake robin. It is from the eastern United States and has wide white flowers on short, arching stems. They are expensive to buy, but once established will form a very pretty clump. Otherwise substitute 10 white anemones *Anemone blanda* 'White Splendour' or some mixed bluebells.

40 litres of John Innes No 2 soil with peat or leaf-mould worked in as well.

Drainage material such as old crocks or pieces of polystyrene.

Method
1. Cover the base of the inner plastic liner or container with 5cm (2″) drainage material and add sufficient soil to bring the level to within 7.5cm (3″) of the rim.
2. Plant the foxglove at the centre-back of the barrel.
3. Plant the two hart's tongue ferns and hostas on either side and the lady fern at the centre-front.
4. Plant the trilliums spaced out across the middle of the container in between the hostas.
5. Fill in the gaps with soil bringing the level to within 2.5cm (1″) of the rim of the container.
6. Water well and firm in the plants. Add more soil if necessary.

Aftercare
This planting scheme likes moist, shady conditions. Do not let it dry out, particularly in the spring and summer months. Remove the flower stalks from the foxglove and hostas after flowering, and cut back growth of the lady fern in the autumn. If the foxglove dies after flowering replace it in the autumn so that you will still get a show the following year. Top-dress with leaf-mould or more compost early each spring. Use a slow-release fertilizer in April. Apply a liquid feed in early June.

Lift and replant in September every third year using new soil. The foxglove can be replaced. The hostas will need dividing. The lady fern will need replanting as its rootball tends to rise out of the ground, and as it gets higher it is more liable to dry out. Try not to disturb the trilliums any more than necessary as they prefer to be left alone.

14   RICH GREENS IN AN ACER POT

This acer makes an outstanding subject for a container and looks particularly handsome underplanted by the bright green carpet of plants.

Site
Sun or partial shade; prefers a moist, cool soil so it is best to keep the pot itself in the shade even if the leaves are in the sun. Take care that the sun does not shine on new leaves if there has been a frost. Protect from cold winds.

Container
Large terracotta pot made by Whichford Pottery: 40cm (16″) in diameter, 25cm (10″) deep.

Planting Time
September, October or March.

At its best
May and June for the fresh green foliage, and then September for the autumnal tints.

Ingredients
1 *Acer palmatum* 'Dissectum'; a slow-growing, lime-tolerant Japanese maple which has very finely-cut light green leaves.

4 *Sempervivum tectorum* or houseleek. Together they will form a dense cluster in two or three years. There are many different colours to choose from.

1 *Rosularia sedoides*; small grey-green rosettes.

1 *Sagina glabra* 'Aurea'; forms a green cushion and bears a mass of tiny white flowers in May and June.

1 *Sedum acre* 'Aureum'; a stonecrop which gently tumbles over the edge of the pot. It has bright, pale yellow shoot tips from March to June. Yellow flowers in June and July.

20 litres of John Innes No 3 soil.

Drainage material such as old crocks or pieces of polystyrene.

Method
1. Cover the base of the container with 5cm (2″) of drainage material and add about 10cm (4″) of soil.

2. Plant the acer so that the top of its rootball sits just 2.5cm (1″) below the rim of the container. Add 5cm (2″) more soil.
3. Plant the sempervivums in a widely-spaced group at the back of the acer.
4. Plant the rosularia in front of the acer.
5. Plant the sagina to the right and the sedum to the left of the acer.
6. Fill in the gaps with soil and adjust the plants so that they sit just below the surface of the pot.
7. Water well, firm in the plants and add more soil if necessary.

Aftercare
Keep the soil moist at all times, particularly in the spring and early summer. Shelter from strong winds, and avoid sites which catch the early morning sun in late spring when there might have been a frost. Top-dress early each spring with a general slow-release fertilizer. The pot will need little attention for two or three years except to curb the growth of the sagina as it threatens to spread over the pot. It can easily be pulled out where not wanted. Restrict the sedum and rosularia as well, if necessary.

The acer is such a valuable tree for a container that it is worth potting on into a bigger pot after three years. Late autumn is the best time to do it.

15   THE SPLENDOUR OF ROSES

This rose pot created a sensation. The pinks and blues complemented each other so well that it was a real joy to behold.

Site
Open and sunny position, although light shade is acceptable.

Container
Large terracotta pot: 35cm (14″) in diameter, 27.5cm (11″) deep.

Planting Time
October or November is best but can still be planted until March.

At its best
June and July when all the flowers are in bloom together.

Ingredients
  2 bush roses *Rosa* 'Pink Bells' from John Mattocks Nursery in Oxford. They make excellent container plants. Other colours are white or crimson-pink.
  1 *Alchemilla mollis* or Lady's mantle; a favourite with flower arrangers for its lime-green flowers and soft, hairy leaves.
  1 *Veronica spicata* 'Blue Fox' with bright lavender-blue spires to set off the pink roses.
20 litres of John Innes No 3 soil.
Drainage material such as old crocks or pieces of polystyrene.

Method
  1. Cover the base of the container with 5cm (2″) of drainage material and add 10cm (4″) soil.
  2. Plant the two roses on either side of the pot, turning them round until the best natural overall shape is created. Adjust the soil level so that the top of the rootball sits about 2.5cm (1″) below the rim of the container.
  3. Plant the alchemilla at the back of the pot and the veronica at the front, keeping the rootballs at the same level as the roses.
  4. Fill in the gaps with soil. Water well. Firm in the plants and add more soil if necessary to bring the level to within 2.5cm (1″) of the rim.

Aftercare
Maintain soil moisture throughout the year, particularly in the late spring and summer. Cut down the veronica to just above soil level in November. Remove the dead stems of the alchemilla after flowering. Apply a well-balanced rose fertilizer in the spring when the new growth begins.

Lightly prune the roses in their third year of growth in February or March. After the third flowering they should probably be discarded. By then the alchemilla and veronica will need dividing. Repot them with two new roses.

With container-grown roses such an excellent display can only be expected during their second and third year. Use a large pot and look after it well with adequate attention to water and feed.

16   A SUMMER POT OF SOFT PINKS AND GREYS

The delicate pink flowers of the lavatera look lovely with the soft greys of the lavender, silver thyme and variegated ivy.

Site
Full sun and sheltered.

Container
Large terracotta pot: 35cm (14″) in diameter, 25cm (10″) deep.

Planting Time
October to March.

At its best
June to October.

Ingredients
1 *Lavatera thuringiaca* 'Barnsley'; a fast-growing but delicately-coloured shrubby mallow which continues to flower from June to October.
1 *Lavandula angustifolia* 'Hidcote'; a compact form with lovely lavender-blue flowers from July to September.
1 variegated ivy *Hedera helix* 'Glacier' with small silver-grey variegated leaves edged with white.
1 *Thymus* × *citriodorus* 'Silver Queen'; a silver lemon-scented thyme which tumbles over the edge of the pot and smells wonderful especially when it has just rained or been watered.
20 litres of John Innes No 2 soil.
Drainage material such as old crocks or pieces of polystyrene.

Method
1. Cover the base of the container with 5cm (2″) of drainage material and add 13cm (5″) of soil.
2. Plant the lavatera at the centre-back of the pot with the lavender in front. Adjust the soil level so that the plants sit with the top of their rootball 2.5cm (1″) below the rim of the pot.
3. Plant the ivy on one side and the thyme on the other so that they also sit 2.5cm (1″) below the rim of the pot.
4. Fill in the gaps with soil. Water well. Firm in the plants and add more soil if necessary.

Aftercare
Maintain soil moisture throughout the year but

particularly in the spring and summer months. Apply a general fertilizer each spring and give a liquid feed in July and August. Trim back the lavender each year after flowering and remove dead flower stems. If you want to dry the lavender flowers cut the stems before the flowers are fully open, then hang them in a cool, airy place to dry. Both the thyme and the lavender can be used in cooking. They also make fragrant and attractive subjects for a small flower arrangement.

Repot in late autumn after three years, using a larger container. You can easily take cuttings from all these subjects; especially useful are the thyme and lavender. These could then replace the older plants when the repotting is done.

17   WHITE AGAPANTHUS

The first agapanthus was brought from the Cape of Good Hope in 1629. Since then it has become a prize subject for a container, best grown on its own and left undisturbed. These days we can choose from deep violet-blue, mid blue, pale blue and the purest white. All of them make a wonderful display but perhaps white is a little more distinctive and it certainly shows up well against a dark or stone background.

Site
Full sun, sheltered.

Container
Old orchid pot: 37.5cm (15″) in diameter, 35cm (14″) deep, with small holes all around it; attractive but not essential. The plants flower best when left undisturbed and crowded, but this eventually causes problems for the pot as the roots become too

restricted and might break it. Gertrude Jekyll suggested that wooden barrels should be used instead, but even they rot.

Planting Time
April.

At its best
July and August.

Ingredients
3 Agapanthus 'Bressingham White' or A. campanulatus 'Albus'; both available by mail order from Bressingham Gardens (see the list of specialist suppliers on page 225). White agapanthus are also available from garden centres supplied by O. A. Taylor Bulbs Ltd.
15 litres of John Innes No 2 soil.
Drainage material such as large crocks or small pieces of polystyrene.

Method
1. Cover the base of the container with 7.5cm (3″) of drainage material and add 10cm (4″) of soil.
2. Space the plants (fleshy roots) around the pot, well away from the sides, and adjust the soil level so that the crowns sit 7.5cm (3″) below the rim of the container.
3. Add more soil so that the level comes to within 2.5cm (1″) of the rim. Water well.

Aftercare
Maintain soil moisture throughout the spring and summer months but allow to become much drier in the autumn. The pot can be brought into a cold greenhouse or garage for the winter to give it extra protection, although this is not essential if hardy bulbs have been planted, but it might help if the weather is very severe. Keep barely moist throughout the winter; never water in frosty weather. Increase the supply when growth starts again in the spring.

The cut flowers will make a stunning indoor flower arrangement, or if left on the plants to go to seed they may be used for dried flower arrangements later in the year. Clear the stems and leaves as they die off in the autumn and winter. The pot is best left undisturbed for several years, as overcrowding is good for flowering. Eventually divide and repot in April. Use a slow-release fertilizer in the early spring each year.

18   AN ALPINE POT

The rich blues and pinks of campanula and thrift dominate this small alpine pot and provide a glorious show of colour.

Site
Full sun.

Container
Small terracotta strawberry pot: 22.5cm (9″) in diameter and 27.5cm (11″) deep, with six holes around the sides.

Planting Time
September to March. All these plants are available in the Bressingham Gardens mail order catalogue or from garden centres which stock the Bressingham plants (for address see page 225).

At its best
May to July but neat and attractive all year round.

Ingredients
1 *Campanula carpatica* 'Wheatley Violet' with deep blue flowers from June to August.
2 *Armeria maritima* 'Dusseldorf Pride'; this thrift flowers from June to August and forms compact evergreen hummocks.
2 *Arabis ferdinandi-coburgii* 'Old Gold' with sprays of white flowers in April and May and golden variegated leaves.
1 *Campanula carpatica* 'Bressingham White' with white flowers from June to August.
1 *Thymus serpyllum* 'Albus', a creeping white thyme.
1 *Sedum* 'Lidakense'; blue-green mat with pink flowers.
1 *Sempervivum* 'Proud Zelda', this one has very tight green rosettes. There are plenty of different ones to choose from.
10 litres of John Innes No 2 soil.
10 handfuls of horticultural grit.
Drainage material such as old crocks or pieces of polystyrene.

Method
1. Cover the base of the container with 5cm (2″) of drainage material and add sufficient soil to bring the level equal to the bottom ring of holes.
2. Plant the blue campanula, one of the armerias and one of the arabis in each of the three bottom holes.
3. Make sure the roots are sitting firmly on the bed of soil. Mix in two handfuls of grit in the centre of the pot and bring the soil level up to the bottom of the top ring of holes.
4. Plant the second arabis in the upper hole between the thrift and the campanula below; the other thrift in between the campanula and the arabis below; and the white campanula in between the thrift and the blue campanula below. It is important to maintain a balanced arrangement and, therefore, to avoid placing the same two plants next to or immediately above each other.
5. Add more grit in the centre and more soil all round, and firm in the roots.
6. Plant the top of the pot with the white thyme over the blue campanula. The sedum and sempervivum will then go side by side above the lower thrift and the lower arabis.
7. Add more grit in the centre of the pot. Fill in the remaining gaps with soil.
8. Firm in the plants and water gently but thoroughly. Add more soil, if necessary, to bring the level to within 2.5cm (1″) of the rim of the pot.

Aftercare
Water regularly but carefully to avoid the soil running through the holes (once the pot is established and the roots have grown this will no longer be a problem). The added grit is to encourage drainage and to stop the soil becoming compacted. Apply a liquid feed sparingly throughout early and mid summer. Deadhead all flowers when they have died down to maintain a neat appearance.

Repot after three years taking the opportunity to divide the plants and renew the soil.

19   AN ALPINE TROUGH

This is a butler's sink to which a mixture of sand and cement has been applied to create the stone effect. Filled with a few choice winter and spring bulbs and a lively variety of summer alpines, it can look extremely attractive.

Site
Full sun.

Container
'Stone' trough created out of a butler's sink: 75cm (30") long, 37.5cm (15") wide, 25cm (10") deep.

Planting Time
September or March. The snowdrops can be bought dry or 'in the green' with leaves intact after flowering in March. The fritillarias can be purchased from most garden centres stocking O. A. Taylor Bulbs. Many of the other plants can be bought from the Bressingham Gardens mail order catalogue or from garden centres which stock their plants. (For addresses, see page 225.)

At its best
April to August; and end January to early February.

Ingredients
(These plants represent just a few of the many alpines available in our garden centres today. You don't have to buy all of them or even the same ones to have a wonderful show in your trough. Use these merely as a guideline. But do take care to purchase low-growing plants, find a few with good foliage colour and choose with regard to flowering times so that you have a good colour span throughout the summer and spring too. Also beware of soil type: choose plants that either all tolerate lime, or all prefer an acid soil.)

1 *Sagina glabra* 'Aurea'; a low carpet of yellow-green studded with tiny white flowers in May and June.
1 *Ajuga reptans* 'Purpurea'; makes a carpet of reddish-purple leaves from which bright blue flower spikes emerge in May and June.
1 *Sedum aizoon*; compact growth with yellow flowers in July.
1 *Dianthus deltoides* 'Albus' or try one of the other cultivars.
1 *Sisyrinchium brachypus*; iris-like with bright yellow flowers from July to October.

1 *Phlox adsurgens* 'Wagon Wheel' with salmon-pink flowers in June and July.
1 white viola *Viola cornuta* 'Alba'; flowering from May throughout the summer.
1 *Sedum reflexum* with yellow flowers opening in June/July.
1 *Campanula cochlearifolia* 'Cambridge Blue' with blue bell-like flowers from July to September.
1 *Penstemon procerus*; a neat mat-forming perennial with blue flowers from May to July.
3 *Fritillaria michailovskyi* with beautiful gold bell-shaped flowers in April. A short, neat and unusual flower. Rather expensive. Available at some garden centres; otherwise buy through a bulb specialist. You could instead try *Fritillaria meleagris* – the snake's head fritillaria – but it is taller.
6 *Galanthus nivalis* 'Magnet'; a rather special snowdrop with tall, large flowers on slender stems, available from specialist bulb suppliers. Best ordered in January/February and purchased through the post or direct in March when they will be sent 'in the green' with their leaves intact. Plant immediately. Expensive. Alternatively, try the common snowdrop.
35 litres of John Innes No 2 soil.
20 litres of horticultural grit: 15 litres to mix in with the soil for added drainage and 5 litres to scatter on the surface of the trough after planting.
Drainage material for base of container in the form of old crocks or small pieces of polystyrene.

Method
1. Cover the base of the container with 5cm (2") of drainage material.
2. Mix soil with half the horticultural grit.
3. Add sufficient soil and grit mixture to the trough to bring the level to within 7.5cm (3") of the top.
4. Take stock of your plants and see which ones will complement each other with regard to foliage, flowering times, colour of flowers, height etc.
5. Around the edge of the trough plant the bright green sagina, contrast the reddish-purple ajuga, the neat sedum aizoon, the neat cushion of the dianthus, the swordlike sisyrinchium, the straggly but lovely pink phlox, the pretty white viola, the trailing sedum reflexum, and complete the edging with the blue campanula.

6. In the centre plant the low penstemon, the fritillarias to the left and – in March – the 'Magnet' snowdrops to the right.
7. Fill in the gaps with soil. Water well and add more soil if necessary.
8. Cover all exposed soil with grit. This will keep the surface free of excess moisture, and also look very attractive.

Aftercare
Maintain soil moisture throughout the year but particularly in the spring and summer months.

Most of these plants prefer their roots to be left undisturbed but inevitably some will grow faster than others and need to be kept in check. Where this occurs be ruthless and cut back excessive growth. This might specifically happen with the ajuga, penstemon, sedum reflexum and sagina. Deadhead unsightly dying flowers except on the sisyrinchium which is best left until the late autumn when you should cut back both leaves and flowering stems to ground level.

Feed sparingly as many of these alpines do not enjoy a rich diet. A general slow-release fertilizer should be applied in early spring but do not put it around the dianthus.

If a plant fails for some reason then simply discard and try another alpine, or perhaps leave the gap to be filled by a neighbour.

20   THE LONGDON GREEN POT

This combination is inspired by a planting scheme which sits beneath a warm, south-facing stable-block wall in the heart of the Midlands. The fern is a native evergreen and so provides interest all the year round. It is underplanted with bulbs. First come the bluebells as a natural companion. Then in the autumn it is transformed by the exquisite pink nerines.

Site
Sunny and sheltered.

Container
Terracotta pot: 30cm (12″) in diameter, 27.5cm (11″) deep.

Planting Time
August or April.

At its best
May; and September to November.

Ingredients
  3 *Nerine bowdenii* 'Fenwick's Variety'; this is a hardy nerine which will only require protection in very severe weather.
  2 evergreen ferns *Polypodium vulgare* 'Cornubiense'; a delightful fern which was originally found wild in Cornwall.
10 bluebells *Hyacinthoides non-scripta (Scilla nutans)*.
10 litres of John Innes No 2 soil.
Drainage material such as old crocks or pieces of polystyrene.

Method
1. Cover the base of the container with 5cm (2″) of drainage material and add 7.5cm (3″) of soil.
2. Plant the nerine bulbs quite widely spaced apart but away from the edges of the pot.
3. Cover with soil until just the tips of the bulbs show.
4. Plant the ferns on either side of the pot with the bluebells spaced in between.
5. Add more soil to bring the level to within 2.5cm (1″) of the rim of the pot.
6. Water well and firm down all the plants, adding more soil if necessary.

Aftercare
Maintain soil moisture throughout the year but particularly in spring and summer. Keep sheltered in severe weather, covered by a loose straw mulch. After the bluebells have died down, remove untidy leaves and begin a fortnightly liquid feed for the benefit of the nerines until flowering is finally over. Keep the pot tidy by removing unsightly nerine flowers when they have died, and old fern leaves.

Only repot when the bulbs appear to be regressing and not producing as many flowers as in previous years.

21   SNOW IN A SUMMER BASKET

Two roses called 'Snow carpet', a sprinkling of lobelia and some parsley provide the basis of this beautiful white hanging basket.

Site
Sunny.

Container
Wire hanging basket: 35cm (14″) in diameter with a sturdy 27.5cm (11″) bracket.

Planting Time
Order the roses in summer or at latest early autumn from a rose specialist. Plant on receipt. The parsley can be added at the same time if it is available then, otherwise wait until early spring and then plant the lobelia in early to mid May. If you manage to find container-grown roses for sale in a garden centre then you can make the basket up at any time, although the results will be better if done well before the main flowering season starts. NB: This basket will be in peak condition in its second and third year, not the first.

At its best
Mid June to July.

Ingredients
  2 dwarf patio roses, *Rosa* 'Snow Carpet'; from R. Harkness and Co Ltd (see the list of specialist suppliers, page 225). This is a charming little rose which produces a dense mass of tiny white flowers. Use the petals to scatter on salads or to decorate cakes. An alternative pink one is 'Fairyland' or try the new rose called 'Suma' from Japan which has rose-red flowers and leaves that turn crimson in autumn.
  2 parsley plants *Petroselinum crispum*; pretty foliage and, of course, good in the kitchen.
  ½ strip of white lobelia *Lobelia erinus* 'White Lady'; this is poisonous so don't try eating it! Odd blue plants often appear amongst the white ones.
10 litres of John Innes No 2 soil.
  2 handfuls of horticultural grit.
  1 basketful of moss bought from a florist's shop.
  1 circle of plastic sheeting, cut about the same size as a dinner plate.

Method

1. Line the basket with a generous thickness of moss, starting at the base and working up the sides so that you form a collar above the rim of the basket.
2. Cut four 2.5cm (1″) slits in the plastic circle and place over the moss lining in the bottom.
3. Spread two handfuls of grit over the plastic circle and then add 7.5cm (3″) of soil.
4. Plant the two roses either side of the basket so that their shape complements each other.
5. Adjust the soil level and add the parsley around the edge between the roses. If not yet available plant two empty plant pots to mark the spot and plant them later in the spring.
6. Water well. Firm in the plants and add more soil to bring the level to within 2.5cm (1″) of the rim. Add more moss if necessary. It is most important to retain the collar right up to the rim of the basket as this helps to retain the soil.
7. The half strip of lobelia should be added in May, tucked in around the front and sides.

Aftercare

Water generously from April through to the end of the autumn; in hot weather this will mean daily or even twice daily. Be patient and careful so that the water really soaks in every time you apply it. It is important to remember to keep the soil moist throughout the winter.

This is a suitable basket for a combined insecticide and feed pellet. Otherwise feed regularly with a liquid fertilizer throughout May, June and early July, and spray for greenfly etc whenever necessary.

The parsley makes a delightful companion plant with roses, and both of course have a use in the kitchen.

These roses will be at their best in their second and third year. Replant each March with fresh soil and moss, new parsley plants and lobelia in due course. Cut out any dead or damaged stems, and prune to keep the shape attractive for the basket. The roots may be lightly pruned at the same time to encourage new growth.

22   SECOND TIME ROUND

Have you ever wished that you did not have to replant your hanging baskets each year? Well, here is one planting scheme that looked really lovely the first year and then had a quiet winter lying dormant in the conservatory. Then, surprisingly, in the second year it gave this wonderful display.

Site
Shade or partial shade; frost-free greenhouse or conservatory for the winter months.

Container
Wire hanging basket: 35cm (14″) in diameter with a sturdy 27.5cm (11″) bracket.

Planting Time
Mid to end May in the first year.

At its best
June to September in the first and second years.

Ingredients
2 strips of pink and white begonias *Begonia semper-florens*. If you choose all red fuchsias then look for red rather than pink begonias. There are some beautiful shades these days and some of them have dark bronze leaves which contrast well with the flowers.
2 strips of pale blue or white trailing lobelia *Lobelia erinus* 'Blue Cascade' or 'White Cascade'. This was planted the first year but not the second.
2 variegated fuchsias *Fuchsia* 'Golden Marinka' with golden foliage and red flowers.
2 pendulous fuchsias *Fuchsia* 'Cascade' make an excellent shape for a basket. 'Swingtime' or 'Snowcap' are handsome basket varieties as well.
10 litres of John Innes No 2 soil.
2 handfuls of horticultural grit.
1 basketful of moss bought from a florist's shop.
1 circle of plastic sheeting, cut about the same size as a dinner plate.

Method
1. Line the basket with a generous thickness of moss, starting at the base and working halfway up the sides.
2. Cut four 2.5cm (1″) slits in the plastic circle and place over the moss lining in the bottom of the basket.
3. Spread the grit over the plastic circle and add 5cm (2″) of soil.

4. Divide the strips of begonias and lobelia and plant about half of them alternately around the top of the moss. Make sure their roots are firmly in contact with the soil.
5. Add 5cm (2″) more moss and soil and repeat the process with more begonias and lobelia leaving three of each for the top.
6. Add more moss so that it forms a collar about 2.5cm (1″) above the rim of the basket.
7. Plant the variegated fuchsias on either side of the basket and the other two on the opposite sides in between.
8. Plant the remaining begonias in the centre of the basket and the lobelia around the edge.
9. Firm down all the plants, fill in the gaps with soil and add more moss if necessary so that it forms an unbroken rim around the top of the basket.
10. Water gently but well so that the soil settles and the plants all get a good drink.

Aftercare
Water generously throughout the summer; in hot weather this will mean once or twice a day. Each week, from June to September, give a liquid feed. Spray for greenfly etc as necessary and deadhead regularly to encourage flowering.

At the end of the summer take the basket into a frost-free greenhouse or conservatory. It will continue to flourish for a few more weeks but then allow it to become dry. Cut off all the begonia stems and remove the dead lobelia (if it is still alive just cut it right back and let it grow again next year).

In late February start to water again, just a little at first until growth is properly underway. Don't bother adding any new lobelia if the first year's plants died – the begonias will put on so much growth its disappearance will never be noticed. There is no need to repot but it will need to be fed. Apply a weak liquid feed every week from early April onwards and then full strength from early May when the basket should be in flower again.

Hang the basket outside towards the end of May when all danger of frost has passed, and if cold nights are still a threat bring it into the shelter of the greenhouse or conservatory again. Spray for greenfly as and when necessary, and deadhead regularly throughout the flowering season.

If you take some fuchsia cuttings during the early part of the second summer, you will have some good plants to make up a basket for the following year when the whole process can begin again.

44

23   A LONGTERM WINTER BASKET

As winter approaches this basket looks more and more festive with its mass of red berries. Furthermore the birds don't seem to like them so they remain until late in the spring when they eventually fall off. This is its third winter and it has never been replanted!

Site
All the plants are hardy but severe frost could still damage the plants in a basket and strong winds would spoil the foliage. A sheltered site is best.

Container
Wire hanging basket: 35cm (14″) in diameter with a sturdy 27.5cm (11″) bracket.

At its best
The gaultheria berries begin to turn red in October and remain until April. In July and August it is covered with lots of dainty white flowers, also very appealing. The ferns, ivy and eunonymus are evergreen so the foliage is attractive all year round.

Planting Time
Spring or autumn.

Ingredients
(if you choose more mature specimens the basket will look fuller)

1 hardy shrub *Euonymus japonicus* 'Aureopictus' (in the centre to add height) with green and gold leaves to give extra interest in winter.

1 hardy fern *Dryopteris erythrosora*. This one has attractive light coppery fronds when they are first sent up in the spring. It is available from some garden centres and by mail order from Fibrex Nurseries Ltd (as are the ivies; see the list of specialist suppliers on page 225).

1 variegated ivy *Hedera helix* 'Sagittifolia Variegata' with arrow-shaped leaves; very distinctive.

2 *Gaultheria procumbens* also known as the partridge berry, with creeping evergreen foliage, shiny dark green leaves, dainty white flowers in July and August and glossy red berries in the autumn and winter. It is said to like an acid soil but these have thrived on John Innes No 3.

1 variegated ivy *Hedera helix* 'Kolibri' with dark pink stems and lots of white in its variegation.

10 litres of John Innes No 3 soil.

2 handfuls of grit for additional drainage.

1 basketful of moss from a florist's shop.

1 circle of plastic sheeting the size of a dinner plate, cut from a black sack for example.

Method
1. Line the basket with a generous thickness of moss, starting at the base and working up the sides to form a collar about 2.5cm (1″) above the rim of the basket.
2. Cut four 2.5cm (1″) slits in the plastic circle for drainage and place over the moss lining in the bottom of the basket.
3. Spread the grit over the plastic circle and then add 10cm (4″) of soil.
4. Plant the euonymus at the centre-back of the basket with the fern immediately in front and the 'Sagittifolia Variegata' ivy at the rear so that it forms a good back to the basket.
5. Plant the gaultherias on either side of the fern.
6. Plant the 'Kolibri' ivy at the front of the basket so that it trails over the sides. Its dark pink stems will look attractive with the dark leaves of the gaultheria and the young fronds of the fern.
7. Fill in the gaps with soil so that the level reaches to within 2.5cm (1″) of the rim of the basket.
8. Water well. Add more soil if necessary. The moss collar should remain intact as it helps to retain the soil. Add extra if needed.

Aftercare
Maintain soil moisture all year round especially in spring and summer but never water in frosty weather. Give extra protection in severe weather and keep well sheltered from strong winds which will damage the foliage.

Apply a liquid feed every two weeks during the summer months. No spraying should be necessary for insects. Cut off any untidy growth or split leaves, particularly if damaged by the wind. This applies mainly to the fern.

My basket is in its third winter and looks very happy. Leave well alone until overcrowding eventually spoils it. Divide the gaultheria, ivy and ferns and replant with new ferns and euonymus.

24   FOUR-IN-ONE POT

A simple planting in rather an unusual pot. Easy to look after, drought resistant and pleasing to the eye, especially in the autumn and winter when its neat appearance remains unchanged by winds or frosts.

Site
Fully exposed to sun and air.

Container
Four-in-one pot (made by Whichford Pottery). Each section is 15cm (6″) wide, 15cm (6″) deep.

Planting Time
October to April.

At its best
Except for flowering, it varies little with the seasons, remaining pleasing to the eye the whole year but, as it matures, the rosettes will begin to spill over the sides creating an attractive cascade.

Ingredients
(There are many sempervivums – commonly known as houseleeks – to choose from. Use the mail order service from Alan Smith, who specializes in these plants, or Bressingham Gardens (see page 225). Otherwise be guided by your nearest big garden centre. Look for different colourings and for some with cobwebbed rosettes.)
 1 *Sedum spathulifolium* 'Cape Blanco'; a low hummock of grey-white rossettes. Easily available.
 1 *Sempervivum arachnoideum* (cobweb houseleek) with silvery cobwebbed rosettes and deep pink flowers. (Seen here is an unnamed cultivar of this species.)
 1 *Sempervivum tectorum*, the common houseleek; compact rosettes with sharp upturned red tips.
 1 *Sempervivum* 'Corsair'; grey-green rosettes which turn claret-red in summer.
5 litres of John Innes No 2 soil.
1 litre of horticultural grit for drainage.

Method
1. Cover the base of each pot with 2.5cm (1″) of drainage material and add 5cm (2″) of soil.
2. Add a little extra grit in the top pot when you plant *Sedum spathulifolium* 'Cape Blanco'.
3. Plant the three sempervivums around the bottom tier.
4. Adjust the plants so that they sit 2.5cm (1″) below the rim of each pot. Carefully fill in the gaps with soil. Water well and add more soil if necessary.

Aftercare
These plants require little attention. They are all quite hardy and can withstand dry conditions, although they will thrive better if the soil is kept just moist.

25   AN ALI BABA POT

Festoons of ivy tumble out of this wonderful pot, joined in spring by golden daffodils and in summer and autumn by handsome trails of Virginia creeper.

Site
Sun or partial shade.

Container
Ali Baba pot: 65cm (26″) deep and only 25cm (10″) in diameter at the top. Or use any large, tall pot.

Planting Time
October to November.

At its best
Its golden crown of daffodils is most attractive in April. When the Virginia creeper turns red in the autumn then the pot takes on another look. But really it is delightful all year round, and always wins admirers.

Ingredients

10 daffodils *Narcissus* 'Binkie'. These make a good container subject with their attractive double cream and yellow flowers.

1 ivy *Hedera helix* 'Cristata' with crinkly edges to its leaves known as the parsley effect. It sometimes goes under the name of 'Rokoko', 'Parsley', and 'Pice Lep'. It is particularly good for a pot (or hanging basket) because it sends out long trails. Very attractive in early summer when the new leaves unfurl.

1 Virginia creeper. This is the Chinese one *Parthenocissus henryana*. It has dark leaves with pink and white variegations which become more obvious when it takes on its autumn colourings. If you live in the north or have an exposed site try the common Virginia creeper from North America which is hardier.

20 litres of John Innes No 3 soil or a peat-based compost which would be lighter and therefore make the whole pot less heavy to move if you needed to.

Drainage material such as pieces of polystyrene which as previously explained, would be lighter than old crocks.

Method

1. Put the container in its permanent position and cover the base with 10cm (4″) of drainage material. Add 37.5cm (15″) of soil.
2. Plant the daffodils well spaced out in the centre of the pot. Cover with soil until just their tips show.
3. Plant the ivy at the front of the pot and the Virginia creeper at the back.
4. Fill in the gaps with soil and bring the level to within 2.5cm (1″) of the rim.
5. Firm in the plants, water well and add more soil if necessary.

Aftercare

Maintain soil moisture throughout the year, but particularly in the spring and summer. The neck of this pot is very small and not much natural rainfall will ever penetrate.

Let the daffodils die down completely before you remove the dead leaves. You may need to trim the ivy and Virginia creeper eventually; they are strong growers and will need to be kept in check. Apply a general slow-release fertilizer in late winter/early spring and add 5cm (2″) of leaf-mould or compost to the top of the soil.

WINTER AND
SPRING SCHEMES

INTRODUCTION TO THE WINTER AND SPRING RECIPES

Once the summer displays are over thoughts turn to spring and the planting of bulbs. There are so many different ones available these days that to select a few is a difficult task. I have deliberately tried to avoid using the same combinations as in my previous book *Creative Container Gardening*, not because I no longer think they are suitable – on the contrary they are well tried and tested – but rather because I wanted to draw on a wider variety of bulbs and other combinations.

TWO-TIER DISPLAY
Small bulbs such as crocuses, anemones, scillas and grape hyacinths all make lovely companion plants to the taller hyacinths, daffodils and tulips. Combinations may be drawn by selecting bulbs from the first group to create a low carpet of colour, and another batch from the second group to provide the spectacle above. The result is a two-tier display which can flower in unison or in two stages to give continuity of colour. Early flowering varieties of daffodils and tulips can be planted to coincide with crocuses, scillas and anemones, while mid-season varieties of daffodils, hyacinths and tulips can be carpeted by anemones and grape hyacinths. The late-flowering tulips and daffodils rely on bedding plants for their lower tier of colour.

Bedding plants include such favourites as primroses, polyanthus, aubrietia, arabis, bellis daisies, little violas, wallflowers, forget-me-nots and winter-flowering pansies. In recent years the pansies have become universally popular, rightly so because of their ability to flower on and off throughout the entire season from the time of planting in the autumn until the spring. They come in a wide variety of colours, but I think the white and yellow and possibly the blue ones show up best in the dull months of the year. All these kinds of winter bedding were popular with the Victorians, but they also used auriculas, double primroses and feverfew as well. The first two are becoming far more widely available again. They are well worth a try and you do not have to be planting a Victorian-style container to use them. Feverfew has never disappeared from use in the garden, largely because it seeds itself so freely. It is sometimes regarded as a weed and is pulled out in handfuls. But if you plant the golden variety and use it for winter bedding you will be amazed at the transformation it can bring to a simple arrangement. Kept clipped it will remain golden all summer.

Of course dwarf conifers, aucubas, golden and dark green euonymus, winter-flowering heathers, golden tree heathers and variegated periwinkles also make important contributions throughout the winter months. Perhaps the most valuable of all is the humble ivy, in both its green and variegated forms. Its leaf shape varies considerably from a heart shape and sharp arrow shape to a curly-edged type: all interesting in their different ways. It is very useful for tumbling over the edge of a large pot or window box, or for providing a carpet of green around a winter hanging basket.

The bedding plants can be planted with any combination of bulbs in the autumn, but at this stage only the pansies, violas and perhaps the bellis daisies will be in flower. If you plant them in September or early October they will have a chance to put on growth before winter sets in, and the amount of flowers should increase as well if it is a mild autumn. This will be even more likely if the container is kept in a sunny, sheltered spot. By early spring they should reward you well, heralding the lovely bulb display which will be just around the corner. Feverfew should be added to this list, not because it will flower at all but because its vibrant foliage makes such a positive contribution to the display throughout the entire period. When the spring comes, the arabis, double and single primroses, some of the auriculas and then the aubrietia will come into flower first, followed by the polyanthus, forget-me-nots and wallflowers.

TIMING OF DISPLAY

When you plan your combinations think of the effect you want to create. Do you want an early or a late display, or both? A combination of early dwarf daffodils and primroses will give you an earlier show. If you plant late wallflowers and late tulips together you will have a magnificent late display. Do you want autumn and winter colour by the use of bedding, or do you just want to wait until the spring? Obviously by adding the winter bedding plants you involve more cost but then you get months of additional pleasure. Your local climate must play a part in your decision here, for in exposed places you run the risk of losing some of these plants either because of severe frost or biting winter winds. Sheltered urban areas are always safer.

BUYING BULBS

Buy your bulbs as early as you can in September so that you are sure of a good choice. Some of the dwarf daffodils, for example, are extremely popular and supplies can run low. You don't have to plant them immediately, as long as they are kept in a cool, dry place. Wait until you have collected your bedding plants and then the fun can begin. All the bulbs mentioned in the following recipes are available at those garden centres which are supplied by O. A. Taylor and Sons Ltd of Holbeach. They serve over 1,000 garden centres throughout the United Kingdom. Of course many of them are available elsewhere in garden centres, hardware shops etc and from mail order suppliers.

SUBSTITUTES

While all the bulbs recommended in the recipes which follow have proved successful in their various combinations, don't feel that you necessarily have to copy the suggestions down to the last detail. You can make various changes by using other bulbs which flower around the same time, as long as they are of a suitable height. Choose the dwarf or shorter ones for most container work. Additionally there may be times when some of these bulbs are not available, or some will be more popular than others and sell far quicker. In these circumstances, too, it is good to know which ones can be substituted.

Of the early dwarf daffodils, 'February Gold', 'February Silver', 'Peeping Tom' and 'Tête-à-Tête' are all reliable and longlasting; they are interchangeable for tub, pot and window box work, although 'Tête-à-Tête' is the best for hanging baskets because it is short and multiheaded. 'February Gold' is well-proportioned and gold throughout and is generally the first of these to flower; 'February Silver' has a cream trumpet and is slightly later than 'February Gold' and far more expensive usually; 'Tête-à-Tête' is multiheaded, excellent for basket work and forcing; 'Peeping Tom' has a good yellow, very long trumpet and is slightly taller and later than 'February Gold'.

Mid-season short daffodils suitable for all window boxes, tubs and pots include 'Minnow' which is a dainty pale yellow; 'Hawera' which is a multiheaded, graceful lemon-flowered daffodil; 'Double Campernelle', a pretty double yellow; 'Pencrebar', a double gold; and 'Thalia' which is slightly taller than the others and multiheaded, and an absolutely beautiful white.

Early dwarf single tulips come in so many shades and colours that it would be relatively easy to substitute one for another; they tend to flower alongside the first batch of daffodils and can be planted together to create a vivid display. The double early tulips tend to be a little later, ranging from yellow, orange, crimson, red and pink. They coincide approximately with the hyacinths and blue grape hyacinths. The taller double tulips, apeldoorns and late tulips flower at the end of the season and are best planted with forget-me-nots and wallflowers. This is, of course, an over-simplified view, but it should at least help to explain how the combinations work and what to substitute for what if one particular bulb is unobtainable.

You may be surprised by the number of bulbs which

are used in some of these recipes. I like to create a full display which is worthy of the container and can become a focal point in the spring. You can see the results for yourself; they are glorious. But, if you want to use less, then do so. You will still get a lovely show.

INSTANT SPRING DISPLAYS
For those who have missed the autumn planting, there are plenty of opportunities for quick colour from cinerarias and calceolarias – these can both be planted outdoors in sheltered containers once the risk of a bad frost has passed. Polyanthus are plentiful, so are primroses and cowslips, bellis daisies and violas, and a whole range of colourful pansies. Mix pink bellis daisies with yellow violas and you will have a wonderful spectacle. Mix blue pansies with them instead and the display will take on a very pretty look. Planted at the end of March or early April, they will make a superb show for many weeks; in fact right up to the time of the summer planting. They are suitable for window boxes, hanging baskets, wicker baskets and tubs. You could have a complete display with them for very little expense if you can find them growing in strips.

WATERING
These winter and spring containers often need watering quite regularly. If they are close to the wall of the house or sitting on a window-sill rain water will never be entirely adequate, particularly once the main growth has begun. Check to see if the soil is moist and if not, then water, although you should never be tempted to do so if frost threatens. They need it in the autumn, too, when the roots are being formed. If they are left too dry their growth will be stunted. The bedding plants require plenty of moisture as well, of course. Forget-me-nots and pansies will soon flag if they are kept too dry.

WINTER PROTECTION
Winter weather is notoriously unpredictable. Severe frosts and deep snows may come and, although hardy, the plants in containers may suffer. Biting cold winds will damage them, too, as the drying effect kills the foliage. You may not notice it at first; only later does it become apparent as the ivy leaves turn brown and wither. While a risk remains, place the containers in sheltered sites, away from north and east winds. Keep them near the house or an outbuilding where the surrounding temperatures will not fall so low at night. In extreme weather be prepared to move the containers inside the greenhouse if you have one, or keep them covered with sacking along the wall of the house. If it is frosty, keep the pots on the dry side. When a milder spell comes you can soon move them again and give them a drink. However, if it is a mild winter, then the winter containers will be safe.

HANGING BASKETS (see also pages 4–6 in the General Introduction)
Hanging baskets are particularly susceptible to damage either by wind or severe frost and may need more winter protection than the tubs and pots. On the other hand they are attractive hung beside a front door in the early spring. I have been experimenting with ways of creating colour around the sides of these baskets so that they do not look as bare as they sometimes do at this time of year. We know that spring bulbs never hang down or trail, so what is the answer? One recommendation is to follow Victorian advice and use ivy to cover the sides and base. Obviously it has to have long trails. These are then pegged in to the sides of the basket to form a ball and where the ivy touches the moss it begins to root so that a green covering is created (see Recipes 111 and 112).

Another method was also gleaned from Victorian gardening books. It is straightforward and very easy. The secret is to leave the planting of the basket until February. By this time the shoots are well advanced, even though they have not felt soil or water the whole winter. It means that they can be planted already poking out of the sides of the basket so that they continue to grow in this way and therefore create a ring of colour around the sides. Normally, if you plant them this way in the autumn only the odd one grows outwards – the rest grow straight upwards towards the light, which is most annoying! I was afraid that the bulbs would have suffered as they had not been planted earlier. But this was not the case: they flowered beautifully. I planted up two hanging baskets in this fashion, the first using crocuses, the second using hyacinths. You can see the results in Recipes 34 and 35. Another year, I would try and save more crocus corms and aim for a greater display. This one was slightly sparse, although it continued for many weeks at a time of year when little else was in flower. And the important point is that this method was successful in providing colour at the sides of the basket, not just at the top. Moreover it avoids the problem of protecting the basket through the winter. By the time the basket is ready to be hung up the worst of the weather should be almost over.

The third experiment involved the creation of an upside-down basket where the planting is done so that the bulbs are pointing outwards through the moss, all round the base and sides of the basket. After planting, a board is placed over the base and the entire basket is turned upside down. It remains like this for the whole winter, tucked away in a sheltered spot in the garden until growth is quite mature. Then it is carefully reverted so that all the leaves and flowers now hang down. After a week or so they begin to curl round. Meanwhile extra bulbs already planted in the autumn are neatly placed in the top of the basket so that the whole forms a ball effect. I used large Dutch crocuses in one basket and in another I used anemones mixed with grape hyacinths. The first was not successful (perhaps if I had used smaller flowering crocuses it might have been better). But the second was a great success – you can see the results in Recipe 36. Anemones have dainty leaves which make a good shape as they turn upwards to the light. They were a good foil for the more untidy grape hyacinth leaves. Moreover the anemones were in flower a good two weeks before the grape hyacinths, so that the display was very longlasting. They were a good combination and I do recommend them.

END OF SEASON CARE

ARABIS AND AUBRIETIA These should both be cut back severely after flowering and moved to a sunny, well-drained position in the garden where they can remain until the autumn. Then they can be lifted and used again.

BULBS On the whole bulbs are best not planted for a second time in containers for a display the following spring. Instead, they are best planted out in the garden where they will recover, if necessary, and then flower for many years. This applies to all daffodils, crocuses, scillas, grape hyacinths, anemones and hyacinths, although the hyacinths will never produce quite the same big blooms again. If you have not enough room in your garden, then either give them to a friend or throw them away. Tulips are more difficult to predict. Those which are closest to the wild species will tend to survive best. The safest approach when you want to keep a very special pot of tulips is to let them die down in the containers themselves, then lift in June or July and store. But

only keep the biggest bulbs (those larger than a tenpence piece). The golden rule with all bulbs which are to be transferred, is to disturb the roots as little as possible and let the foliage die down naturally in June and July. This means that they must not be allowed to dry out until this has happened. All the goodness must be allowed to go back into the bulb for the following year's growth. You may pick the flowers to bring indoors but don't gather the leaves; this is especially true of the tulip, which means that for some kinds you can only cut short stems.

FEVERFEW Use for a summer container. Keep well clipped throughout the season and the foliage will remain golden. Only allow it to flower and seed if you want seedlings to appear.

IVIES AND PERIWINKLE These can both look good in summer displays as well, especially if they are trained over the front of a chimney pot, for example. Don't be afraid to cut them back if they have become straggly during the winter. This will neaten the plants and encourage them to thicken out. Alternatively, plant them out in the garden and then lift them in the autumn for more container work. If the roots grow too large, don't worry. They can be cut back quite severely and the plant will come to no harm, although it is better, on the whole, to do this in summer rather than autumn.

PRIMULA DENTICULATA, GOLD-LACED, DOUBLE AND SINGLE PRIMROSES, AURICULAS AND POLYANTHUS These should be planted out in the garden where they can mature and be used for another display in the autumn. In time you may wish to divide them, but for another season keep them as larger plants.

SEDUM ACRE 'AUREUM' This is worthy of a summer display in a wicker basket, or try growing it for a winter hanging basket, using it as a liner instead of moss. This will mean that it should be encouraged to grow either in a very large circle or through an upturned hanging basket. It propagates very easily.

THYME Transfer to a herb pot or a sunny spot in the garden. It can be used again in the autumn.

26   PEEPING TOM

These dwarf daffodils known as 'Peeping Tom' are an excellent window box subject, reliable and early. They combine well with the rich blue pansies. This container is both easy to plant and look after. It is suitable for a child to try because it is simple and has instant colour.

Site
Pansies will perform best where there is some sun.

Container
Small terracotta window box: 40cm (16″) long, 15cm (6″) wide, 15cm (6″) deep.

Planting Time
September to October.

At its best
The pansies should flower in all but the worst weather during the winter, joined by the daffodils in early spring.

Ingredients
12 early dwarf daffodils *Narcissus cyclamineus* 'Peeping Tom'; its trumpet is long and narrow, its petals are reflexed.
 3 blue winter-flowering pansies *Viola* × *wittrockiana* 'Universal'.
 9 litres John Innes No 2 soil.
Drainage material such as grit or small pieces of polystyrene.

Method
1. Cover the base of the container with 2.5cm (1″) of drainage material and add 5cm (2″) of soil.
2. Plant the twelve bulbs in two rows along the front and back of the window box.
3. Cover with soil.
4. Space the pansies along the centre of the box.
5. Check that the plants are well balanced, then fill in the remaining gaps with soil. Firm in.

6. Water well. Add more soil if necessary to bring the level to within 2.5cm (1″) of the rim.

Aftercare
Maintain the soil moisture throughout the autumn, winter and particularly in spring, but never water in frosty conditions. The pansies are thirsty drinkers and will soon flag if they are dry. Feed them regularly throughout the flowering period with a liquid plant feed so that they make a wonderful blue carpet for the golden daffodils in the spring.

 'Peeping Toms' are good for naturalizing in the garden, so after flowering plant them out either in a border or in the lawn. Be careful to leave their roots intact as much as possible. Keep them watered until the leaves turn yellow and die down. Discard the pansies.

27 BRIGHT AND CHEERFUL

A mixture of daffodils and tulips flowering together to create a cheerful splash of colour in early spring. Peeping out from underneath is the little viola 'Johnny Jump-Up'.

Site
The violas and tulips will prefer some sun.

Container
Medium green plastic window box: 60cm (24″) long, 15cm (6″) wide, 15cm (6″) deep.

Planting Time
September to October.

At its best
Little 'Johnny Jump-Up' should flower on and off throughout the winter, depending on how cold it is, joined by the daffodils and tulips in early spring.

Ingredients
10 early dwarf daffodils *Narcissus cyclamineus* 'February Gold'.
10 early dwarf tulips *Tulipa kaufmanniana* 'Stresa'.
1 golden feverfew *Tanacetum parthenium* 'Aureum'.
2 pots of yellow and blue violas *Viola tricolor* 'Johnny Jump-Up'. 10 litres John Innes No 2 soil.
Drainage material such as grit or small pieces of polystyrene.

Method
1. Cover the base of the container with 2.5cm (1″) of drainage material and add 5cm (2″) of soil.
2. Plant the daffodils in a row along the back of the window box.
3. Plant the tulips in a line along the centre of the box.
4. Cover the bulbs with soil.
5. Plant the feverfew at the centre-front and the two violas on either side. Make sure they are firmly in place and that the box looks well balanced. Fill any remaining gaps with soil.
6. Water well. Add more soil if necessary to bring the level to within 2.5cm (1″) of the rim.

Aftercare
Maintain the soil moisture throughout the autumn, winter and particularly in the spring, but never water in frosty conditions. Give an occasional liquid feed so that the violas flower well throughout the season.

After the bulbs have finished flowering they may be planted out in the garden; however, make sure the leaves do not dry out until they die down in June or July. 'February Gold' is a good daffodil for naturalizing and should give many years of pleasure. 'Stresa' is not so adaptable but it may be worth a try.

The violas and feverfew should be planted out as well. The violas should continue to flower over a long period, especially if you keep using the little flowers for salads or decorating pâtés etc.

28   SPRING SALMON

First a winter carpet of pansies, joined in spring by dainty white hyacinths and crowned by rich salmon tulips.

Site
A sunny, sheltered window-sill.

Container
Large terracotta window box: 80cm (32″) long, 20cm (8″) wide, 17.5cm (7″) deep (don't use anything shallower).

Planting Time
September through to November.

At its best
The pansies should flower in all but the worst winter weather, joined by the hyacinths and then by the tulips in early to mid spring.

Ingredients
12 multiheaded salmon tulips *Tulipa* 'Toronto'.
 2 white dainty multiheaded Roman hyacinths *Hyacinthus orientalis albulus* 'Snow White'. If unavailable buy the ordinary white bedding type.
 4 white winter-flowering pansies *Viola* × *wittrockiana* 'Universal'.
25 litres of John Innes No 2 soil.
Drainage material such as small pieces of polystyrene or horticultural grit.

Method
1. Cover the base of the container with 2.5cm (1″) of drainage material and add 5cm (2″) of soil.
2. Plant eight tulips in a line along the back of the box and four spaced out along the front.
3. Plant the two Roman hyacinths on either side at the front of the box.
4. Cover the bulbs with soil and then plant the four pansies along the centre of the box. Check that they are well balanced.
5. Fill in the remaining gaps with soil. Firm in the pansies.
6. Water well. Add more soil if necessary to bring the level to within 2.5cm (1″) of the rim.

Aftercare
Maintain the soil moisture throughout the autumn, winter and particularly in spring, but never water in frosty conditions. The pansies will soon flag if they become too dry. Feed them regularly throughout the flowering period with a liquid plant feed so that they make a good carpet for the bulbs in spring.

   After the hyacinths have finished flowering, carefully remove them from the box and plant them out in the garden where they should continue to flower for years to come. You can try planting out the tulips but they are not so adaptable. Be sure to keep all leaves, stems and roots intact. Make sure they are not allowed to dry out before the leaves die down naturally in June and July. Discard the pansies.

29 SPRING IN A CHIMNEY POT

'February Gold' daffodils and purple crocuses make striking bedfellows in any pot but particularly when underplanted by this bright little stonecrop (see it arranged as part of a group scene on page 220).

Site
Any.

Container
Tall chimney pot into which a plastic pot 22.5cm (9″) in diameter, 22.5cm (9″) deep is lowered.

Planting Time
September to October.

At its best
Early spring.

Ingredients
12 early dwarf daffodils Narcissus cyclamineus 'February Gold'.
 8 purple crocuses Crocus vernus 'Purpureus Grandiflorus'.
 1 large pot of stonecrop Sedum acre 'Aureum'.
10 litres of John Innes No 2 soil.
Drainage material such as small crocks or pieces of polystyrene.

Method
1. Cover the base of the container with 2.5cm (1″) of drainage material and add 5cm (2″) of soil.
2. Plant the daffodils in two layers towards the centre-back of the pot. Plant the first six and then cover over with enough soil so that just their tips show. Then plant the next six on top in between the tips of those underneath.
3. Plant four crocus corms on either side.
4. Plant the stonecrop at the centre-front of the pot so that new growth will begin to fall over the rim.
5. Fill in any remaining gaps with soil.
6. Water well. Add more soil if necessary to bring the level to within 2.5cm (1″) of the rim.

Aftercare
Maintain soil moisture throughout the autumn, winter and particularly in the spring, but never water in frosty weather.

After the bulbs and corms have finished flowering they may be planted out in the garden; however, make sure the leaves do not dry out until they die down naturally in June or July. 'February Gold' naturalizes well, so it should adapt well to garden conditions; likewise the crocuses. The stonecrop is worth using again for a summer display (see Recipe 63) or saving for another autumn/spring planting.

30   A GOLDEN WALLPOT

Full of colour and interest, this is a simple planting which benefits from being at eye level where you can fully appreciate the combined effect of the sparkling gold-laced primroses and the dainty golden daffodils. Gold lemon-scented thyme provides a good carpet for this arrangement. It smells wonderful when you water it and, of course, the herb can be used in the kitchen.

Site
Any wall, although the sunnier the better.

Container
Terracotta wallpot: 35cm (14″) long, 15cm (6″) wide, 17.5cm (7″) deep.

Planting Time
September to October.

At its best
Early spring.

Ingredients
10 early dwarf multiheaded daffodils *Narcissus cyclamineus* 'Tête-à-Tête'; this is prolific, long-flowering and reliable.
2 gold-laced primroses, *Primula* 'Gold Laced'. Alternatively, *Primula* 'Wanda' or a wild primrose.
1 golden lemon-scented thyme *Thymus* × *citriodorus* 'Aureus'.
8 litres of John Innes No 2 soil.
Drainage material such as crocks or small pieces of polystyrene.

Method
1. Cover the base of the container with 2.5cm (1″) of drainage material and add 5cm (2″) of soil.
2. Plant the daffodil bulbs in a group at the centre-back of the wallpot.
3. Plant the gold-laced primroses on either side of the bulbs.
4. Plant the golden thyme at the centre-front so that it reaches over the rim. Adjust the soil level underneath if necessary.
5. Fill in the gaps with soil. Firm in the plants.
6. Water well. Add more soil if necessary to bring the level to within 2.5cm (1″) of the rim.

Aftercare
Wallpots can become very dry, so check regularly to make sure the soil is moist. Never water in frosty conditions.

When the daffodils have finished flowering, remove them from the pot and plant in the garden where they will flower well in following years, so long as you make sure they do not dry out until the leaves have died down naturally in June or July. Plant out the primroses so that they can be lifted and used again the next autumn. Plant the golden thyme in a sunny spot where you can enjoy its foliage and use it for the kitchen.

31 MINNOWS IN A WALLPOT FOR MID SPRING

Creamy 'Minnow' daffodils and lilac bedding plants combine beautifully to produce a cheery spring wallpot.

Site
Any sunny wall.

Container
Terracotta wallpot: 37.5cm (15″) long, 20cm (8″) wide, 17.5cm (7″) deep.

Planting Time
September to October.

At its best
Mid spring.

Ingredients
10 mid-season dwarf multiheaded daffodils *Narcissus tazetta* 'Minnow'.
 2 stonecrops *Sedum acre* 'Aureum' with pale yellow shoot tips from May to June.
 1 golden aubrietia *Aubrietia deltoidea* 'Aurea'.
 2 lilac drumstick primulas *Primula denticulata*. I had a surprise when one pot produced two plants of different colours, a happy bonus. They come in pretty shades from pale lilac to deep purple, pink and ivory. The choice is yours.
 8 litres of John Innes No 2 soil.
Drainage material such as crocks or small pieces of polystyrene.

Method
1. Cover the base of the container with 2.5cm (1″) of drainage material and add 5cm (2″) of soil.
2. Plant the daffodil bulbs in a group along the centre-back of the wallpot. Barely cover with soil.
3. Plant the stonecrops at each corner, the aubrietia at the centre-front and the drumstick primulas in between.
4. Fill in the gaps with soil. Firm in the plants. Check to see that the planting is well balanced.
5. Water well. Add more soil if necessary to bring the level to within 2.5cm (1″) of the rim.

Aftercare
Wallpots tend to become very dry because they get very little natural rainfall. Check regularly to make sure the soil is moist but never water in frosty conditions.

When the 'Minnows' have finished flowering they may be moved to the garden where they will increase well. Plant the aubrietia in a sunny spot. Place the primulas somewhere moist so that they will grow much bigger, be divided and used again the following autumn. The stonecrops will have begun to shape themselves around the edge of the wallpot. Treat them carefully so that they may be used again either immediately for a summer container or divided, planted out and saved for the autumn.

32 PEACH BLOSSOM IN A CHIMNEY POT

The scented white viburnum will welcome you home right through the depths of winter if you place it in a chimney pot by your front door. It will be joined in the spring by these beautiful pink tulips.

Site
Any, but take advantage of the scent and place it close to somewhere that you walk by regularly.

Container
Tall chimney pot with a 22.5cm (9″) diameter plastic pot fitted inside the top.

Planting Time
September to November.

At its best
The viburnum will flower throughout the winter, joined by the tulips from early to mid spring.

Ingredients
1 *Viburnum tinus* with white, pink-budded flowers which open from November through to May. This is an evergreen, lime-loving shrub which is excellent for winter containers. Choose one with plenty of buds, about 2 feet high.
8 early dwarf tulips *Tulipa* 'Peach Blossom'. I chose pink tulips because of the pink viburnum buds.
1 mature variegated ivy *Hedera helix* 'Chester' or 'Eva'
5 litres of John Innes No 2 soil.
Drainage material such as small crocks or pieces of polystyrene.

Method
1. Cover the base of the container with 2.5cm (1″) of drainage material and add 5cm (2″) of soil.
2. Plant the viburnum towards the centre-back of the pot.
3. Plant the tulips on either side of the viburnum.
4. Place the ivy to trail over the front of the pot.
5. Cover the bulbs and fill in any remaining gaps with soil.
6. Water well. Add more soil if necessary to bring the level to within 2.5cm (1″) of the rim.

Aftercare
Maintain soil moisture throughout the autumn, winter and particularly in the spring, but never water in frosty weather.

After the tulips have finished flowering, the contents of the pot may be removed. Replant the viburnum and ivy either in the garden or in another larger pot so that they may be used again the following autumn. Discard the tulips.

Hanging Baskets

See notes on pages 4–6.

33   A CHEERY BASKET FROM AUTUMN THROUGH TO SPRING

The yellow violas and pink daisies were in flower from October onwards providing welcome colour throughout the depths of winter. By spring they were as pretty as a picture when joined by these pink tulips.

Site
Sheltered and sunny.

Container
Wire hanging basket: 35cm (14″) in diameter with a sturdy 27.5cm (11″) bracket.

Planting Time
September to October – the earlier the better, then the bedding plants can get well established before the winter.

At its best
Depending on the severity of the winter, it should be in flower from planting time onwards and be at its best in mid spring.

Ingredients
2 strips of yellow violas *Viola cornuta* 'Prince John'.
6 pink early dwarf tulips *Tulipa* 'Peach Blossom'.
2 strips of pink daisies *Bellis perennis* 'Dresden China'.
10 litres of John Innes No 2 soil.
1 basketful of sphagnum moss or ordinary wreath moss from a florist.
1 circle of plastic sheeting, cut about the same size as a small dinner plate.

Method
1. Line the basket with a generous thickness of moss, start at the base and bring it a third of the way up the sides.
2. Cut five 2.5cm (1″) slits in the plastic lining and put it in place at the bottom of the basket.
3. Cover the base of the lining with 5cm (2″) of soil.
4. Carefully divide up the strips of plants.
5. Using the yellow violas, plant eight of them evenly around the base of the basket by passing the roots through a hole you have made in the moss. Be sure they make good contact with the soil.
6. Close any gaps with moss, and bring the level up around the sides by another 5cm (2″).
7. Plant the tulip bulbs in the middle of the basket and add another 5cm (2″) of soil.
8. Now use eight pink daisies to make another ring of plants, using the same method as described above.
9. Again plug any gaps in the moss and bring the level to the rim of the basket. Add more soil.
10. Now using a mixture of violas and daisies plant another eight alternately through the moss in a ring just underneath the rim.
11. Add any final bits of moss to make sure there are no remaining gaps in the wall of moss.
12. Plant the remaining violas and daisies around the edge at the top of the basket.
13. Water well. Add more soil and moss if necessary.

Aftercare
Maintain soil moisture throughout the autumn, winter and particularly in spring, but never water in frosty weather. Protect in severe weather. Feed the basket regularly throughout the flowering period so that it makes a good carpet for the bulbs in early spring. After flowering is complete, discard all the plants.

34   A BASKET OF GOLDEN CROCUSES

This is a simple experiment based on a Victorian gardening book which suggested making up a hanging basket of crocuses in the late winter when the shoots were already growing. The result is that the sides of the basket are attractive as well as the top.

Site
Full sun or partial shade.

Container
Wire hanging basket: 35cm (14″) in diameter with a 27.5cm (11″) bracket.

Planting Time
Keep the crocus corms in a cool dry place throughout the autumn and early winter and then be ready to plant end January to mid February.

At its best
March. Each corm produces several flowers which means the flowering period is prolonged for a full month at least.

Ingredients
30   yellow crocuses *Crocus aureus* 'Dutch Yellow'. 40 would have produced a denser mass of colour. By this stage of the winter their shoots should be quite long. *Crocus chrysanthus* 'E. A. Bowles' would provide a smaller neater flower.
  3   red and yellow primroses *Primula vulgaris*.
10 litres of John Innes No 2 soil.
1 basketful of moss, preferably sphagnum, or ordinary wreath moss from a florist.
1 circle of plastic sheeting the size of a dinner plate, cut from a plastic bag.

Method
  1. Line the basket with a generous thickness of moss: start at the base and bring it a third of the way up the sides.
  2. Cut five 2.5cm (1″) slits around the centre of the plastic lining and put it in place at the bottom of the basket.
  3. Cover the base of the lining with 5cm (2″) of soil.
  4. Take eight crocuses and plant them around the sides of the basket through the moss, taking care not to damage any of the shoots.
  5. Bring the moss a further 7.5cm (3″) up the sides of the basket and add more soil.
  6. Take another eight crocuses and repeat the

operation, but staggering the pattern so that one crocus does not sit directly above another.
  7. Add more moss to form a thick rim around the top of the basket. Add more soil to bring the level to within 2.5cm (1″) of the rim.
  8. Plant another six crocuses out through the sides near the top of the basket, again avoid planting directly on top of one another.
  9. Plant the primroses around the centre-top of the basket and the last six crocuses in between them.
10. Water well. Add more moss or soil as necessary.

Aftercare
Maintain the soil moisture throughout the late winter and spring but never water in frosty weather.

After flowering, dismantle the basket and plant the contents in the garden where they should bloom again the following spring.

35   HYACINTHS IN A HANGING BASKET

I tried a late planting of hyacinths, also based on the Victorian practice of letting the tips grow before making up the basket. This way the hyacinths grow in the direction you want them to rather than straight up towards the light. It was full of wonderful scents and made a splendid basket to hang beside the front door.

Site
Any, but if you like the smell of hyacinths put it by your front door.

Container
Wire hanging basket: 35cm (14″) in diameter with a 27.5cm (11″) bracket.

Planting Time
Keep the hyacinth bulbs in a cool, dry place throughout the autumn and early winter. Be ready to plant them up sometime in February when the tips are about 5cm (2″) long.

At its best
Early to mid spring.

Ingredients
14 bedding hyacinths of mixed colours:

    6 salmon-pink *Hyacinthus orientalis* 'Gypsy Queen'.

    3 white *Hyacinthus orientalis* 'L'Innocence'.

    5 yellow *Hyacinthus orientalis* 'City of Haarlem'.

    Salmon-pink, pale yellow and white combine well together, but so too would pink, blue and white. The choice is yours.

  2 white drumstick primulas *Primula denticulata*; these also appear in mauves, lilacs and purples.

  3 pink primroses *Primula vulgaris*; these come in many other wonderful shades.

10 litres of John Innes No 2 soil.

1 basketful of moss, preferably sphagnum, or ordinary wreath moss from a florist.

1 circle of plastic sheeting, cut about the same size as a dinner plate.

Method
1. Line the basket with a generous thickness of moss: start at the base and bring it right the way up the sides of the basket.

2. Cut five 2.5cm (1″) slits around the centre of the plastic lining and place it in the bottom of the basket.
3. Add 5cm (2″) of soil.
4. Make a small gap in the moss about halfway up the side of the basket and carefully pass the shoot of one of the 'Gypsy Queen' hyacinths outwards. Make sure the bulb rests firmly on the soil. Close up the gap in the moss, adding more if necessary.
5. Repeat the process with the other five 'Gypsy Queens' so that they form a semi-circle around the front of the basket.
6. Add 5cm (2″) more soil.
7. Space the three white hyacinths so that they, too, form a semi-circle pointing out underneath the rim of the basket. Again be sure to close up any gaps left in the moss.
8. Plant the three pink primroses around the top of the basket and the two white drumstick primulas in the centre.
9. Finally plant the yellow hyacinth bulbs in between the primroses and primulas, pushing the bulbs well down into the soil.
10. Top up with more soil. Make sure the plants are firmly in place and that there is a good collar of moss around the edge of the basket.
11. Water well. Add more soil or moss as necessary.

Aftercare
Maintain the soil moisture throughout the growing period but never water in frosty weather. Protect in very severe weather.

After flowering, dismantle the basket and plant the contents in the garden where they will bloom the following year. Only the primroses may not survive the next winter, if they were hothouse-grown when you first bought them.

36 AN UPSIDE-DOWN BASKET

Bulbs will never trail down usually, but if they are planted upside-down and the basket reversed they will naturally grow out of the bottom and sides of the basket towards the light. The anemones were very graceful and flowered particularly early followed by the pretty grape hyacinths. The pink tulips provided the final touch; they were added in early spring.

Site
Sunny, or partial shade.

Container
White wire hanging basket: 35cm (14″) in diameter with a 27.5cm (11″) bracket, and two shallow plastic pots about 20cm (8″) in diameter.

Planting Time
October to November for the planting of the upside-down part of the basket and the separate planting for the top. This is added in early spring when the basket is turned the right way up.

At its best
The basket was in flower from early spring with the anemones right through to the second half of April with the grape hyacinths and tulips. It changed as the weeks went by reaching its climax at the beginning of April. The combination of bulbs complemented each other beautifully giving a longlasting and colourful display.

Ingredients
30 white, blue and pink anemones *Anemone blanda* (mixed).
40 muscari or grape hyacinths *Muscari armeniacum* 'Heavenly Blue'.
10 pink early double tulips *Tulipa* 'Peach Blossom'.
10 litres of John Innes No 2 soil.
1 basketful of sphagnum moss or wreath moss from a florist.
A wooden board (or shallow plastic drip tray) which is larger than the top of the basket.
A small amount of drainage material such as pieces of polystyrene.

4. Cover with a thin layer of soil and then bring more soil up the sides of the basket.
5. In alternate fashion, plant another ten anemones and ten grape hyacinths in a wide band around the middle of the basket.
6. Now place one of the shallow 20cm (8″) pots into the centre of the basket. Fill it with soil and also in between the pot and the sides of the basket.
7. Plant another mixture of ten anemones and ten grape hyacinths around the top of the basket between the rim and the pot.
8. Firm down, water well and add more soil or moss as necessary.
9. Place the board over the top of the basket, and carefully turn it upside-down. Place in a sheltered outdoor spot for the winter.
10. Lastly plant up the second 20cm (8″) pot. Put a shallow covering of broken polystyrene over the base and add 5cm (2″) of soil.
11. Plant five tulip and five grape hyacinths bulbs at the bottom. Barely cover with soil so that the tips of the bulbs still show and then plant the others on top.
12. Cover with soil and bring the level to within 2.5cm (1″) of the rim. Water well and add more soil if necessary. Place beside the basket.

Aftercare

Make sure the soil remains moist throughout the autumn, winter and spring but never water in frosty conditions.

When the bulbs have begun to shoot and are visible through the moss, the basket can be turned the right way up. Hold the board steady and invert the basket. Remove the dummy pot and carefully transfer the contents of the other 20cm (8″) pot. It should fit perfectly. Now the basket can be hung up in its final position where it will soon provide a mass of colour.

After flowering, dismantle the basket and plant the anemones and grape hyacinths in the garden. Keep the bulbs well watered until the foliage dies down naturally in early summer. Discard the tulips.

Method
1. Line the basket with a generous thickness of moss: start at the base and bring it right the way up the sides.
2. Add 5cm (2″) of soil.
3. Take ten anemones and ten grape hyacinths and plant them in a mixed pattern UPSIDE-DOWN around the bottom of the basket. Make sure the growing tips are all pointing out towards the bottom of the basket.

37   THE WISHING-WELL BASKET

Inspired by the story of the little girl picking flowers for her grandmother, this basket contains a tulip called 'Red Riding Hood' and a mass of white anemones. Brimming with colour, it is full of gaiety and life.

Site
The sunnier the better.

Container
Wicker basket: 32.5cm (13″) in diameter, 15cm (6″) deep; almost any wicker basket can be used as long as it is sturdy and has a minimum depth of 12cm (5″). It must be given three good coats of yacht varnish to preserve it outdoors.

Planting Time
September to late October.

At its best
This planting may be enjoyed for many weeks. First the anemones will begin to bloom very early in the spring. They have such a natural habit and look charming in the basket. At the same time the tulips are beginning to emerge and as they do so their leaf colouring becomes evident. The leaves have purple stripes running through them which provide a striking background to the white anemones. By mid spring the basket is teeming with brilliant red tulips surrounded by a lacy white collar.

Ingredients
20 *Tulipa greigii* 'Red Riding Hood', a bright red tulip with striking purple veins in its leaves.
30 white anemones *Anemone blanda* 'White Splendour'.
12 litres of John Innes No 2 soil.
4 handfuls of horticultural grit as drainage material.
Black plastic lining cut to fit inside the basket.

Method
1. Line the basket with the black plastic sheeting and make six 2.5cm (1″) slits along the bottom to provide drainage holes.
2. Cover the lining with grit and add 5cm (2″) of soil.
3. Gently firm the tulip bulbs into the soil, trying to avoid contact with each other or the sides of the basket.
4. Cover the bulbs with soil until just the tips show.
5. Plant the anemones between the tulips but concentrate them mainly around the outer edge.
6. Add more soil and bring the level to within 2.5cm (1″) of the rim.
7. Water lightly and add more soil if necessary.
8. Any odd bits of plastic lining still showing should be trimmed off or tucked under the soil. Find a sheltered spot for it to sit during the winter eg. near the wall of the house; it needs moisture so don't cover it up but do raise it off the ground slightly so that the bottom can remain dry. Protect it further in very severe weather.
9. In early March bring the basket into a sunny spot where you can enjoy it to the full.

Aftercare
Maintain the soil moisture throughout the autumn, winter and particularly in spring, but never water in frosty conditions. After flowering the bulbs may be planted out in the garden. The tulips may not do well but the anemones should flower for years. The basket can now be used again for a summer planting but give it another coat of yacht varnish first.

38   A BASKET OF DAINTY DAFFODILS

Creamy daffodils and pretty blue and white grape hyacinths make a charming basket together. It would make a wonderful Easter present.

Site
Any.

Container
Wicker basket: 38cm (15″) long, 25cm (10″) wide, 15cm (6″) deep. Almost any wicker basket can be used as long as it is sturdy and has a minimum planting depth of 12cm (5″). Before use, apply three coats of yacht varnish to preserve it outdoors.

Planting Time
September to October.

At its best
From early to mid spring, a longlasting display.

Ingredients
25 *Narcissus tazetta* 'Minnow'; multiheaded cream and yellow bicoloured daffodils. They are very dainty, and being multiheaded are excellent in a basket where planting space is at a premium. Alternatively, use 'Hawera'.
20 *Muscari botryoides* 'Album'; a white grape hyacinth which is sweetly scented and sometimes called Pearls of Spain.
10 *Muscari armeniacum* 'Heavenly Blue'; a beautiful blue grape hyacinth included to add a touch of stronger colour to the display. If you prefer you could just use all white muscari.
15 litres of John Innes No 2 soil.
4 handfuls of horticultural grit or other drainage material.
Black plastic lining cut to fit inside the basket.

Method
1. Line the basket with the black plastic sheeting and make six 2.5cm (1″) slits in the centre to provide drainage holes.
2. Cover the lining with grit and add 5cm (2″) of soil.
3. Gently firm the daffodil bulbs into the soil, trying to avoid contact with each other or the sides of the basket.
4. Cover the bulbs with soil so that just the tips show.
5. Plant the grape hyacinths between the daffodils, mixing the two colours as you do so.
6. Add more soil and bring the level to within 2.5cm (1″) of the rim.
7. Water lightly and add more soil if necessary.
8. Any plastic lining still showing should be trimmed off.
9. Find a sheltered, sunny spot for this basket during the winter eg. near the wall of the house but don't cover it up as it needs moisture. Raise it off the ground slightly so that water is not trapped underneath. Protect it in very severe weather by bringing it into a cold garage or barn.
10. In early March put the basket into its final flowering position, somewhere sunny and near to the house where you can enjoy it for many weeks.

Aftercare
Maintain soil moisture throughout the autumn, winter and early spring, but never water in frosty conditions.

After flowering, all the bulbs may be planted in the garden where they will flower for many years.

39 MAUVES, LILACS AND PURPLES IN A STRAWBERRY POT

I find strawberry pots quite difficult subjects to choose plants for, but this arrangement of violas, aubrietia and oxalis has worked well. This can be adapted to make a longterm planting.

Site
Sun or partial shade.

Container
Strawberry pot: 27.5cm (11″) in diameter, 35cm (14″) deep. This one has eight holes around the sides.

Planting Time
September.

At its best
Mid to late spring. This photograph was taken when the oxalis were just beginning to flower.

Ingredients
1 strip of *Aubrietia deltoidea*. It comes in many shades of lilac, pink and purple. Any would be pretty here.
1 strip of violas. Here I have used *Viola tricolor* 'Prince Henry' which is deep purple. Alternatively, use 'Johnny Jump-Up' which has a large splash of yellow.
6 *Oxalis adenophylla*. This has a curious fibrous rhizome which produces attractive grey foliage and pretty lilac-pink flowers.
22 litres of John Innes No 2 soil.
Drainage material in the form of plenty of gravel and some large crocks.

Method
1. Cover the base of the container with a few large crocks. To help drainage further try to build up a column of gravel in the centre of the pot so that as the soil level rises there is a concentration of gravel in the middle.
2. Add more soil to bring the level up to the bottom ring of holes. Divide the strips of aubrietias and violas.
3. Alternate the planting so that each hole has either an aubrietia or a viola and so that the four viola holes also have an oxalis.
4. Plant the bottom layer of holes first, making sure that the plants have their roots firmly placed in the soil and that the oxalis are well covered.

5. Bring the level of soil and centre core of gravel up the top layer of holes and repeat the planting process.
6. Add more soil and gravel to bring the level to within 2.5cm (1″) of the rim.
7. Plant the rest of the violas and aubrietias around the top of the pot with the two remaining oxalis in the centre.
8. Water carefully to minimize loss of water through the holes. Once the plants get established this problem will diminish.

Aftercare
Maintain soil moisture throughout the autumn, winter and spring, but never water in frosty weather.

Apply liquid feeds regularly during the spring. After flowering, trim the aubrietia so that it remains neat if you decide to leave it in the pot. Viola flowers can be eaten; use them to decorate a meringue or a spring salad. Deadhead any fading ones in order to encourage further production of flowers.

The pot could be replanted in the autumn using new violas. Alternatively, the aubrietias and oxalis could be planted in the garden where they should flower for many years. Discard the violas.

40   APRICOT BEAUTY

'Apricot Beauty' is one of my favourite tulips. As the flower matures the colour changes subtly to a deeper shade of apricot and as the bloom opens in the sunlight all sorts of delicate salmons, pinks and apricots are revealed inside. It is wonderful as a cut flower . . . if you can spare the odd one from the pot!

Site
Sunny.

Container
Large terracotta pot: 30cm (12″) in diameter, 27.5cm (11″) deep.

Planting Time
Late September to November.

At its best
The pansies should flower throughout the winter in all but the worst weather joined by the tulips in early to mid spring. This would make a lovely display for a mid spring wedding.

Ingredients
12 apricot tulips *Tulipa* 'Apricot Beauty'. Alternatively, use delicate pink, slightly later-flowering 'Douglas Bader'.
 3 white winter-flowering pansies *Viola* × *wittrockiana* 'Universal'. Alternatively, use cream-coloured pansies but no strong colours.
20 litres John Innes No 2 soil.
Drainage material such as large crocks or pieces of polystyrene.

Method
1. Cover the base of the container with 7.5cm (3″) of drainage material and add 5cm (2″) of soil.
2. Plant the tulip bulbs firmly in the soil so that they form a balanced group. Space them out well so that they are not touching each other or the sides of the container.
3. Cover with more soil to bring the level to within 5cm (2″) of the rim.
4. Plant the three pansies around the edge of the pot.
5. Water well. Firm in the plants and add more soil if necessary.

Aftercare
Maintain soil moisture throughout the autumn, winter and spring. The pansies will soon flag when they are thirsty, but never water in frosty weather.

These tulips do not transplant well. If you want to save them for another season it is best to let them mature and dry off in this pot in early to mid summer.

Then lift, dry, clean and store until the autumn. Save only the largest bulbs (those bigger than a tenpence piece). Discard the pansies.

41 ONE FOR THE CONNOISSEUR

Tulips with variegated leaves are becoming more widely available. 'Unicum' has a delicate creamy-yellow margin which combines majestically with the brilliant red flower. It is further enhanced by the bright green foliage of the feverfew plants which are regarded almost as weeds by some gardeners, but if used thoughtfully they can be extremely valuable as spring bedding.

Site
Sunny.

Container
Oval Tudor planter made by Renaissance Casting Company Ltd (see the list of specialist suppliers on page 226): 62.5cm (25″) long, 30cm (12″) wide, 25cm (10″) deep. Lead provides a marvellous background for rich red flowers.

Planting Time
October to November.

At its best
The feverfew will remain bright all through the winter, but the real joy comes when you see the first creamy-yellow tips of the tulips emerge. By early to mid spring the pot will look sensational.

Ingredients
10 *Tulipa praestans* 'Unicum' with a creamy-yellow margin to the leaves and multiheaded bright red flowers. It is very expensive. A good alternative without the leaf interest is its parent *Tulipa praestans* 'Fusilier'.
 4 golden feverfew *Tanacetum parthenium* 'Aureum'.
30 litres of John Innes No 2 soil.
Drainage material such as small pieces of polystyrene.

Method
1. Cover the base of the container with 5cm (2″) of drainage material and add 5cm (2″) of soil.
2. Space the tulip bulbs around the container, taking care to keep them well away from the sides.
3. Cover with soil so that just the tips show.
4. Plant the feverfew around the edge of the container. Avoid placing it directly over any bulbs.

5. Add more soil to bring the level to within 2.5cm (1″) of the rim.
6. Water well. Firm in the plants. Add more soil if necessary.

Aftercare
Maintain soil moisture throughout the autumn, winter and spring, but never water in frosty weather.

After flowering, very carefully plant the tulips in a sunny spot in the garden. Do not allow to dry out until the foliage has died down naturally in the early summer. Alternatively, let them stay in the container until they have died down naturally, lift and store the largest of them (those bigger than a ten-pence piece) for use in the garden in the autumn. Plant the feverfew in the garden. If you allow it to flower and go to seed you will find lots of small plants in the autumn to use for winter schemes. On the other hand you may prefer to keep it clipped back. This way it will retain its fresh foliage and remain neat.

42 THE ORANGE EMPEROR

This is a simple but effective planting scheme which combines the rich orange of the tulip with the brilliant blue of the grape hyacinth.

Site
Sun or partial shade.

Container
Terracotta pot: 30cm (12″) in diameter, 25cm (10″) deep.

Planting Time
October to November.

At its best
Mid spring.

Ingredients
12 *Tulipa fosteriana* 'Orange Emperor'; a rich orange tulip with a large flower and sturdy, short stem. Alternatively, use 'Red', 'White' or 'Yellow Emperor'.
20 *Muscari armeniacum* 'Heavenly Blue' commonly known as grape hyacinths.
18 litres of John Innes No 2 soil.
Drainage material such as small pieces of polystyrene or crocks.

Method
1. Cover the base of the container with 5cm (2″) of drainage material and add 5cm (2″) of soil.
2. Space the tulip bulbs in the middle of the container. Take care that they do not touch each other or the sides of the pot.
3. Cover with soil so that just their tips show.
4. Plant the grape hyacinths in between the tulips but concentrate most around the edge of the container.
5. Cover with soil and bring the level up to within 2.5cm (1″) of the rim.
6. Water well and add more soil if necessary.

Aftercare
Maintain the soil moisture throughout the autumn, winter and spring, but never water in frosty weather.

After flowering, plant the contents in a sunny part of the garden. Be careful not to disturb the roots. The grape hyacinths will cheerfully reappear year after year. The tulips may not perform so well.

43   TEN SALMON PARROTS

As they open, these tulips reveal an exotic mixture of yellow and pink, orange, green, red and peach. The heads are heavy and in bright sunshine they are apt to flop. In the 1920s they were grown in hanging baskets where they would look splendid falling over the sides! Either you accept this part of their nature, or put them in light shade where they will remain more upright. Try two or three cut very short for a table decoration.

Site
Sun or partial shade, very sheltered.

Container
'Florentine Square' pot: 30cm (12″) cube. Any medium to large pot would be appropriate.

Planting Time
October to November.

At its best
The anemones will be in flower from early spring joined by the tulips in mid spring.

Ingredients
10 *Tulipa* 'Salmon Parrot'. There are many alternative colourings including violet, white-flamed red, cherry-edged yellow.
20 mixed blue and white anemones *Anemone blanda* (blue) and 'White Splendour'. With the salmon-coloured tulips all-white might be better.
25 litres John Innes No 2 soil.
Drainage material such as small pieces of polystyrene.

Method
1. Cover the base of the container with 5cm (2″) of drainage material and add 10cm (4″) of soil.
2. Plant the tulip bulbs so that they do not touch either each other or the sides of the pot.
3. Add more soil to bring the level to within 2.5cm (1″) of the rim and then plant the anemones about 4–5cm (1.5–2″) deep, all around the pot but concentrate them mainly near the edge.
4. Water well.

Aftercare
Maintain soil moisture throughout the autumn, winter and spring, but never water in frosty weather.

Protect in windy and very wet conditions when in flower.

After flowering, plant the tulips and the anemones in a sunny spot in the garden with as little root disturbance as possible. Allow the foliage to die down naturally. The anemones should do well for many years but the tulips will be more difficult to keep flowering.

44 SCARLET TULIPS AND PRIMULAS

Some of these primulas are a perfect match for the scarlet tulips and provide a dazzling carpet to show off the rich tones of the upper blooms with their dark black centres.

Site
Sunny.

Container
Erin planter: 40cm (16″) in diameter, 32.5cm (13″) deep. Any medium to large pot would be appropriate.

Planting Time
Late September to November.

At its best
Mid to late spring.

Ingredients
 8 *Tulipa* 'Olaf' with scarlet flowers and contrasting black centres. Alternatively, use 'Abu Hassan' which is dark red with a gold rim.
 5 mixed polyanthus. Try and find the best hardy varieties.
40 litres John Innes No 2 soil.
Drainage material such as large crocks or pieces of polystyrene.

Method
1. Cover the base of the container with 5cm (2″) of drainage material and then add 12cm (5″) of soil.
2. Plant the tulip bulbs well spaced out so that they are right away from the sides of the container and are not touching each other.
3. Add more soil to bring the level to within 5cm (2″) of the rim and plant the polyanthus around the edge of the container.
4. Water well. Firm in the plants and add more soil if necessary to bring the level to within 2.5cm (1″) of the rim.

Aftercare
Maintain soil moisture throughout the autumn, winter and early spring. Apply a liquid feed in early spring once the polyanthus begin to flower and need the extra boost.

After the bulbs have finished flowering, empty the contents of the pot. Plant the polyanthus in a moist part of the garden where they will grow and multiply for use in the autumn. The tulips may not fare well another year but if you have light soil and want to try them in a sunny spot, plant out with minimum disturbance to their roots. Do not allow to dry out until the leaves have died down naturally in the early summer.

45 ANYONE AT HOME?

This planting scheme was inspired by Monet who loved to see red and yellow tulips planted with a carpet of red daisies in his garden. Simple but effective, especially seen against a yellow door.

Site
Sunny.

Container
Medium to large pot (this is a handthrown terracotta 'pastry' flower pot made by Whichford Pottery): 47.5cm (19″) in diameter, 32.5cm (13″) deep.

Planting Time
October.

At its best
In a mild winter the daisies will continue to flower throughout joined by the tulips from mid to late spring.

Ingredients
16 mid-season Darwin hybrid tulips including 8 yellow *Tulipa* 'Golden Apeldoorn' and 8 scarlet *Tulipa* 'Apeldoorn'.
 1 strip of red daisies *Bellis perennis* 'Lilliput'.
50 litres John Innes No 2 soil.

Drainage material such as large crocks or pieces of polystyrene.

Method
1. Cover the base of the container with 5cm (2″) of drainage material and add 12cm (5″) of soil.
2. Plant the tulip bulbs in two circles, red on the outside, yellow in the centre. Try to make sure they are well spaced so that they are neither touching the sides of the pot nor each other.
3. Add more soil to bring the level to within 2.5cm (1″) of the rim.
4. Divide the strip of daisies – there should be eight plants – and plant them around the edge of the pot. Firm in.
5. Water well. Top up with more soil if necessary.

Aftercare
Maintain soil moisture throughout the autumn, winter and spring. Apply liquid feeds during the flowering times of the daisies, particularly in the autumn and again in early spring.

After the tulips have finished flowering, they may be carefully lifted and planted in the garden. Make sure the leaves do not dry out until they die down naturally in June or July. These varieties should perform quite well in the garden another year. Discard the daisies.

46 THE LOVELY ANGELIQUE

'Angelique' has the softest pink flowers which look very pretty rising out of a bed of blue anemones.

Site
Sheltered and sunny.

Container
Large handthrown terracotta pot (made by Whichford Pottery): 47.5cm (19″) in diameter, 32.5cm (13″) deep.

Planting Time
Late September to November.

At its best
The anemones will be in flower from early spring onwards joined by the tulips in mid to late spring.

Ingredients
20 *Tulipa* 'Angelique'; tall double pink. For the same colour combination but earlier flowering try the early double tulip 'Peach Blossom'.
20 blue *Anemone blanda*. Forget-me-nots would give a similar carpet effect.
50 litres John Innes No 2 soil.
Drainage material such as large crocks or pieces of polystyrene.

Method
1. Cover the base of the container with 5cm (2″) of drainage material and add 12cm (5″) of soil.
2. Plant the tulip bulbs well spaced out, right away from the sides of the container and so that they are not touching each other.
3. Add more soil to bring the level to within 2.5cm (1″) of the rim.
4. Plant the anemones about 4–5cm (1.5–2″) deep, all around the pot but concentrated mainly near the edge.
5. Water well.

Aftercare
Maintain soil moisture throughout the autumn, winter and spring, but never water in frosty weather.

Protect in windy and very wet weather when the tulips are in flower. They have large heads and can be damaged easier than single tulips. Placed in a sheltered spot, however, this should not be a problem.

After flowering, plant the anemones in the garden where they will multiply. The tulips may not do so well another year but you may like to try them in light soil in a sunny spot. Try not to disturb the roots too much when you replant and keep them watered until the leaves die down naturally in the early summer.

47   A TRADITIONAL BARREL OF TULIPS AND WALLFLOWERS

Rich yellows and oranges radiate forth from this simple planting of tulips and wallflowers. It makes a warm welcome to any front door where it can be enjoyed not only for its colours but also for its delicious scent.

Site
Sunny; ideally somewhere you can enjoy the fragrance from the wallflowers.

Container
Wooden half barrel or large pot: 60cm (24″) in diameter, 40cm (16″) deep. I have used a plastic tub to sit inside the barrel so that the wood does not come into contact with the soil.

Planting Time
Early October.

At its best
Mid to late spring.

Ingredients
12 mid-season Darwin hybrid tulips *Tulipa* 'Beauty of Apeldoorn' with rich streaks of yellow and orange. Alternatively use scarlet 'Apeldoorn' or yellow 'Golden Apeldoorn'.
8 wallflower plants *Cheiranthus cheiri* 'Persian Carpet'; a mixture of subtle shades. You might have to buy a bunch of ten and choose the best eight. Look for strong, sturdy plants that have branched out well – not tall, limp, straggly ones. As soon as you have purchased them, open the bunch and give them all a good drink before planting.
100 litres of John Innes No 2 soil.
Drainage material such as large crocks or pieces of polystyrene.

Method
1. Cover the base of the container with 5cm (2″) of drainage material and add 20cm (8″) of soil.
2. Plant the tulips in two wide circles, eight in the outer one and four in the inner one. Mark their shape with sticks.
3. Add more soil to bring the level to within 5cm (2″) of the rim.
4. Plant five wallflower plants in between the two circles of tulips, saving the last three for the centre. By planting the wallflowers close together they seem better protected during the winter.

5. Water well. Firm down the plants and top up with more soil where necessary, leaving at least a 2.5cm (1″) gap between the soil and the rim of the container.

Aftercare
Maintain soil moisture throughout the autumn, winter and spring, but never water in frosty weather. Wind seems to damage wallflowers more than heavy frost or snow, so keep the barrel in a sheltered area. Don't despair if you wake up to see the leaves all floppy after a bad frost the night before. By midday they will probably look as perky as they normally do. They can actually withstand quite low temperatures.

Discard the wallflowers after flowering. Remove the tulips, keeping the roots intact as much as possible, and plant them in the garden. They should flower well another year. Make sure they do not dry out until their leaves die down naturally in June or July.

48   RED, WHITE AND BLUE

These days plastic pots can be bought in very cheerful colours. Here we see a bright red one filled with dainty white daffodils and brilliant blue grape hyacinths. An easy planting scheme, but a striking combination.

Site
Any, but best if it is not too exposed during the winter.

Container
Red plastic pot with matching drip tray: 32.5cm (13″) in diameter, 27.5cm (11″) deep. Any medium-sized pot would be appropriate.

Planting Time
September to October.

At its best
Mid spring.

Ingredients
12 multiheaded white daffodils *Narcissus triandrus* 'Thalia'.
20 blue grape hyacinths *Muscari armeniacum* 'Heavenly Blue'.
16 litres of John Innes No 2 soil.
Drainage material such as small pieces of polystyrene.

Method
1. Cover the base of the container with 5cm (2″) of drainage material and add 10cm (4″) of soil.
2. Plant eight daffodils in a wide outer circle and four more in a well-spaced centre group. Cover with soil so that just the tips show.
3. Plant the grape hyacinths around the edge, leaving just a few for the middle.
4. Cover with soil and bring the level up to within 2.5cm (1″) of the rim.
5. Water well. Add more soil if necessary to regain the former level.

Aftercare
Maintain soil moisture throughout the autumn, winter and spring, but take care never to water in frosty weather.

After the bulbs have finished flowering, plant them in a sunny, sheltered spot in the garden. Make sure that the leaves do not dry out until they die down naturally in June or July. The grape hyacinths in particular should multiply and give a good show for many years to come.

49   THE GAUDY PROFESSOR

We don't often intermingle daffodils and wallflowers but here is a daffodil called 'Professor Einstein' which has a deep orange cup. It is flowering just as the orange wallflowers in the pot are beginning to bloom. The wallflowers will outlast the daffodils, providing colour and interest over a long period.

Site
Any, but preferably sheltered from cold winter winds.

Container
Medium to large pot (this is an old sea-kale pot turned upside-down): 37.5cm (15″) in diameter, 42.5cm (17″) deep. Terracotta acts as a good background colour for this planting scheme.

Planting Time
September to early October.

At its best
Mid to late spring.

Ingredients
15 orange trumpet daffodils Narcissus 'Professor Einstein'. Alternatives with a red cup would be 'Delibes' or 'Orangery'.

6 dwarf wallflowers Cheiranthus cheiri 'Orange Bedder'. If you prefer a taller one, 'Fireking' would be appropriate. You might have to buy a bunch of ten and choose the best six, planting the others elsewhere. Look for strong, sturdy plants that have branched out well and have a good root system. Upon purchase, open up the bunch and give them a drink.

28 litres of John Innes No 2 soil.

Drainage material such as large pieces of crocks or polystyrene.

Method
1. Cover the base of the container with 5cm (2″) of drainage material and add 20cm (8″) of soil.
2. Plant the daffodils in two circles, the outer one with ten daffodils and the inner one with five. Mark them with sticks.
3. Add more soil to bring the level to within 5cm (2″) of the rim.
4. Plant five wallflowers between the two circles of bulbs and one in the centre of the pot. Don't worry about planting them close together; by doing so they will give each other protection during the winter.
5. Water well. Firm down the plants and top up with more soil where necessary to bring the level to within 2cm (1″) of the rim.

Aftercare
Maintain soil moisture throughout the autumn, winter and spring, but never water during frosty weather.

Wind seems to do more damage to wallflowers than heavy snow or severe frost, so keep the pot in a sheltered position throughout the worst of the winter. Don't despair if you wake up just after a sharp frost to see the plants looking floppy as if they are dead. By midday they will probably have perked up. They can stay like that for several days and come to no harm.

Discard the wallflowers after flowering. The daffodils can be planted in the garden where they can be enjoyed next year.

50   A CHERUB POT

This is an unusual daffodil called 'Binkie' which has delicate shades of lemon and cream on its trumpet and perianth. It combines rather well with the strong blue of the grape hyacinths. Very easy to plant and look after.

Site
Any.

Container
Tall terracotta 'Cherub' pot: 30cm (12") in diameter, 35cm (14") deep. Any medium to large pot would be appropriate.

Planting Time
September to October.

At its best
Mid spring.

Ingredients
15 lemon daffodils *Narcissus* 'Binkie'. Alternatively, use 'Spellbinder'.
15 blue grape hyacinths *Muscari armeniacum* 'Heavenly Blue'.
20 litres of John Innes No 2 soil.
Drainage material such as small pieces of polystyrene.

Method
1. Cover the base of the container with 5cm (2") of drainage material and add 10cm (4") of soil.
2. Plant the daffodils in two wide circles, touching neither each other nor the sides of the pot. Cover with soil so that just their tips show.
3. Plant the muscari in between the two circles of daffodils and also around the edge of the pot.
4. Cover with soil and bring the level to within 2cm (1") of the rim.
5. Water well. Add more soil if necessary to regain the former level.

Aftercare
Maintain soil moisture throughout the autumn, winter and spring, but never water in frosty weather.

After flowering, all the contents may be removed and planted in the garden. Make sure the leaves of the daffodils in particular are not allowed to dry out before they die down naturally in June or July. The grape hyacinths should adapt well and multiply.

SUMMER AND AUTUMN SCHEMES

INTRODUCTION TO THE SUMMER AND AUTUMN RECIPES

Summertime offers the widest choice of plant material for container work with the opportunity of continuous colour from May to September. All the hard work is done in May, then there are weeks of pleasure as the plants mature.

AVAILABILITY
Most of the recipes which follow use traditional summer and autumn bedding plants such as geraniums, fuchsias, busy lizzies, petunias, begonias, French marigolds, lobelia, alyssums, dahlias and chrysanthemums. Nearly all of them are easily available from a good garden centre, but where some cultivars might be more difficult to find, the supplier's name is given. However if you prefer not to order it through the post, then choose a substitute. Look closely at the description as to the type of plant; whether, for example, in the case of a geranium it is an upright rather than an ivy-leaved trailing kind. Secondly take note of the colour; if the recipe demands a salmon-pink kind you might substitute pale pink, white, apricot or an orange-red but a lilac would be hopeless, unless you wanted an entirely different colour scheme. Look along the benches at the garden centre and see what you can find.

You may have a frustrating time deciding upon fuchsias which are sometimes difficult to buy because the labelling is so poor. You might get a brief description as to 'bush' and 'upright', or 'cascade', 'trailing' and 'basket', but names and even colour analysis is often sorely lacking. Your best bet is to buy plants already in flower, or to squeeze open a bud! There are a great many colours to choose from, ranging from the typical fuchsia pink, bright crimson, through to blues and lilacs, whites and salmon. They are one of the daintiest of flowers and make excellent container plants, particularly for areas of partial shade.

Some summer bedding plants are sometimes not usually sold in the garden centres. You might find white lobelia, pale yellow nasturtiums, yellow or white trailing begonias, yellow canary creeper, dwarf sweet peas and scented mignonette difficult to find. With the exception of begonias, they can all be grown from seed quite easily following the instructions on the packet. You won't need expensive equipment. A seed catalogue or a good garden centre will provide them all and if you plant in March or April you will have good plants for containers by the end of May. Begonias may be bought as dry tubers in February or March and started into growth soon after. They are not much trouble at all, but they are infinitely cheaper purchased this way and the choice of colour will be much greater.

HEALTHY PLANTS
There are some plants which are more prone to whitefly and greenfly than others. Petunias, nico-

tiana, fuchsias and white marguerites are particularly susceptible so check the plants are pest-free before you buy them: you don't want to import aphids, if you can avoid it. They can also suffer from drought and will soon look withered and pathetic if they have missed a drink. Go to a garden centre where the stock looks healthy and the foliage perky. Don't be tempted to buy a tall, straggly plant just because it has flowers on it. Choose its smaller but bushier neighbour, even though it may still be in bud stage. The 'leggy' plant will never do as well as the well-shaped one. Garden centres often have weekly deliveries in April and May. Try and find out when these are made and go the same day or the day after, then your choice will be greater and the plants in a first-class state.

At some stage during the summer you are bound to discover aphids on your plants. Be prepared to spray immediately with one of the many insecticides available. Some these days use natural pyrethrum which makes them safer to other friendly insects like bees and butterflies. If you are intending to crop your containers, then use one which is intended for fruit and vegetables. Other remedies are French marigolds and basil which are reputed to deter aphids, and planted generally amongst your containers will help to keep them free from infestation. It's certainly worth a try and if you don't want to introduce the French marigold colours into your schemes, plant several together in a pot and place strategically around the patio. They come in a lovely range of russets, reds, oranges and primrose-yellow and can certainly look very colourful.

HANGING BASKETS

Hanging baskets are now an intrinsic part of any summer patio display. For detailed advice on types of baskets and siting etc, see pages 4–6 in the General Introduction.

SUN AND SHADE

Some plants will tolerate shade better than others. Fuchsias, busy lizzies, mimulus, creeping jenny, lobelia and begonias all do well in partial shade and are particularly useful for the basement and north-facing sites. Mix them with ferns and ivies and you will have some lovely displays. Sun-lovers include all types of geraniums, petunias, alyssums, livingstone daisies, echeverias, gazanias and heliotropes. These all love to bask in the sun and will thrive in hot summers. Begonias and busy lizzies seem able to cope with both sun and shade. They are among our most precious container plants. They are generally trouble-free and

as long as they have plenty of food and water will perform admirably.

COLOUR THEMES

There is such a wide variety of plants to choose from for our summer planting schemes that the task can seem rather daunting. Why not consider a colour theme for your containers. First work out the overall design and the numbers of containers involved, consider the positions as to sun and shade and then choose your colours.

You might want an all-white display using white geraniums, both upright and trailing, white verbena, white busy lizzies, white alyssums, white lobelia, white daisy-like marguerites, white begonias; non-stop, double or cascade. You could add grey foliage plants like *Lotus berthelotii*, *Helichrysum microphyllum* and *Cineraria maritima*.

On the other hand you may prefer a yellow theme, although you will have a more restricted choice. There will be no geraniums, fuchsias, or busy lizzies. You will be forced to rely on yellow begonias, yellow nasturtiums, creeping jenny, yellow petunias, yellow mimulus, gazanias, yellow French and African marigolds. Foliage plants such as the lime-green *Helichrysum petiolare* 'Limelight', dark perilla or flame-coloured coleus would make exciting companions. Any of the white flowers listed above would all blend beautifully with the yellow theme and combine to make an unusual but striking summer display.

Pinks are easy to find within the range of summer plants. Your decision will rest on whether you prefer pale pinks or salmon shades or perhaps the stronger bright cerise or mauve pinks etc. Geraniums, fuchsias, busy lizzies and petunias will all oblige, whatever colour you choose. There will be lots of choice with lobelia too. White, dark and pale blue lobelia blend well with all shades of pinks. Only the mixed lobelia is difficult to put with salmon or apricot pinks; save it for the cerise and mauve shades.

Red is one of the favourite colours for summer work. Red geraniums make a wonderful splash of colour and are hard to beat for impact. Mix them with red petunias or red begonias, red nasturtiums and red busy lizzies and you will have a vibrant collection. Dark blue petunias make a good contrast, particularly those with a white stripe or frill. So does dark blue lobelia, especially 'Mrs Clibran' or 'Sapphire'; both types have a white eye.

Some container gardeners might prefer a riot of colour to the restriction of any one mentioned above. Mix them all up together and enjoy the sumptuous riches which they will exude. I think this way of dealing with colour works particularly well if you are planting a large area. Create a whole series of containers which are close to each other; perhaps a series of window boxes on top of a wall, or one window box with matching hanging baskets on either side.

BUDGET

Before you buy your plants, draw up a budget. Do you want to save money? – in which case buy seeds and begonia tubers, as well as lots of strips of plants to use as edgers. You will spend much more wisely if you stick to your plan and buy all your new plants as part of a predetermined scheme. Going to the garden centre is like going to the supermarket – you have to stick to your list if you want to stay within budget! You will have to decide whether to buy strips of busy lizzies, petunias etc or mature plants in pots. Usually there are eight plants in a strip, so compare the price of a strip to the equivalent of eight pots. Summer bedders are all fast-growing plants and will only take two or three weeks longer to reach the same size as the potted versions. One drawback might be that you won't get the individual colour choice in strips as you would in pots.

THREE RULES

Three key factors will determine whether you have good displays or not. First, you must be prepared to water them often. This will mean daily attention in hot weather. Water in the early morning or evening when the sun is not on the containers so there is no risk of scorch. Water at soil level, then the water will not run off the leaves onto the ground but will penetrate down to the roots where it is needed. Be patient while you water. Let it soak in and then water the same pot again. In high summer the demands will be great: water is the lifeline. Second, remember to feed regularly. A great deal is expected of each container display and the original soil nutrients will soon be used up. Constant watering will have a leaching effect and will wash them through. Approximately four to six weeks after planting, apply a liquid feed to almost all the pots once a week. Don't give more than the recommended dose on the manufacturer's packet or bottle, but do make feeding a habit. Third, keep the plants in good health. If you notice greenfly etc then spray immediately, and then again soon afterwards to break the cycle of reproduction. Also, keep them neat and tidy. Trim off any damaged stalks or leaves and deadhead any flowers to prevent them setting seed and having a rest from flowering.

This is particularly helpful with fuchsias, petunias, sweet peas, begonias and some geraniums.

BEGINNING AND END OF SEASON CARE

AGAVE Overwinter at a temperature of 5°C (41°F). Keep dry until mid spring.

BEGONIAS (tuberous): Spring Start new or old tubers into growth again in early spring by planting them in individual pots or spare window boxes filled with moist peat-based compost. The tubers should be bedded into the top of the soil, hollow side uppermost, so that they are nestling into it without being entirely covered. Put the pot or window box into your airing cupboard or any other warm place until the tubers have started into growth. The soil needs to be kept quite moist during this period. Once a few leaves have appeared, bring the plants into the light. No artificial heat is now needed but they should remain indoors until all risk of frost has passed. Harden off gradually. Any tubers which are shy to start shooting should remain in the warmth.

Autumn Their leaves will start to turn yellow which indicates the beginning of the drying off process. Label them and lift them in early October so as to avoid any frost damage. Plant them temporarily in some moist peat. Gradually reduce their supply of water. When the foliage has died down completely, remove the tubers, clean the soil off and store them in a cool frost-free environment 7–10°C (45–50°F) covered with dry peat until around Christmas. Keep them well labelled. You should then give the occasional light watering to prevent the tubers from shrivelling.

CAMPANULA ISOPHYLLA Overwinter in a frost-free greenhouse. Take 7.5cm (3") cuttings in April or May, several to an 7.5cm (3") pot.

CHRYSANTHEMUM (ARGYRANTHEMUM) FRUTESCENS Commonly known as white marguerites, these may be overwintered in a frost-free greenhouse. In early spring, the old plants will provide a source of useful cuttings for the following summer. Take 5–7.5cm (2–3") stem cuttings off a non-flowering shoot.

ECHEVERIAS Overwinter at a temperature of 5°C (41°F) and keep barely moist. Separate the offsets in the spring and pot up individually in 7.5–10cm (3–4") pots of John Innes No 2 soil. Alternatively, leaf cuttings may be taken in spring or early summer and used as propagating material.

FUCHSIAS Spring Prune back the old wood to within two or three nodes of the old season's growth. When new signs of life appear, this is the time to water again. By mid May the plants will be ready to be hardened off before being planted out for the summer.

Autumn Remove the plants from their summer containers and pot them up into 15–23cm (6–9″) pots. Don't forget to label them. Keep in a frost-free greenhouse, shed or loft over the winter. Gradually reduce their water supply until their leaves drop off. The plants need hardly any water from now until the spring.

GERANIUMS (PELARGONIUMS) Spring When new growth begins gradually increase the water supply. Take cuttings, and put them in 7.5cm (3″) pots full of John Innes seed compost. Harden off the plants gradually before end May when they can be planted out for the summer.

Autumn Remove the plants from their summer containers, cut back the top growth to 10–15cm (4–6″), remove any remaining leaves and trim the roots. Label them, and plant individually in John Innes No 2 soil in a 10cm (4″) pot. Keep them in a frost-free but light position such as the greenhouse or on a window-sill inside the house. Water them well to begin with and then only when absolutely necessary. You will know when they need a drink because the new leaves will start to flag.

There may be many other successful ways of keeping geraniums but this method ensures that the old leaves, which may be harbouring insects and disease, are stripped off and destroyed, leaving the plants clean. The new growth which is then made in the autumn is hardier than the summer growth which has now been removed. By trimming the roots you encourage new root hairs to grow which will strengthen the plant ready for when growth really gets going in the spring. In the spring you will soon have lots of cuttings material available.

HELICHRYSUMS Overwinter in a frost-free greenhouse, keep barely moist until growth begins again in the spring, then take 7.5cm (3″) cuttings.

LILIES: Late winter/early spring On buying new bulbs plant them up individually into 15cm (6″) pots of John Innes No 1 soil. Keep in a cool, dark place until top growth shows, when they can be brought into the daylight and given more moisture. By mid May they should have made a good start and be ready to plant out in a summer arrangement.

Autumn The old growth has to die down completely to ensure a good plant for next year; therefore premature lifting would not be advised unless the lily was being transferred permanently to the garden where the natural dying-off process could continue.

PLECTRANTHUS Overwinter in a frost-free greenhouse, and keep barely moist until growth begins again in the spring. Take tip cuttings in March.

SEDUM SIEBOLDII 'MEDIO-VARIEGATUM' Overwinter in a frost-free greenhouse. Divide plants in the spring. Take cuttings between April and September, planting several to a pot.

HANGING BASKETS

See notes on pages 4–6.

51 A SYMPHONY OF YELLOW AND WHITE

This basket was much admired for its unusual colour combination which looked cool and refreshing throughout the long hot summer.

Site
Eye level, sheltered in shade or sun.

Container
Wire hanging basket: 35cm (14″) in diameter with a sturdy 27.5cm (11″) bracket.

Early Preparation
You will find it difficult to buy trailing white and yellow begonias in May, but if you purchase the corms in February or early March you can start them into growth yourself. (Follow the instructions on page 85.) White lobelia is available at some garden centres in May, but not all. However, it is easy to grow from seed. Sow in March and follow the instructions on the packet.

Planting Time
Mid to end May (unless you have a greenhouse or conservatory, in which case plant from mid April and keep it inside until end May).

At its best
June to September.

Ingredients
 1 *Lysimachia nummularia* known as creeping jenny with long dark green trails and yellow flowers.
 2 *Lysimachia nummularia* 'Aurea' with golden leaves and yellow flowers. The two variations make a good contrast.
 1 strip of white lobelia *Lobelia erinus* 'Snowball' (or 8 clumps of plants).
 2 white trailing begonias *Begonia* × *tuberhybrida*.

 2 yellow trailing begonias *Begonia* × *tuberhybrida*.
 1 yellow non-stop begonia *Begonia* × *tuberhybrida*.
 1 *Helichrysum petiolare* 'Limelight' with spreading foliage.
10 litres of peat-based compost or John Innes No 2 soil.
 2 handfuls of grit.
 1 basketful of moss, sphagnum preferably, or wreath moss from a florist.
 1 circle of plastic sheeting about the size of a dinner plate, cut from a strong plastic bag.

Method

1. Line the basket with a generous thickness of moss, starting at the base and working a third of the way up the sides.
2. Cut four 2.5cm (1") slits in the plastic circle and place over the moss lining in the bottom of the basket.
3. Spread two handfuls of grit over the plastic circle and then add 5cm (2") of soil.
4. Plant one lysimachia (creeping jenny) in the middle-front of the basket and the other two on either side.
5. Add another layer of moss, making sure that it fits snugly around the lysimachias and then add more soil.
6. Plant the lobelia all around the basket. Make sure the roots have good contact with the soil.
7. Add more moss so that it now forms a collar above the rim of the basket. Add more soil so that the lobelia roots are just covered.
8. Plant the two white trailing begonias on either side of centre, arranging them so that the growth falls naturally outwards.
9. Plant the two yellow trailing begonias in the centre-front and back, arranging them in a similar way.
10. Plant the non-stop yellow begonia in the centre-front of the basket and the helichrysum at the centre-back.
11. Carefully fill in the gaps with soil.
12. Water well. Firm in the plants and add more soil and moss if necessary.

Aftercare

Water generously. In hot weather you must be prepared to do it daily. Use a long-spouted watering can or a low-pressure hose so that you can water under the leaves at soil level. Otherwise the water will just run off the leaves and onto the ground. Never water with the sun shining on the basket as the foliage will scorch and look terrible. The best time to do it is in the evening when the colours change and look particularly beautiful. As the summer progresses, the basket fills out and the lysimachia becomes ever more effective.

Once a week give a liquid feed. Deadhead all begonias regularly. They should not be troubled by greenfly etc, but if they are then spray immediately.

Before the first frosts, dismantle the basket. Discard the lobelia. The lysimachia is quite hardy and should be planted out in the garden ready for another planting scheme next year. The begonias may be overwintered and used again next year as well; likewise the helichrysum, from which cuttings may be taken (see pages 85–6).

52 TRADITIONAL REDS AND BLUES

The mix of colours in this basket would show up particularly well beside a dark blue door. The variegated leaves of the plectranthus and the white stripes in the geranium and busy lizzie flowers give a welcome lift and help to create an attractive and lively arrangement.

Site
Eye level, sheltered and sunny.

Container
Wire hanging basket: 35cm (14″) in diameter with a sturdy 27.5cm (11″) bracket.

Planting Time
Mid to end May (unless you have a greenhouse or conservatory, in which case plant from mid April and keep it inside until end May).

At its best
June to September.

Ingredients
3 red and white striped busy lizzies *Impatiens* F1 Hybrids.
½ strip of trailing white lobelia *Lobelia erinus* 'White Cascade'.
1 strip of trailing dark blue and white lobelia *Lobelia erinus* 'Sapphire'.
1 red upright geranium *Pelargonium* 'Bruni'. This was bought from a garden centre but was culture virus indexed. The result is larger flowers and brighter colours. It was a large plant and certainly worth the extra money.
2 scarlet and white trailing ivy-leaved geraniums *Pelargonium* 'Rouletta'. These two were large as well. If you can only find medium-sized ones buy three and put one in the centre-front underneath the fuchsia.
1 *Fuchsia* 'Snowcap' with its red and white flowers.
1 *Plectranthus hirtus* 'Variegatus' known as Swedish ivy; a prostrate foliage plant with white edges to its leaves.
1 *Helichrysum petiolare* 'Limelight'; another spreading foliage plant of a more upright bushy character. This one has attractive lime-green leaves.
2 dark blue petunias *Petunia* × *hybrida*, Grandiflora type.
10 litres of John Innes No 2 soil.
2 handfuls of grit.
1 basketful of moss, sphagnum preferably, or wreath moss from a florist.
1 circle of plastic sheeting about the size of a dinner plate, cut from a strong plastic bag.

Method
1. Line the base of the basket with a generous thickness of moss and then bring it halfway up the sides.
2. Cut four 2.5cm (1″) slits in the plastic circle and place over the moss lining in the bottom of the basket.
3. Spread the grit over the plastic circle and add 7.5cm (3″) of soil.

4. Plant one of the busy lizzies in the centre of the basket sides, carefully passing the foliage through the wire rings. Plant the other two on either side, leaving a small space in between.
5. Divide both lobelias, plant one clump of white next to the central busy lizzie and another six or seven clumps of blue in between the other plants so that they form a ring around the basket. Make sure all the roots have good contact with the soil.
6. Add more soil so that the roots are covered. Firm down all the plants so that there is no chance of them falling out.
7. Add more moss so that it now forms a thick collar above the rim of the basket.
8. Plant the upright geranium in the centre-back of the basket and the two trailing geraniums on either side.
9. Plant the fuchsia at the centre-front with the plectranthus and helichrysum centre-right and left near the rim of the basket. Plant the petunias just behind them on either side of the fuchsia.
10. Plant the remaining lobelia all round the rim of the basket wherever you can find a space. Save a clump of white for the centre-front.
11. Fill in the gaps with soil. Water well.
12. Firm in the plants and add more soil and moss if necessary. The soil level should now be just below the rim of the basket, not equal to it.

Aftercare
Water generously. In hot weather you must be prepared to do it daily. Never water when the sun is shining on it as the leaves will scorch and look unattractive. Evening is best, then it is refreshed for the next day. It is best to water at soil level; otherwise the petunia flowers will be damaged. It is very densely planted and needs to be carefully looked after. Apply a liquid feed once a week. Deadhead the geraniums and petunias regularly and at the end of the summer trim back the helichrysum if it is getting too straggly. You will need to spray for greenfly etc. Keep watch and act quickly.

At the end of the summer, dismantle the basket. Discard the petunias, busy lizzies and lobelia. Overwinter the helichrysum and plectranthus so that you can take cuttings next spring (see p. 86). Pot up the geraniums and fuchsias and bring indoors (see pages 85–6).

53   AN ORANGE BALL

Orange tagetes and the intricate coleus leaves make a striking combination, a perfect colour for this background. With two circles of small plants around the sides, and the rest in the top, this basket is reasonable in cost and easy to look after.

Site
Eye level or slightly below, sheltered and sunny.

Container
Wire hanging basket: 35cm (14″) in diameter with a sturdy 27.5cm (11″) bracket.

Planting Time
Mid to end May (or earlier if you have a greenhouse or conservatory, but don't put it out until mid May).

At its best
June to September.

Ingredients
  3 strips of *Coleus blumei*. You will find a wonderful mixture of colours. Much cheaper and easier to plant here than pots.

  3 strips of dwarf double French marigolds *Tagetes patula* 'Spanish Brocade' or any other one that you especially like for its colours – either russet, yellow, gold or red.

10 litres of John Innes No 2 soil.

2 handfuls of horticultural grit.

1 basketful of moss, sphagnum preferably, or wreath moss from a florist.

1 circle of plastic sheeting about the size of a dinner plate, cut from a strong plastic bag.

Method

1. Line the basket with a generous thickness of moss, starting at the base and working a third of the way up the sides.
2. Cut four 2.5cm (1″) slits in the plastic circle and place over the moss lining in the bottom of the basket.
3. Spread two handfuls of grit and add 5cm (2″) of soil.
4. Carefully divide the strips of coleus and tagetes. Plant eight coleus in a circle through the sides of the basket, one third of the way up from the bottom so that they rest snugly on top of the moss. Try and put plants of different colours next to each other. Then plant eight tagetes in between them. Discard any with extra long stems.
5. Make sure all the roots have good contact with the soil and that the plants are not sticking out further than they need to.
6. Build up the wall of moss so that it comes two-thirds of the way up the sides. Make sure the bottom row of plants is firmly secured by the moss and that no gaps have been left. Add more soil and bring it level with the moss.
7. Repeat the operation with the coleus and tagetes using another two strips. This time position all the tagetes so that they are placed over a coleus and vice versa. This will ensure a good mixture of colours and leaf patterns.
8. Add more moss so that it forms a collar above the rim of the basket. Then add more soil to bring the level to within 2.5cm (1″) of the rim.
9. Plant the remaining tagetes and coleus around the top of the basket, again alternating them so that the plants around the sides are different from the ones immediately below.
10. Water well. Gently firm down the plants and add more soil and moss if necessary. Make sure there are no weak spots in the moss around the top of the basket; otherwise water will escape through the sides rather than soak into the basket.

Aftercare

Water regularly; you must be prepared to do it daily in hot weather. Apply a liquid feed once a week. You should not be troubled by greenfly etc but if you are then spray immediately. Deadhead regularly to maintain a neat appearance and encourage further flowering.

To keep the ball of coleus and tagetes in shape you must pinch out the growing tips every two or three weeks. Aim to keep the whole basket looking even. This photograph was taken at the end of July. By the end of August you might let nature take its course and give up the task of pinching out. I like the coleus flowers which appear as blue spikes. Allow them to grow and in the autumn you will have a new look. If by then the bottom of the basket is looking less interesting than the top, simply take it off its bracket and put it on the floor. It can still be enjoyed for its glorious colours, even if it is no longer so neat.

Dismantle the basket in late September and discard all the plants.

54   A PINK AND BLUE BALL

Begonias and lobelia create a tight ball. It remains neat and attractive throughout the season, it is reasonable in cost and the plants are easy to find and to look after. You could vary the shades or colours to suit your own taste. Try pale pink begonias and deep blue lobelia. Or you could even make an all-white basket.

Site
Eye level, sheltered, sunny, partial shade or full shade.

Container
Wire hanging basket: 35cm (14″) in diameter with a sturdy 27.5cm (11″) bracket.

Planting Time
Mid to end May (or earlier if you have a greenhouse or conservatory, but don't put it out until mid May).

At its best
June to September.

Ingredients
3 strips of fibrous-rooted begonias *Begonia semper-florens* with pink, white or red flowers and green or bronze foliage. Sometimes the strips are mixed, sometimes they will be a single colour. Hunt around and buy just what you want.
3 strips of compact lobelia. *Lobelia erinus* 'Cambridge Blue' is pale blue as used here, or you could try 'Crystal Palace' with its deep blue flowers and bronze foliage.
10 litres of peat-based compost or John Innes No 2 soil.
2 handfuls of horticultural grit.
1 basketful of moss, sphagnum preferably, or wreath moss from a florist.
1 circle of plastic sheeting about the size of a dinner plate, cut from a strong plastic bag.

Method
1. Line the basket with a generous thickness of moss, starting at the base and working a third of the way up the sides.
2. Cut four 2.5cm (1″) slits in the plastic circle and place over the moss lining in the bottom of the basket.
3. Spread two handfuls of grit and add 5cm (2″) of soil.
4. Carefully divide the strips of begonias and lobelia. You would expect to find about eight plants or clumps of plants to a strip.
5. Plant eight begonias in a circle through the sides of the basket, one-third of the way up from the bottom so that they rest snugly on the moss. Then plant eight clumps of lobelia in between.
6. Make sure all the roots have good contact with the soil and that the plants are not sticking out further than they need to.
7. Build up the wall of moss so that it now comes two-thirds up the sides of the basket. Make sure the bottom row of plants is firmly secured by the moss and that no gaps have been left. Add more soil and bring it level with the moss.
8. Repeat the operation with the begonias and lobelia using another two strips. This time

position all the begonias so that they are placed over the lobelia and vice versa. This will ensure an even distribution over the whole basket.

9. Add more moss so that it forms a collar above the rim of the basket. Then add more soil to bring the soil level to within 2.5cm (1″) of the rim.

10. Plant the remaining begonias and lobelia around the top of the basket, again alternating them so that the plants around the edge are different from those immediately below.

11. Water well. Gently firm down the plants and add more soil and moss if necessary. Make sure there are no weak spots in the moss around the top of the basket; otherwise water will escape through the sides rather than soak into the basket.

Aftercare

Water regularly; be prepared to do it daily in hot weather. Apply a liquid feed once a week. You should not be troubled by greenfly etc but if you do notice them, then spray immediately. Deadhead the begonias to maintain a neat appearance. No pinching out should be necessary – the plants should grow together and maintain the ball effect.

Dismantle the basket in late September. Discard all the plants unless you want to try and keep one or two of the begonias as houseplants (the roots may be very difficult to separate). Pot them up, trim back the top growth and bring them inside onto a warm window-sill. They will soon grow on again.

55   FOUR IN A ROW

This delightful group of matching hanging baskets made a great impact. Why not try two identical ones on either side of your front door?

Site
Sheltered, sun or partial shade is best for these two baskets.

Container
Wire hanging basket: 35cm (14″) in diameter with a sturdy 27.5cm (11″) bracket.

Planting Time
Mid to end May (or earlier if you have a greenhouse or conservatory, but don't put it out until mid May).

At its best
June to September.

Ingredients
2 strips of *Lobelia erinus* 'Cascade Mixed'.
1 upright pink geranium such as *Pelargonium* 'Brenda Kitson' or 'Burgenland Girl'.
1 *Fuchsia* 'Aintree' or any other bush variety which matches the colour scheme.
2 dark blue *Petunias* × *hybrida*, Grandiflora type. You could substitute 2 white, or find mixed blue and white striped ones.
2 pink busy lizzies *Impatiens* F1 hybrids; a similar shading to the geraniums. If this basket is to be in partial shade rather than full sun, try 4 busy lizzies and miss out the petunias.
3 trailing pink ivy-leaved geraniums *Pelargonium* 'Helena'; a double with deep pink flowers. Alternatively, try the softer pink 'Madame Crousse'.
10 litres of John Innes No 2 soil.
2 handfuls of grit.
1 basketful of moss, preferably sphagnum or wreath moss from a florist.
1 circle of plastic sheeting about the size of a dinner plate, cut from a strong plastic bag.

Method
1. Line the basket with a generous thickness of moss and then bring it halfway up the sides.
2. Cut four 2.5cm (1″) slits in the plastic circle and place over the moss lining in the bottom of the basket.
3. Spread the grit over the plastic circle and add 7.5cm (3″) of soil.
4. Divide the strips of lobelia and plant about eight clumps around the middle of the basket, carefully passing the foliage through the wire rings. Make sure all the roots have good contact with the soil.
5. Add more moss so that it forms a collar above the rim of the basket. Add 5cm (2″) more soil.
6. Plant the upright geranium at the centre-back of the basket and the fuchsia in centre-front.
7. Plant the petunias (and/or busy lizzies) on either side.
8. Plant the biggest trailing geranium in the centre-front between the fuchsia and rim, and one at each side.
9. Plant the remaining lobelia around the edge of the basket.
10. Fill in the gaps with soil. Water well.
11. Firm in the plants and add more soil and moss if necessary. The soil level should now be just below the rim of the basket – not equal to it – whereas the moss should be just above it. In time the moss will sink down and you don't want gaps appearing through which water can escape.

Aftercare
Water generously. In hot weather be prepared to do it every day; it would be difficult to give too much. Never water when the sun is shining on the basket as the leaves will scorch. It is much better to water in the evening and to apply it at soil level so the flowers won't be marked. The basket is very densely planted and needs lots of attention. Apply a liquid feed once a week. Deadhead the geraniums and petunias and watch out for greenfly, particularly on the petunias. Spray immediately you see them.

At the end of the summer, dismantle the basket. If you want to overwinter the geraniums and fuchsia see page 86. Discard the other plants.

56 A COLOUR MATCH

This basket was planted to complement the pot shown in Recipe 70. The strong apricot-orange of the geranium 'Deacon Suntan' is very similar to that of the busy lizzies. Add white verbena and lobelia, grey trailing helichrysum and the attractive foliage of sedum sieboldii and you have a striking combination.

Site
Eye level, sheltered and sunny.

Container
Wire hanging basket: 35cm (14″) in diameter with a sturdy 27.5cm (11″) bracket. (This scheme could be easily adapted to a solid plastic hanging basket: reduce the number of plants according to size eg. three busy lizzies, just one sedum, no white geranium.)

Planting Time
Mid to end May (or earlier if you have a greenhouse or conservatory, but don't put it out until mid May).

At its best
June to September.

Ingredients
3 *Sedum sieboldii* 'Medio-variegatum' with spreading grey and creamy-yellow foliage, so good with salmons and whites.
5 salmon-pink busy lizzies *Impatiens* F1 Hybrids.
1 strip of white lobelia *Lobelia erinus* 'White Lady'. White lobelia often has a few blue seeds in it (as seen in the photograph).
1 white upright geranium *Pelargonium* 'Immaculata'.
1 white verbena *Verbena* × *hybrida*.
2 apricot-orange geraniums *Pelargonium* 'Deacon Suntan'. A striking colour, it smothers itself with flowers, especially in a very hot summer. Available from the Vernon Geranium Nursery (see the list of specialist suppliers on page 225). If pale pink, lilac or red appeals more, look for geraniums of that colour and buy matching busy lizzies.
2 *Helichrysum microphyllum*, a trailing foliage plant with small grey leaves.
10 litres of John Innes No 2 soil.
2 handfuls of horticultural grit.
1 basketful of moss, sphagnum preferably or wreath moss from a florist.

1 circle of plastic sheeting about the size of a dinner plate, cut from a strong plastic bag.

Method
1. Line the basket with a generous thickness of moss, starting at the base and working up the sides.
2. Cut four 2.5cm (1″) slits in the plastic circle and place over the moss lining in the bottom of the basket.
3. Spread two handfuls of grit and add 7.5cm (3″) of soil.
4. Carefully plant one of the sedums in the centre-front of the basket, and plant two busy lizzies on either side. Add half the strip of lobelia in between these plants.
5. Add more moss so that it forms a collar above the rim of the basket. Check that there are no gaps around the plants in the centre of the basket. Cover their roots with soil and make sure they are firmly in place.
6. Plant the white geranium at the centre back of the basket, with the white verbena in front. Plant the two 'Deacon Suntan' on either side.
7. Plant one busy lizzie at the front of the basket and

the other two further back around the sides with the two helichrysum and sedums in between.

8. Use up the rest of the lobelia in any spaces around the rim or in the top of the basket.
9. Fill in the gaps with soil. Water well and add any more soil or moss as necessary. Make sure there are no weak spots in the moss around the top; otherwise water will escape through the sides rather than soak into the basket.

Aftercare

Water regularly; be prepared to do it daily in hot weather. It is best done at soil level so the flowers remain unspoilt. Do not water in direct sunlight, wait until the evening. Apply a liquid feed once a week. Deadhead the geraniums and verbena frequently. Spray against greenfly as necessary.

Dismantle the basket in September. To overwinter the geraniums, helichrysum and sedums see pages 85–6. Discard the lobelia, verbena and busy lizzies.

57 BRIGHT AND CHEERFUL

A vivid mixture of colours brightens up a north-facing wall. Begonias, busy lizzies and lobelia all thrive in shade, and the French marigolds seem quite happy too!

Site
Eye level, sheltered, shade or partial shade.

Container
Solid green plastic hanging basket: 27.5cm (11″) in diameter, only 10cm (4″) deep. This has less than half the volume of the 35cm (14″) diameter wire baskets used elsewhere and allows no planting in the sides. However, it is simple to plant up, and has the advantage that the plastic lip attached to the base of the basket acts as a small reservoir.

Early Preparation
If you purchase the begonia tubers in February or early March you can start them into growth yourself. This way you will save a considerable amount of money. (Follow the instructions on page 85.) On the other hand you should be able to buy plants of these colours in a garden centre in May.

Planting Time
Mid to end May (unless you have a greenhouse or conservatory in which case plant from mid April and keep it inside until mid to end May).

At its best
June to September.

Ingredients
1 yellow non-stop begonia *Begonia* × *tuberhybrida*.
2 orange or salmon trailing begonias *Begonia* × *tuberhybrida*. (I made a mistake here and planted a salmon-pink non-stop. By the time I realized it was too late to change.)
2 salmon-pink busy lizzies *Impatiens* F1 Hybrid.
$\frac{1}{2}$ strip of dwarf French marigolds *Tagetes patula* 'Leopard' or 'Fireflame'. There are so many to choose from.
1 strip of trailing lobelia *Lobelia erinus* 'Sapphire'. This one is dark blue with a white eye. It makes a good contrast with the oranges and yellows.
4 litres of a multipurpose peat-based compost.

Method

1. Cover the base of the basket with 5cm (2″) of compost.
2. Plant the yellow non-stop begonia in the centre with the two trailers on either side positioned so that they fall naturally over the edge of the basket.
3. Plant one busy lizzie on each side of the central begonia.
4. Split the tagetes and plant them around the busy lizzies.
5. Divide the lobelia and tuck it in between all the plants around the rim of the basket so that it forms a complete circle.
6. Fill in the gaps with soil so that the level comes just below the rim of the basket.
7. Water well, firm in the plants and add more soil if necessary.

Aftercare

Food and water is what this basket needs most! Be prepared to water generously in hot weather and feed weekly. If it is in a north-facing site as here, the time of day when watering is unimportant; otherwise never water when the sun is shining on it as the leaves will get scorched and look very unsightly. Water at soil level to prevent all the moisture running off the leaves.

It should not be troubled by greenfly etc but if it is, spray immediately. Deadhead the begonias and tagetes.

At the end of the summer, dismantle the basket. Discard the lobelia, tagetes and busy lizzies. If you want to save the begonias for another year follow the instructions on page 85.

58   A WEDDING OR CHRISTENING ARRANGEMENT

White anemones and white alyssum make a wonderful display fit for any wedding reception or christening party in May or early June.

Site
Partial shade, best in full sun.

Container
Wire hanging basket: 35cm (14″) in diameter. I placed it on this lovely white urn to show how baskets can be so easily used for other purposes than hanging. By planting up the basket rather than the urn I had a much bigger planting area and could make maximum use of the pretty white alyssum, planting it in the sides of the basket to create a white frill around the anemones. It is much less susceptible to cold weather than many other summer bedding plants and so is particularly suitable.

Early Preparation
Buy the anemone corms in February or March. They are rather a strange shape but don't be put off! Buy large ones. Plant them about three months before you want them to flower. Spring weather can be so unpredictable; you would probably be safer planting another batch early and another one rather later. However, they do continue flowering for several weeks and they are reasonably priced.

Planting Time
Plant the anemones in March in a shallow plastic container about 25cm (10″) in diameter and 10cm (4″) deep (a green solid plastic hanging basket would be ideal) and add the alyssum at the end of April.

At its best
May or early June depending on time of planting and weather.

Ingredients
3   strips of white alyssum *Lobularia maritima*. (This photograph shows the sides planted with white lobelia as well but it was not in flower by end May/early June. Alyssum is better for this time.)
10 white anemones *Anemone* 'De Caen'; the height should be 15–30cm (6–12″) although mine grew higher. This is a single white with several flowers to each corm. 'St Brigid' is the double or semi-double strain but it has less flowers per plant. There were lots of flowers still to come out in this arrangement. The photograph was taken before it looked its best as it had a wedding to attend the next week!
10 litres of a multipurpose peat-based compost.
2 handfuls of horticultural grit.
1 basketful of moss, sphagnum preferably, or wreath moss from a florist. If difficult to find at this time of year locate some ordinary lawn moss. I wouldn't normally recommend it for summer baskets but any growth from grass seeds here will not be too obvious.
1 circle of plastic sheeting about the size of a dinner plate, cut from a strong plastic bag.

Method
1. Use the green solid plastic container to begin with. Fill it with soil and plant the anemone corms 5cm (2″) deep. Water gently, firm the soil down lightly and place in a light, cool, frost-free area. Maintain the soil moisture and increase the water supply gradually as the foliage begins to grow.
2. When the alyssum becomes available towards the end of April, buy the moss and prepare the wire basket.
3. Cover the base of the wire basket with a generous thickness of moss, starting at the base and working a third of the way up the sides.
4. Cut four 2.5cm (1″) slits in the plastic circle and place over the moss lining in the bottom of the basket.
5. Cover with grit and then add 5cm (2″) of soil.
6. Divide the alyssum and plant about eight plants in a circle around the basket, carefully passing the foliage through the wire rings. Make sure the roots have good contact with the soil and that the plants are not sticking out any further than they need to.
7. Add more moss so that it now comes two-thirds of the way up the sides of the basket. Make sure the bottom row of plants is firmly secured by the moss and that no gaps have been left. Add more soil and bring it level with the moss.
8. Plant a second circle of alyssum following the same method as described above.
9. Bring the wall of moss right above the rim of the basket, so that it forms a thick collar.
10. Now for the slightly tricky part: it is like unmoulding a jelly! Gauge the depth required to put the anemones in the centre of the basket. Make a well 25cm (10″) in diameter and 10cm (4″) deep in the centre of the basket.
11. Carefully remove the anemones from the first container and put them straight into the wire basket. The easiest way is simply to turn the first container upside-down on the palm of your hand and then quickly revert and pop them in their final resting place. Alternatively, divide the anemones into two or three sections and move each one in turn.
12. Plant the remaining alyssum in a circle around the rim of the basket. Fill any remaining gaps with soil. Water well.

Aftercare
Water regularly (daily in hot weather) and apply a liquid feed once flowering has begun. Spray for greenfly as necessary. Deadhead all fading flowers.

Enjoy the wonderful honey scent of the alyssum and the delicate flowers of the anemones. You don't need a special occasion for an excuse to plant them!

After flowering plant them out in a sunny spot in the garden. They should flower another year and with luck the alyssum will seed itself: happy reminders!

59   SALMON IN HIGH SUMMER

This simple planting of salmon geraniums and matching salmon busy lizzies provided a bright display throughout the summer. The tall spikes of the white antirrhinum added extra interest and were echoed in the terracotta pot in Recipe 66.

Site
Sunny.

Container
Medium wooden window box: 90cm (36″) long, 20cm (8″) wide, 20cm (8″) deep.

Planting Time
Mid to end May.

At its best
June to September.

Ingredients
  1 antirrhinum or snapdragon *Antirrhinum* 'White Wonder'; of medium height.
  2 strong upright salmon geraniums *Pelargonium* 'King of Denmark'.
  3 salmon busy lizzies *Impatiens* F1 Hybrids.
  1 strip of lobelia either all the same colour or a rich mixture of different blocks of colour as here: *Lobelia erinus* 'Mrs Clibran' is dark blue with a white eye; 'Crystal Palace' is dark blue with bronze foliage; 'Cambridge Blue' is pale blue; and 'Snowball' is white.
30 litres of John Innes No 2 soil.
Drainage material such as pieces of polystyrene.

Method
1. Cover the base of the window box with 2.5cm (1″) of drainage material and add 7.5cm (3″) of soil.
2. Plant the antirrhinum in the centre towards the back with the geraniums on either side.
3. Plant the busy lizzies in a row in the centre-front.
4. Fill in the gaps with soil, bringing the level to within 2.5cm (1″) of the rim of the box.
5. Add the lobelia along the front edge.
6. Water well. Firm in the plants and add more soil if necessary.

Aftercare
Water regularly; in hot weather this will mean a daily routine. Apply a liquid feed weekly from end June. Deadhead the geraniums and antirrhinum. Spray for greenfly etc as necessary, although you might have no problem with this combination.

    At the end of the summer, pot up the geraniums if you want to keep them for another year (following the instructions on page 86). Discard the other plants.

60 SUBTLE SHADES FOR AUTUMN

There is a gap between the main summer displays and those of winter. Chrysanthemums are excellent container plants for this time of year and are available in so many colours. Here is a combination of pink chrysanthemums and trailing blue campanula which create a very restful and pleasing picture.

Site
Sunny.

Container
Small to medium wooden window box: 75cm (30") long, 20cm (8") wide, 20cm (8") deep.

Early Preparation
Chrysanthemums are available in mid to late summer in many florists and garden centres but they will be hothouse plants and they will not be hardy. If you would like to try hardy cushion chrysanthemums from Thompson and Morgan Ltd (see the list of specialist suppliers on page 225) order by mid March. Delivery of young plants is in April. Grow them on according to the instructions supplied with the order and plant in the window box in July. There is a minimum order of ten plants. Either plant the rest in hanging baskets or pots for a full autumn display or split the order with a friend. These are hardy so you can keep them for another year.

Planting Time
July or early August.

At its best
End August to early October.

Ingredients
1 *Hebe* 'La Seduisante' with dark green leaves to contrast with the variegated one below. This is not reliably hardy but treated in the same way as described below it has a good chance of survival.
2 *Hebe* × *andersonii* 'Variegata'. It has lavender flowers in autumn. This is not reliably hardy, but should survive most winters if kept in a sheltered spot.
2 hardy 'cushion' *Chrysanthemum*; 'The 1000 Flowers' sold by Thompson and Morgan Ltd. Otherwise try the hothouse chrysanthemums or pink cyclamen.
3 blue trailing campanula *Campanula isophylla*.
2 *Sedum sieboldii* 'Medio-variegatum', a trailing foliage plant with fleshy grey and creamy yellow leaves.
20 litres of John Innes No 2 soil.
Drainage material such as old crocks or pieces of polystyrene.

Method
1. Cover the base of the container with 2.5cm (1″) of drainage material and add 7.5cm (3″) of soil.
2. Plant the plain dark green hebe in the centre-back of the box with the two variegated hebes spaced on either side.
3. Plant the two pink chrysanthemums towards the front of the box on either side of the central hebe.
4. Along the front edge of the box plant the three campanulas with the two sedums in between.
5. Fill in the gaps with soil, bringing the level to within 2.5cm (1″) of the rim of the box.
6. Water well. Add more soil if necessary.

Aftercare
Water regularly to maintain a moist soil and apply a liquid feed every week. Deadhead the chrysanthemums, hebes and campanulas. Spray if necessary. At the end of the flowering season remove the chrysanthemums and plant in the garden so that they can be enjoyed another year. Pot up the campanulas and sedums so that they can be overwintered in the protection of a greenhouse (see pages 85–6). Leave the hebes in place but plant a row of yellow pansies and pink bellis daisies along the front for a winter and spring display. Make sure you put the window box in a sheltered sunny place and with luck the hebes should survive.

61   A RICH TAPESTRY OF COLOURS

This window box is teeming with a variety of strong colours both in the flowers and foliage.

Site
Sheltered; sun or partial shade. Begonias can be easily broken. Mishaps do happen, as seen here with one missing trailing begonia on the left.

Container
This is an unusually long box: 120cm (48″) long, 20cm (8″) wide, 20cm (8″) deep.

Early Preparation
If you buy begonia tubers in February or early March you can start them into growth yourself. This will give you a wider choice of colours and save money. (See page 85 for instructions.)

Planting Time
Mid to end May.

At its best
June to September.

Ingredients
2 white marguerites *Chrysanthemum (Argyranthemum) frutescens* once known as the Paris daisy.

3 double upright begonias – 2 dark pink and 1 yellow – *Begonia* × *tuberhybrida*.

2 dark pink trailing begonias (only one showing in the photograph) *Begonia* × *tuberhybrida*.

2 variegated leaved geraniums *Pelargonium* 'Lady Plymouth'.

3 white trailing geraniums *Pelargonium* 'L'Elegante'.

2 *Perilla frutescens*, a handsome bronze foliage plant which provides a good contrast to others. It was a Victorian favourite. If unobtainable in garden centres, substitute more coleus.

3 *Coleus blumei* with richly coloured leaves.

½ strip of *Lobelia erinus* 'Cambridge Blue' and 'Snowball'.

30 litres of a soil-less peat-based compost or John Innes No 2 soil.

Drainage material such as small pieces of polystyrene.

Method
1. Cover the base of the container with 2.5cm (1″) of drainage material and add 7.5cm (3″) of soil.
2. Along the back of the box, from left to right, plant the white marguerite, double pink begonia, double yellow begonia, double pink begonia and white marguerite.
3. Along the front of the box, from left to right, plant the geraniums 'Lady Plymouth' and 'L'Elegante', coleus, perilla, coleus, geranium 'L'Elegante', perilla, coleus and lastly geraniums 'L'Elegante' and 'Lady Plymouth'.
4. Fill in any remaining gaps with soil, bringing the level to within 2.5cm (1″) of the rim. Plant the lobelia around the sides of the box and along the front edge.
5. Water well. Add more soil if necessary.

Aftercare
Water regularly at soil level; in hot weather water daily (in the evening). Begonia leaves are particularly susceptible to leaf scorch, so do the watering in the evening when the sun is not shining on them. Water at soil level so that you are sure the water can soak right in rather than run off the large leaves onto the ground. Apply a liquid feed once a week. Deadhead the geraniums and begonias regularly. Support the double begonias if they are not on a window-sill. Spray for greenfly etc as necessary.

At the end of the summer discard the lobelia, perilla and coleus. To keep the begonias, geraniums and the marguerites (see pages 85–6).

62   A BRIDAL WALLPOT

This is the simplest of all combinations and could grace any summer wedding whether the style was Victorian or modern. The name of the geranium is 'L'Elegante' and it has been a favourite for the last hundred years.

Site
Full sun outdoors or in a conservatory.

Container
Terracotta wallpot: 32.5cm (13″) wide, 15cm (6″) deep. (This is a particularly large pot so scale down the planting if you are using a smaller one.)

Planting Time
Mid to end May.

At its best
June to September.

Ingredients
3 white trailing ivy-leaved geraniums *Pelargonium* 'L'Elegante'. It has very attractive variegated leaves which turn mauve around the edges if the plant gets dry.
1 strip of white alyssum *Lobularia maritima*.
7 litres of John Innes No 2 soil.
Drainage material such as old crocks or pieces of polystyrene.

Method
1. Cover the base of the container with 2.5cm (1″) of drainage material and add 5cm (2″) of soil.
2. Plant the three geraniums around the rim of the wallpot.
3. Add more soil to bring the level to within 2.5cm (1″) of the rim and plant the alyssum all around the wallpot in between the geraniums and in the corners and around the back.
4. Water well. Gently firm in the plants.

Aftercare
The geraniums will survive quite well without too much water but the alyssum will soon wither away, so water regularly; this might mean every day in hot weather. Apply a liquid feed once a week. Deadhead the geraniums. The alyssum may be subject to downy mildew; spray with Zineb.

At the end of the summer discard the alyssums and if you want to keep the geraniums through the winter follow the instructions on page 86.

63   GOLDEN ORF IN SUMMER

'Golden Orf' is a striking dwarf geranium. Its golden foliage and delicate coral-pink flowers creates a magnificent show all summer long. The sedum clothes the basket and provides an excellent underplanting, especially early in the season when its golden tips match the geranium leaves.

Site
Full sun.

Container
An old wicker basket: 30cm (12″) long, 25cm (10″) wide, 15cm (6″) deep. Almost any wicker basket will do; however, it is vital that it receives three good coats of yacht varnish to preserve it outdoors.

Planting Time
Mid to end May.

At its best
June to September.

Ingredients
2 coral-pink dwarf geraniums *Pelargonium* 'Golden Orf'; yellow leaf with bronze zone.
2 stonecrops, *Sedum acre* 'Aureum' with golden tips from March to June. Growth is rapid.
6 litres of John Innes No 2 soil (or less if the sedums are large plants).
Drainage material such as small pieces of polystyrene.
Black plastic sheeting, cut from a refuse sack, to use as a liner; this will help to keep the basket dry on the inside and prevent soil escaping through the wickerwork.

Method
1. Cut some black plastic sheeting to fit inside the basket so that it covers the base and comes right up the sides. Make six 2.5cm (1″) slits in the bottom area to allow excess moisture to drain away.
2. Cover it with 2.5cm (1″) of drainage material and add 5cm (2″) of soil.
3. Plant the two geraniums either side of the handle.
4. Plant the sedums at either end of the basket.
5. Fill in the gaps with soil, bringing the level to just beneath the rim of the basket. Cut off any excess plastic sheeting which may still show, or tuck it under the soil.
6. Water carefully. Add extra soil if necessary.

Aftercare
Water regularly, although this planting scheme will stand the odd day of neglect! Apply a liquid feed once a week. Deadhead the sedums and geraniums to keep the basket tidy. Trim the growth on the sedums if it becomes too long.

At the end of the summer empty the contents of the basket. If you want to pot up the geraniums see page 86. Use the sedum for an outdoor winter display (see Recipe 29). Revarnish and plant up the basket again for either outdoor or indoor use.

64   SUMMER BEDDING IN A STONE TROUGH

Stone troughs look attractive but some are so shallow that they are difficult to plant. Often simple patterns can be the most effective. Succulents make ideal partners in this scheme.

Site
Full sun or light shade.

Container
Stone trough: 90cm (36″) long, 47.5cm (19″) wide, 10cm (4″) deep. Make sure there is a drainage hole, and that the trough is tilted slightly towards it.

Planting Time
End May/early June.

At its best
It will remain attractive all summer. I like the flowers on the echevarias which appear in mid summer; however you might prefer to cut them off to retain the simplicity.

Ingredients
2 *Agave americana* 'Marginata' with sword-shaped leaves arranged in a rosette. Choose small ones.
6 strips of *Echeveria secunda*; like a little agave with grey rosettes. It produces orange flower spikes in June and July. Masses of offsets are formed by late summer making it a very easy plant to propagate. To buy six strips would be extremely expensive so why not buy just a few plants, say six in total this year, overwinter them in a greenhouse, remove the offsets and pot up in March and then by May you will have plenty for this scheme. The next year you could make a hanging basket out of them for the conservatory. You could substitute house-leeks for the echeveria.
25 litres of John Innes No 2 soil.
10 litres of horticultural grit.
Large crocks to cover the drainage hole.

Method
1. Place the large crocks over the drainage hole. Pour some water into the trough to check that it all drains towards the hole.

2. Cover the base of the trough with a thick layer of grit. Add 7.5cm (3″) of soil.
3. Plant the two agaves in the middle of the trough, either side of centre.
4. Depending on how many echeverias you have available, plant them around the edge of the trough and in a central group between the agaves. Don't worry if you only have a few echeverias. As long as the pattern is symmetrical it will be attractive.
5. Add more soil if necessary to bring the level just below the rim of the trough. Water carefully to remove any soil on the foliage.
6. Add the remaining grit so that it forms a complete cover over the arrangement.

Aftercare
Water regularly. These succulents will survive the odd day of drought but they will thrive far better on loving care and attention. No spraying is necessary. Deadhead the echeverias to keep the trough tidy.

In September pot up the agaves and echeverias. Agaves have very large, fleshy roots and I was amazed to see how far they had spread out in this shallow trough. The echeverias can be planted several to a pot and then divided in the spring when the offsets are potted up separately.

65   A DONKEY CART

A rich variety of gay summer bedding plants tumble out of this colourful old donkey cart. You could try painting an old wheelbarrow or a wooden beer barrel and using that instead.

Site
Sun or partial shade.

Container
An enamel sink 52.5cm (21″) long, 40cm (16″) wide, 15cm (6″) deep, acts as the real container in this display. Several drainage holes were drilled into the base. It is simply placed inside the donkey trailer and raised up slightly. If you planted a wheelbarrow you could find a smaller container to place inside it or cut out black sheeting (don't forget the slits in the bottom) and use as a liner.

The great advantage of both these items is that you can move the displays around your garden for maximum impact.

Early Preparation

Try growing the begonia tubers yourself. Buy in February or early March and start into growth following the instructions on page 85. The nasturtiums can be sown in late March or early April to get strong early plants, but you could leave them until the main planting in May. If you have a greenhouse this display could be planted together at the end of April and put out in mid May.

Planting Time

Mid to end May (or end April if planted in a greenhouse).

At its best

June to September. The begonias make a wonderful display all summer. But it is interesting to watch the emphasis shift from the white to the yellow daisies in mid summer, and to see the nasturtiums making more and more of an impact as autumn grows nearer. By then they were completely entwined around the shafts of the cart. These were May sown, and would have made a bigger display earlier if I had brought them on earlier. This photograph was taken in late July.

Ingredients

There is such a wide range of coloured begonias to choose from. The doubles are tall with very large flowers. The non-stops are more compact, and the trailers are low-spreading plants with more elongated flowers. Orange trailers seem to trail lower than white for some reason.

1 white double begonia *Begonia* × *tuberhybrida*.
2 salmon non-stop begonias *Begonia* × *tuberhybrida*.
2 yellow daisies *Chrysanthemum (Argyranthemum) frutescens* 'Jamaica Primrose'. These tend to flower best from mid to late summer.
2 white daisies *Chrysanthemum (Argyranthemum) frutescens*; the popular white marguerite or Paris daisy of old. These tend to flower best from early to mid summer.
3 orange trailing begonias *Begonia* × *tuberhybrida*.
½ strip of trailing lobelia *Lobelia erinus* 'Sapphire' with dark blue and white flowers which contrast well with these rich colours.
4 semi-trailing nasturtiums *Tropaeolum majus*

'Double Gleam Mixed'; semi-double flowers in orange, scarlet, and yellow. They are sweetly scented and the young blooms look marvellous on a summer salad or in a vase at the harvest supper!
20 litres of a multipurpose peat-based compost or John Innes No 2 soil.
Drainage material such as pieces of polystyrene.

Method

1. Cover the base of the container with 2.5cm (1″) of drainage material and add 7.5cm (3″) of soil.
2. Plant the large white double begonia towards the centre-back with the two salmon non-stops at the front on either side.
3. Plant the yellow and white daisies in a line through the middle of the display.
4. Plant the three orange trailing begonias near the edge of the container, one on each side at the front and the third at the back.
5. Divide the lobelia and plant at the front and back.
6. Fill in the gaps with soil, bringing the level to within 2.5cm (1″) of the rim of the container.
7. Firm in the plants. Water well.
8. Sow the nasturtium seeds in four pairs around the front, back and sides. When they have germinated remove the weakest one.

Aftercare

Water regularly. This is closely planted and needs to be looked after well. Be prepared to water daily in hot weather. Never water when the sun is shining on it as you will scorch the leaves. Wait until evening and then water at soil level; otherwise some of the water will simply run off the large begonia leaves on to the ground.

Apply a weekly liquid feed. Deadhead the daisies, nasturtiums and begonias to keep a tidy appearance and encourage further flowering. Spray for greenfly and blackfly as soon as necessary. The daisies in particular seem to attract greenfly and the nasturtiums attract blackfly.

In the late autumn dismantle the container. The white daisies can be overwintered and used for cutting material the following spring (see page 85). The begonias can be dried off and overwintered ready to start into growth the following spring (see page 85). Discard the nasturtiums and lobelia.

66 THRIFTY SALMON

This pot is based on the same colour theme as the salmon-pink window box in Recipe 59 but it does not contain any geraniums. It just goes to show that you can have a colourful and longlasting display without spending very much money.

Site
Sun or partial shade.

Container
Terracotta pot: 36cm (14″) in diameter, 12cm (5″) deep. Any tub, pot or barrel would be suitable.

Planting Time
Mid to end May.

At its best
June to September.

Ingredients
1 white antirrhinum or snapdragon *Antirrhinum* 'White Wonder'. Easily grown from seed or available as strip bedding at most garden centres. Buy a strip and plant the remainder in other window boxes or pots.
3 salmon busy lizzies *Impatients* F1 Hybrids.
1 strip of lobelia; it might be the same colour or in mixed groupings as here. Planting a variety creates a rich and colourful effect. *Lobelia erinus* 'Mrs Clibran' is dark blue with a white eye; 'Crystal Palace' is dark blue with bronze foliage; 'Cambridge Blue' is pale blue and 'Snowball' is white. You can buy lobelia mixed in strips but that gives a different effect to mixed groupings. With salmon-pink I think groups of dark blue and of white make particularly good partners.

25 litres of a soil-less peat-based compost or John Innes No 2 soil.
Drainage material such as pieces of polystyrene.

Method
1. Cover the base of the container with 5cm (2″) of drainage material and add sufficient soil to bring the level to within 5cm (2″) of the rim.
2. Plant the antirrhinum in the centre of the pot with the three busy lizzies around it near the edge.
3. Plant the lobelia all round the edge of the pot.
4. Water well. Firm in the plants and add more soil if necessary to bring the level to within 2.5cm (1″) of the rim.

Aftercare
Water regularly; be prepared to do it daily in hot weather. Apply a liquid feed once a week. Remove old antirrhinum spikes after flowering. Spray for greenfly if necessary, but it will probably remain quite free of pest trouble.

At the end of the summer discard all the plants unless you want to try and grow the antirrhinum for another year, in which case plant it out in a sunny spot in the garden.

67   A BEGONIA POT

Begonias are excellent value in summer pots, not only because their season lasts for such a long time but because they provide a wide choice of colours, including yellow, which shows up so well in summer arrangements.

Site
Sun, partial or full shade, but a fairly sheltered site.

Container
Ali Baba pot (made by Whichford Pottery): 43cm (17″) in diameter, 50cm (20″) deep.

Early Preparation
Try growing the begonia tubers yourself. Buy in February or early March and start into growth (following the instructions on page 85). You will have a greater choice of colours and they will prove much cheaper. For well-established nasturtium plants sow seeds in March or early April and transfer to the begonia pot in May.

Planting Time
Mid to end May.

Ingredients
   2 yellow double begonias *Begonia* × *tuberhybrida*.
   3 yellow trailing begonias *Begonia* × *tuberhybrida*.
   2 yellow non-stop begonias *Begonia* × *tuberhybrida*. There is a red and yellow begonia called 'Marginata Crispa' which would have looked lovely here.
   2 cherry-red nasturtiums *Tropaeolum* 'Dwarf Cherry Rose' (which would have combined beautifully with 'Marginata Crispa'). With all-yellow begonias you could use any ordinary mixed semi-trailing varieties, or for a really special display use 'Peach Melba' which is a lovely, soft yellow blotched with scarlet.
$\frac{1}{2}$ strip of blue lobelia *Lobelia erinus* 'Crystal Palace'.
25 litres of a soil-less peat-based compost or John Innes No 2 soil.
Drainage material such as pieces of polystyrene.

Method
1. Cover the base of the container with 5cm (2″) of drainage material and add sufficient soil to bring the level three-quarters of the way up the pot.
2. Plant the double begonias in the centre of the pot, adjusting the soil level as necessary so that the top

of their rootball is sitting about 2.5cm (1″) below the rim of the container.
3. Plant the trailers around the edge and then the two non-stop begonias in between at the front.
4. Plant the nasturtiums on either side with the lobelia around the edge.
5. Fill in the gaps with more soil to bring the level to within 2.5cm (1″) of the rim.
6. Water well. Add more soil if necessary.

Aftercare
Water regularly; be prepared to do it daily in hot weather. Apply a liquid feed once a week. Use cane supports for the double begonias. Spray for blackfly etc as necessary. Deadhead the begonia and nasturtium flowers.

   At the end of the summer discard the lobelia and nasturtiums, but if you want to overwinter the begonias follow the instructions on page 85.

Opposite: Yellow begonias – upright, trailing and non-stop – create the link between the two containers

68   A WEB OF LIME-GREEN

Lime-green is an unusual colour for high summer but it is very pleasing mixed with pinks and dusky reds. The lead trough acts as an excellent base colour. This is an adaptable planting which will thrive in almost any site, and it is scented.

Site
Sun, partial shade or full shade.

Container
Oval lead trough (made by Renaissance Casting Company Ltd): 62.5cm (25″) long, 30cm (12″) wide, 15cm (10″) deep.

Planting Time
Mid to end May.

At its best
June to September.

Ingredients
1 *Helichrysum petiolare* 'Limelight'; a spreading foliage plant with lime-green leaves which become even more striking when wet.
1 strip or 5 plants of tobacco plant *Nicotiana* 'Domino F1 Mixed'; these are dwarf and compact. If you want taller plants then try 'Sensation Mixed'. They come in a delightful range of pinks, creams, white, lime-green and reds. They are all fragrant.
30 litres of a multipurpose peat-based compost or John Innes No 2 soil.
Drainage material such as small pieces of polystyrene.

Method
1. Cover the base of the container with 5cm (2″) of drainage material and add sufficient soil to bring the level to within 5cm (2″) of the rim.

2. Plant the helichrysum in the centre of the trough.
3. Plant the tobacco plants all around, trying to mix the colours. Don't use the whole strip as they will grow into quite large plants.
4. Water well. Firm in the plants and add more soil to bring the level to about 2.5cm (1″) of the rim of the container.

Aftercare
Water regularly; in hot weather be prepared to do it daily. Apply a liquid feed every week from the end of June. If the bottom leaves of the tobacco plants get untidy, cut them off. Deadhead regularly. You will need to spray against greenfly. Act as soon as you see the evidence.

   At the end of the summer, pot up the helichrysum so that it may be overwintered and have cuttings taken from it the following spring. Discard the tobacco plants.

69 GRANDMA'S POT OF PINK AND MAUVE

A simple planting of matching pink geraniums, busy lizzies and fuchsias. They are surrounded by trailing mixed lobelia which blends so well with this colour scheme.

Site
Partial shade, or sun.

Container
Terracotta pot: 30cm (12″) in diameter at top, 28cm (11″) deep. Any medium to large container would be suitable.

Planting Time
Mid to end May.

At its best
June to September.

Ingredients
2 pink upright geraniums *Pelargonium* 'Mary Wilkes' or 'Olympia'. The cultivar is not particularly important but try and choose a colour where you can match a fuchsia and busy lizzie to it.
2 matching pink fuchsias; *Fuchsia* 'Aintree' is a lovely one with dainty white and pink flowers.
2 matching pink busy lizzies *Impatients* F1 Hybrids.
1 strip of mixed lobelia *Lobelia erinus* 'String of Pearls'.
14 litres of a multipurpose peat-based compost or John Innes No 2 soil.
Drainage material such as small pieces of polystyrene.

Method
1. Cover the base of the container with 5cm (2″) of drainage material and add 13cm (5″) of soil.
2. Plant the two geraniums on opposite sides of the pot, centre-front and centre-back.
3. Plant the two fuchsias to the centre-right and centre-left.
4. Plant the busy lizzies by the geraniums.
5. Fill in the gaps with soil, bringing the level to within 2.5cm (1″) of the rim of the container.
6. Carefully divide the lobelia and plant all round the edge.
7. Water well. Add more soil if necessary.

Aftercare
Water regularly; in hot weather be prepared to do it daily. Apply a liquid feed once a week from end June. Spray for greenfly etc as necessary. Deadhead geraniums and fuchsias.

At the end of the summer discard the lobelia and busy lizzies. If you want to keep the geraniums and fuchsias pot them up according to the instructions on page 86.

70   BRONZE AND APRICOT

The dramatic bronze leaves of the perilla contrast well against the rich apricot-orange of the geranium and salmon-orange fuchsia. They make a striking combination. See Recipe 56 for a hanging basket idea using the same geraniums.

Site
Sunny.

Container
Terracotta pastry flower pot (made by Whichford Pottery): 37.5cm (15″) in diameter, 27.5cm (11″) deep.

Planting Time
Mid to end May.

At its best
June to September.

Ingredients
1 *Fuchsia* 'Thalia' with distinctive long and narrow salmon-orange flowers. It is widely available.
2 apricot-orange upright geraniums *Pelargonium* 'Deacon Suntan' supplied by the Vernon Geranium Nursery (see the list of specialist suppliers on page 225). Otherwise choose a salmon-pink geranium.
2 dark bronze foliage plants *Perilla frutescens*; available at some garden centres (if not substitute coleus).
1 white verbena *Verbena* × *hybrida*.
$\frac{1}{2}$ strip of white lobelia *Lobelia erinus* 'Snowball'.
$\frac{1}{2}$ strip of dark blue lobelia *Lobelia erinus* 'Mrs Clibran'.
25 litres of a multipurpose peat-based compost or John Innes No 2 soil.
Drainage material such as pieces of polystyrene or old crocks.

Method
1. Cover the base of the container with 5cm (2″) of drainage material and add sufficient soil to bring the level about three-quarters of the way to the top.
2. Plant the fuchsia in the middle of the pot with the two geraniums on either side.
3. Plant the perilla on the opposite sides.
4. Plant the verbena in the front of the pot.
5. Fill in the gaps with soil, bringing the level to within 2.5cm (1″) of the rim of the container.

6. Plant some white lobelia at the edge of the pot in front of the verbena. Plant the rest of the blue and white lobelia alternately around the pot.
7. Water well. Add more soil if necessary.

Aftercare
Water regularly. In hot weather you must be prepared to do it daily. Always water at soil level so as not to spoil the blooms. Never water when the sun is shining on the pot as it will cause the leaves to scorch. Evening is the safest time. Apply a liquid feed once a week from end June. Deadhead the verbena, fuchsia and geraniums. Spray for greenfly etc as necessary.

At the end of the summer discard the verbena and lobelia, but keep the geraniums and fuchsia (for instructions see page 86).

71   A BARREL OF DAHLIAS

Dahlias create a marvellous show in tubs where they can spread out and exhibit their brilliant flowers. They are good for a late summer display, adding a new dimension of colour and form.

Site
Sunny.

Container
Wooden half barrel traditionally painted. To preserve the wood use a plastic pot to fit inside the barrel; this one is 40cm (16″) in diameter, 30cm (12″) deep. Raise it slightly off the floor.

Early Preparation
To save money and if you want a particular named variety, buy the tubers in February or March when they are available in the garden centres and start into growth by mid April, placing them 10cm (4″) deep in dry peat. Once they have started into growth water them gently. Or buy them in growth from a garden centre in May.

Planting Time
Outdoors, mid to end May.

At its best
July to September or October.

Ingredients
3 bedding dahlias *Dahlia* 'Little William'.
1 mature ivy *Hedera helix* 'Eva'.
½ strip of lobelia *Lobelia erinus* 'White Lady'.
40 litres of a multipurpose peat-based compost or John Innes No 2 soil.
Drainage material such as small pieces of polystyrene.

Method
1. Cover the base of the plastic liner or barrel with 5cm (2″) of drainage material and add sufficient soil to bring the level about halfway up the barrel.
2. Plant the dahlia tubers resting on the soil with their sprouting growths spaced so as to encourage a well-balanced display.
3. Cover gently with soil.
4. Plant the mature ivy at the front of the barrel.
5. Add more soil to bring the level to within 2.5cm

(1″) of the rim of the container and add the white lobelia around the edge.
6. Water well.

Aftercare
Water regularly; this needs to be done daily in hot weather. Apply a liquid feed once a week from early July. Deadhead the dahlias to encourage further flowering and to keep the display tidy. Destroy any earwigs which appear.

Wait until the frost has blackened the dahlias, and then a week later cut the stems to within 15cm (6″) of soil level. Remove and place the tubers upside-down for a week to allow moisture to drain out of the hollow stems. Then put them, stem up, in a box of barely moist peat so that the peat surrounds them but does not cover their crowns. Store in a frost-free place at a temperature of 5°C (41°F). Start into growth in the spring.

72   A POT OF CHRYSANTHEMUMS

A heady display of chrysanthemums is especially welcome at a time of year when summer plants are fading. Mixed with colourful coleus they can create a dazzling display.

Site
Sunny.

Container
Medium to large pot. This one is an old sea-kale pot turned upside-down: 37.5cm (15″) in diameter, 42.5cm (17″) deep.

Early Preparation
Chrysanthemums are available in mid to late summer from many florists and garden centres but most of them will be hothouse plants and they will not be hardy. If you want to try hardy 'cushion' chrysanthemums from Thompson and Morgan Ltd (see the list of specialist suppliers on page 225) order by mid March. Delivery of young plants is in April. Grow them on according to the instructions supplied with the order and plant in the final container in July. There is a minimum order of ten plants. Either plant the rest in window boxes, hanging baskets or individually in the conservatory, or split the order with a friend. Being hardy you can keep them for another year.

Planting Time
End July.

At its best
End August to early October.

Ingredients
  4 hardy 'cushion' chrysanthemums; two colours, either russet and white or russet and gold, *Chrysanthemum* 'The 1000 Flowers' sold by Thompson and Morgan Ltd. Otherwise try hothouse chrysanthemums or white cyclamen.
  4 *Coleus blumei*; choose the ones with the most interesting leaf colourings.
28 litres of John Innes No 2 soil.
Drainage material such as large crocks or pieces of polystyrene.

Method
  1. Cover the base of the container with 5cm (2″) of drainage material and add sufficient soil to bring the level three-quarters of the way up the sides.

  2. Plant the chrysanthemums with the two colours opposite each other.
  3. Plant the coleus in between.
  4. Fill in the gaps with soil, bringing the level to within 2.5cm (1″) of the rim.
  5. Water well.

Aftercare
Water regularly to maintain a moist soil and apply a liquid feed every week from end August. Deadhead the chrysanthemums to keep them tidy and encourage more flowering. It is a personal choice but you can pinch out the flower buds on the coleus to prevent flowering and to maintain a neat shape. If the frost kills the coleus before the chrysanthemums have finished flowering, simply remove the dead foliage – the chrysanthemums will remain unharmed. After the display is over, plant the chrysanthemums in the garden where they will bloom another year. Discard the coleus if it is not already dead or you can try potting up one or two and keeping it indoors on a sunny window-sill.

CONSERVATORY SCHEMES

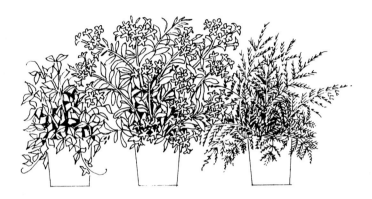

INTRODUCTION TO THE CONSERVATORY RECIPES

Conservatories are deservedly popular these days and are used as much as a living space as a plant house. Getting the right balance is sometimes difficult and much will depend on which way the conservatory faces and how much natural shading it gets from trees or houses outside. A south-facing conservatory with an open aspect can be a big problem in summer as temperatures soar up to and well over 40°C (104°F). The atmosphere becomes very dry and few plants enjoy such excessive heat and bright light.

SHADING
Shading is essential for all but north-facing conservatories not only in summer but in spring and autumn too. Ideally you want to be able to adjust it to suit the weather. Interior blinds fixed to the apex of the roof are extremely useful (the sort that can be easily rolled down and removed for cleaning). Side blinds are very helpful, too, but not as vital as the top ones. Climbing plants growing on the outside of the conservatory can do much to create shade around the sides; one of my favourites for this is the passion flower with its finely divided leaves which look so attractive from behind as well as in front, to say nothing of its exquisite flowers and fruit. If you have no bed around the outside of the conservatory you can always grow it in a pot. Large foliage plants placed judiciously inside can also create shade but

they take up rather a lot of room as well. Depending on the size of your conservatory, just one or two large specimens of the ficus family or a palm or fatshedera can produce good shade, plus a feeling of luxuriant growth. At the same time they will provide a good grouping to show off smaller and more colourful plants.

VENTILATION
Ventilation is as important as shading. Automatic vents which open the top windows when the temperature reaches a predetermined level are most helpful, indeed essential, if nobody is at home all day to open the doors and lower windows. Not only does ventilation help to moderate temperatures, it also allows excess humidity to escape. You may notice the conservatory windows are covered with moisture each morning in spring and early summer. On a dull day this would remain all day and create a dank atmosphere. Adequate ventilation will improve this. The opposite problem can occur during summertime when the plants suffer because the air is too dry. Red spider mites thrive in these conditions and do untold damage. It is important then to keep the pots well watered daily and if necessary keep a watering-can full of water at ground level to increase the humidity. (This is a good tip anyway because it means the water is at air temperature when you give the plants their drink.) Another tip is to splash water over the floor

but this can obviously only be done where it is tiled.

PEST CONTROL

Pest control can be a problem in conservatories where reproduction rates can make the mind boggle. Smoke cones are an effective means of dealing with most insects and mites but the smell is unpleasant and may creep into the house. Always put a mat between the conservatory door and the house and remember to block the keyhole! A safe alternative is to use an organic spray or buy a batch of parasitic or predatory insects. Just as ladybirds should be encouraged to fly in and gobble up lots of the greenfly, on a more sophisticated level special insects may be introduced which thrive in the greenhouse or conservatory environment where the temperature is over 20°C (68°F). These include tiny predatory beetles, wasps and midges which will live off the mealy bug, red spiders, whitefly, greenfly and blackfly. They do not bite or sting and are quite harmless to humans and animals. They are purchased in individual lots and are all available by mail order through Thompson and Morgan Ltd, as advertised in their seed catalogue. They are expensive, but they will repeat their life cycle throughout the summer and so give long-lasting protection.

A much cheaper method of pest control is to grow lots of basil and special tagetes (a particular French marigold suggested by Thompson and Morgan Ltd) in the conservatory. Both plants are insect-repellant and aromatic, colourful in the case of the tagetes, while the basil is very useful in the kitchen. The basil leaves can be crushed to form an organic pesticide. One seed packet of each produced large quantities of plants which I grew in my solardome in the very hot summer of 1989. The results were amazing; I had very little problem from insects at all. I will certainly repeat the experiment again.

WATERING

Regular attention to watering is essential. A healthy plant is far less likely to be troubled by insects. Be prepared to check and possibly water daily for up to six months of the year. An automatic watering system can be invaluable, particularly if you like to go away at weekends or are out most of the day. Some plants will obviously need more water than others and this is allowed for by simply putting more feeder tubes in some pots than others. You can put fertilizer capsules into the supply at regular intervals as well so it can do two jobs effectively. Another advantage is that the water is given at soil level, which avoids any splashing on the leaves and potential scorching. If

watering by hand, never do it in full sun but wait till the evening so that the plants can enjoy a good drink through the cool of the night and be refreshed the next day.

TEMPERATURE CONTROL

Temperature control is important both in summer and winter. Don't be surprised to find a noon temperature of 30°C (86°F) on a sunny day in November or February. Ventilation is vital under these circumstances, even at this time of year. But beware: a sunny day in winter can bring clear skies at night, with temperatures dropping below freezing point. Plants near the window or raised up near the top of the conservatory are especially vulnerable, particularly where they like a minimum temperature of 7°C (45°F), which seems to apply to quite a wide range of conservatory specimens. However, less harm will come to these plants if they are kept on the dry side and moved to ground level near an interior wall. It is important to have some form of heating in the conservatory, often an extra radiator run off the central heating system in the house, but complete with its own thermostat. Additional night-time heaters may be necessary in some conditions. If your conservatory is well stocked, you will have quite a valuable investment in terms of the plant stock alone. It is worth conserving if at all possible.

ARRANGEMENT OF PLANTS

You have a wide choice of plants throughout the year. Create a backcloth of greenery by using a few choice palms, some of the ficus family, fatshederas, ivies, ferns or spider plants, for example. Against this place more colourful combinations which will stand out against the darker background of these other plants and add highlights of colour. The verbena and plumbago arrangement will show off beautifully. So, too, the seasonal colours provided by the bulbs. Dwarf daffodils can be underplanted by primroses, hippeastrum can be carpeted by selaginella, and lilies can be planted with sweet-scented mignonette. These are all charming combinations which are suggested in some of the recipes which follow.

Fragrant plants are so important in the conservatory. It is wonderful to open the door in the morning and smell the primroses or pansies, the mignonette or the verbena; or to brush past the rose scented geranium in the wallpot and smell roses! You might enjoy the aroma of herbs; water the early herb pot and pinch the lemon balm or variegated mint. Try growing the tomato, basil and tagetes hanging basket or window box in the conservatory in the early summer and come to know the wonderful aromas which arise when you water them.

Consider carefully before you place your plants. You want to create a composition so that the plants show each other off well and you have one or more focal points. One of the wicker basket arrangements placed on a central table would set off the whole room. Always put the plants which have finished flowering somewhere out of the main view; tuck them away behind something bigger or more colourful. Tidy up any dead leaves or flowers; don't allow them to detract from the main scene. Keep all the surfaces and windows clean.

Height is an important element and can give the conservatory a more spacious feeling if plants are positioned at eye level or above. Make good use of climbers such as the passion flowers or the lapagerias and introduce hanging baskets either in spring or summer (although not included in this section see Recipes 122 and 123 which would give colour from May to November). Don't forget wallpots which can create great cascades of greenery or bring specimen plants within close proximity.

VICTORIAN STYLE

If you want to echo the style of a modest Victorian conservatory you can make use of the terrariums, ferns and selaginellas, zantedeschias, hippeastrums and lilies. Wonderful lapagerias should be added as a Victorian favourite. Mignonette is a must for its scent. A whole chapter could be devoted to the theme, but let it suffice to give just a few ideas which you will find amongst the recipes which follow.

Concentrate on a few main schemes, some for each time of the year, and you will soon have a room that excites the eye and is a joy to be in. The more care you give the plants the greater your rewards. Here are just a few ideas to start you off!

73   A RUSTIC SPRING BASKET

The yellow and pink in the basketry is echoed by the bright spring flowers. The little daffodil is called 'Tête-à-Tête' and is longlasting, reliable and one of the best for indoor work.

Site
Conservatory, kitchen window-sill, porch or patio table.

Container
Rustic wooden basket: 27.5cm (11″) in diameter, 12.5cm (5″) deep. It has been varnished three times with a good quality yacht varnish so that it can also stand outdoors.

Planting Time
September to October for the bulbs, February for the primroses.

At its best
February to March, depending on whether you force it or not.

Ingredients
15 dwarf daffodils *Narcissus cyclamineus* 'Tête-à-Tête'; these are short, multiheaded and longlasting – ideal for this kind of planting. If you want an April basket try 'Hawera'; also dwarf and multiheaded but in flower a month later.

 4 primroses *Primula vulgaris*; these were chosen with pink to echo the basket and a yellow eye to reflect the daffodils. There are lots of beautiful shades to choose from in the early spring.

6 litres of a peat-based compost or John Innes No 2 soil.

Drainage material such as horticultural grit or small pieces of polystyrene.

1 large circle of black plastic sheeting (taken from a refuse or soil sack) to fit inside the basket and act as a liner. It will stop moisture from the soil coming into contact and so rotting the basket; it will also prevent the soil from escaping through any gaps in the sides. Choose black so it won't show through the wicker work.

Method
1. Line the basket with the black plastic so that it fits snugly round the bottom and comes well up the sides right to the rim of the basket. Cut six 2.5cm (1″) slits in the base of the liner to allow excess moisture to escape.
2. Cover the liner with 2.5cm (1″) of drainage material and add 5cm (2″) of soil.
3. Plant four empty flower pots around the edge of the basket to mark the spot where the primroses will go in the spring. (Two either side of the handle will look pretty later on.)

4. Plant the daffodil bulbs in the centre of the basket and around the pots so that they will form an attractive group in the spring.
5. Fill in the gaps with soil and firm it down lightly.
6. Water well and then place in a cool, dry shed outdoors, or in a sheltered but protected part of the garden if the basket has been varnished.
7. The soil should be kept just moist throughout the winter.
8. When the shoots are about 5cm (2″) high and the buds are clearly seen, remove the empty flower pots and plant the primroses.
9. If you bring the basket indoors at this stage you will probably have a February display. If you leave it outdoors in a sheltered position on the porch or patio you will probably have an early March display. You can of course move the basket about at your will to provide the colour wherever you want it. That's one of its many advantages!

Aftercare
Keep the soil moist at all times, but increase the water as the daffodils begin to grow. After planting the primroses, give a liquid feed every week.

The display will last longer if the basket isn't subjected to too much heat. Conservatories can warm up very quickly even in February. The warmth won't kill the plants but it will shorten their flowering period. Keep them in a light, shady spot for most of the time if possible.

Immediately after flowering is over, carefully remove the contents and plant them out in the garden where they should give pleasure in future years. The daffodils need to be watered until their foliage has died down naturally. The primroses may not be hardy, but it is worth taking the risk. Choose a sheltered site. The basket can now be replanted (see Recipe 77).

74   A PERIOD PIECE

If you look at a hippeastrum (amaryllis) flowering in a pot by itself, it often appears rather naked. But surround it with mossy selaginella and the planting becomes transformed into a period piece straight out of Mollison's book *The New Practical Window Gardener* published in 1879.

Site
Conservatory or light window-sill indoors, but if you want to prolong the flowering period then keep out of direct sunlight for most of the day.

Container
Ordinary clay pot: 17.5cm (7″) in diameter, 17.5cm (7″) deep.

Planting Time
September to November.

At its best
February and March (or earlier if specially treated bulbs are used, but you may have difficulty buying the selaginella in mid winter).

Ingredients
1 pink *Hippeastrum* bulb commonly known as amaryllis. The hybrids are available in red, pink or white with stripes and even frills. Choose one to match your colour scheme.
2 low-growing *Selaginella apoda*; most easily available in the early spring.
1 litre of John Innes No 2 soil.

Drainage material such as a few crocks or small pieces of polystyrene.

Method
1. Cover the base of the container with 2.5cm (1″) of drainage material and add 5cm (2″) of soil.
2. Plant the bulb in the centre of the pot. Add more soil, leaving the top third of the bulb exposed.
3. Water the pot, then put in a warm place such as a sunny indoor window-sill near a radiator, or in the airing cupboard, until such time as a green shoot appears. Keep soil barely moist until this happens.
4. Once the shoot has begun to grow it is time to plant the two selaginellas on either side of the amaryllis.
5. Water carefully and then put the pot into its permanent position – light but not too sunny.

Aftercare
Maintain the soil moisture throughout the growing period. Staking may be required as the flowers are very large and heavy. Apply a liquid feed weekly from the time the flower spike appears until the leaves have yellowed and died down. Remove the selaginellas at this stage and transplant elsewhere in the conservatory (see the zantedeschia pot in Recipe 79). Allow the hippeastrum to stay in its pot, quite dry, until growth begins again in the late autumn. Then you can start the whole cycle again. There is no need to repot but feeding will be essential.

75   A TERRARIUM

Terrariums were a popular form of indoor gardening in mid Victorian times and once again they are very much in favour. If the window is kept closed they need no additional watering. They are particularly suitable for plants that love a moist atmosphere.

Site
A north-facing or shady conservatory would be ideal.

Container
Octagonal terrarium: 30cm (12″) across, 35cm (14″) deep. It has a removable glass window.

Planting Time
Early spring onwards when the plants are available in the garden centres.

At its best
Remains attractive throughout the year.

Ingredients
2 small selaginellas; fern-like plants which love damp conditions and were much used in Victorian plant cases. Choose two of contrasting colour and shape: there are upright, golden, variegated and trailing varieties. Seen here is the upright *Selaginella martensii* and the low *Selaginella apoda*.
1 central palm *Chamaedorea (Neanthe) bella*; the common Parlour Palm.
1 *Helxine (Soleirolia) soleirolii* commonly known as Mind Your Own Business or Baby's Tears! The silver variegated cultivar 'Argentea' has been used here, but there is also a golden-green one called 'Aurea'.
1 box of charcoal.
1 litre each of silver sand and horticultural grit.
2 litres of John Innes No 1 soil.

Method
1. With the window of the terrarium facing towards you, first cover the base with a layer of charcoal, then grit, then sand, in total just over 2.5cm (1″).
2. Add 7.5cm (3″) of soil and then another layer of sand. The soil layer need not be even, in fact it will look more interesting if you raise it up higher on one side and show off the different texture of the charcoal, grit, soil and sand.
3. Plant the selaginellas around the back and on either side of the terrarium, the palm in the centre and lastly the helxine at the front.
4. Firm in the plants gently. Water lightly and very

carefully so as not to splash soil on the glass or plants.
5. Close up the window and place in a light but shaded position. Regulate the window opening for the first few days until a balanced atmosphere is achieved. From this stage onwards little additional watering should be necessary.

Aftercare
The atmosphere in the terrarium will have achieved a good balance when there is only a little condensation on the glass. If there is too much you will need to open the window and let some of the moisture escape into the atmosphere in the room.

Check regularly to see that none of the plants have damaged leaves or stems. If they have, remove them immediately. If one plant grows fast and threatens to smother another, trim it back or replace with a cutting or smaller plant. You will see that the helxine has grown rampant here and needs a haircut!

A minimum winter temperature of 10–13°C (50–55°F) is required. If the temperature threatens to fall below this, bring the terrarium into a warmer spot in the house.

76 EARLY HERBS

Take advantage of the warm spring temperatures inside the conservatory and 'force' a pot of herbs to produce tender, fragrant leaves at least a month earlier than under outdoor conditions.

Site
Conservatory from February until end April; sun or partial shade.

Container
Small to medium clay pot: 30cm (12″) in diameter, 12.5cm (5″) deep.

Planting Time
September to November outdoors or lift from garden in February. Bring pot indoors from February to end April.

At its best
March and April in the conservatory, but will flourish outdoors from then onwards for the rest of the summer.

Ingredients
1 pot or clump of chives *Allium schoenoprasum*; grass-like leaves with a mild onion flavour. Excellent on salads or used with cold eggs and potatoes. Lilac-pink flowers in early summer may be used for scattering on salads or making a mild onion sauce.
1 golden marjoram *Origanum vulgare* 'Aureum'; this has golden yellow leaves when young and pink flowers. Both are aromatic and useful in stuffings, salads, soups and garnishings.
1 *Mentha rotundifolia* 'Variegata'; excellent for culinary and decorative purposes and lasts longer into winter than many of the other mints.
1 golden balm *Melissa officinalis* 'Variegata' with strong lemon-scented leaves which are good for stuffings, salads or cold drinks. Keep clipped for a neat appearance.
6 litres of John Innes No 2 soil.
Small amount of drainage material such as broken crocks or pieces of polystyrene.

Method
1. Cover the base of the container with 2.5cm (1″) of drainage material and add 5cm (2″) of soil.
2. Plant the four herbs around the edge of the pot with the chives at the back, marjoram at the front and the mint and balm on either side.
3. Fill in the gaps with soil, bringing the level to within 2.5cm (1″) of the rim of the container.
4. Firm in the plants. Water well and add more soil if necessary.

Aftercare
Maintain soil moisture throughout the growing period. There will be a rapid take-up of water as growth is made. Apply a liquid fertilizer from early March onwards. Crop the chives when they are about 7.5–10cm (3–4″) high, half at a time if you wish, and then after two or three cuts leave to mature so that you can harvest the flowers. Use the lemon balm as often as you can to prevent it from growing more than 5cm (2″) high. In this way it will remain neat and fresh. The mint can be picked as early as you like; it will continue to make fresh growth so long as it is kept moist and fed. The marjoram makes a lovely fresh garnish on pâtés and salads; use it frequently to enjoy the tender leaves.

Place the pot outdoors after the end of April, keep harvesting the contents regularly and you will be rewarded for many weeks by tender new growth. Divide and plant the contents out at the end of the summer into permanent positions in the herb garden.

77   A SIMPLE BASKET OF DAISIES AND PANSIES

Here is another easy idea for a rustic basket. Pansies and daisies thrive together in this simple arrangement which is as happy in the conservatory in March and April as it would be outdoors in May. It would make a lovely Easter present.

Site
Conservatory, shaded if in direct sunlight all day long. By May it would probably be happier outside.

Container
Varnished rustic wooden basket: 27.5cm (11″) in diameter, 12.5cm (5″) deep. Preserve it with three good coats of yacht varnish so that it can stand outdoors as well as inside the conservatory. The same planting scheme could be adapted to other conservatory containers such as terracotta wallpots, tubs, pots or window boxes.

Planting Time
Early to end March for an Easter display although the basket could be made up any time to the end of April (the earlier the better, especially if you have a south-facing conservatory).

At its best
Two or three weeks after planting it will be a lovely show and continue for several weeks. It will last longer if kept partially shaded or put outside in May.

Ingredients
4 pretty pansies of your choice. Here I have used violet and cream ones *Viola* × *wittrockiana* with dainty, small faces in keeping with the size of the daisies.
1 strip or 6 pots of pink daisies *Bellis perennis* 'Dresden China'. These pinks and blues are good with the colours in the basket but you might prefer bolder yellow pansies and red daisies or some other combination.
6 litres of a peat-based compost or John Innes No 2 soil.

Drainage material such as horticultural grit or small pieces of polystyrene.
1 large circle of black plastic sheeting (taken from a refuse or soil sack) to fit inside the basket and act as a liner. It will stop moisture from the soil coming into contact with the basket and so, in time, rotting it. It will also prevent the soil from escaping through any gaps in the sides. Choose black so it won't show through the wickerwork.

Method
1. Line the basket with the black plastic so that it fits snugly around the bottom and comes well up the sides right to the rim of the basket. Cut six 2.5cm (1″) slits in the base of the liner to allow excess moisture to escape.
2. Cover the liner with 2.5cm (1″) of drainage material and add 5cm (2″) of soil.
3. Plant two pansies on each side of the handles. Add a little more soil.
4. Divide the strip of daisies and plant around the edge of the basket.
5. Fill in the gaps with soil, bringing the level to within 2.5cm (1″) of the rim of the basket.
6. Water well. Gently firm in the plants and add more soil if necessary.

Aftercare
Water regularly – this is most important – and apply a liquid feed every week. Deadhead both the pansies and daisies to keep them neat and to encourage further flowering.

This basket has been planted for the conservatory where it will thrive in March and April. By early May you may find it will be happier outside, as by then the temperatures in the conservatory will be getting rather high, depending on its aspect. Of course, this basket can be placed outside on the patio or in the porch at any time from planting onwards as all the plants are quite hardy.

At the end of May, empty the basket, discard all the plants and refill with miniature geraniums.

78   A CASCADING GREEN WALLPOT

Combine a spider plant and an asparagus fern and you will have cascades of elegant greenery for many years to come. Simple to plant and easy to look after.

Site
A light position in the conservatory or house but out of direct sunlight; can be placed outdoors in summer.

Container
Medium to large terracotta wallpot: 25cm (10″) long, 20cm (8″) wide, 20cm (8″) deep.

Planting Time
April ideally but can be planted at any time of year.

At its best
Attractive all year round, particularly once the plantlets have formed on the spider plant. You may also have red berries on the asparagus fern in the winter months.

Ingredients
1 *Asparagus sprengeri* with arching feathery foliage.
1 *Chlorophytum comosum* 'Mandaianum'; the common spider plant with a central yellow stripe to its leaves. Small plantlets are formed in mid summer which trail down gracefully below the plant.
8 litres of a peat-based compost or John Innes No 2 soil.
Drainage material such as a few small crocks or pieces of polystyrene.

Method
1. Cover the base of the container with 5cm (2″) of drainage material and add 7.5cm (3″) of soil.
2. Plant the asparagus fern to one side of centre and the spider plant on the other.
3. Fill in the gaps with soil and bring the level to within 2.5cm (1″) of the rim of the container.
4. Firm in the plants. Water well and add more soil if necessary.

Aftercare
These plants need to be kept barely moist in late autumn and winter. They require a minimum winter temperature of 7°C (45°F). Water more frequently during early spring and summer and from end May to early autumn apply a liquid feed once a week.

If the mature fronds of the asparagus fern show a yellowing at the tips, cut them off back to the base. Remove any leaves on the spider plant that show a browning at the ends; it is a sign of neglect. Be sure to keep up the feeding and watering.

Repot in April each year and after two or three years divide the plants.

79   SPOTTY FOLIAGE

The foliage of the yellow arum lily is wonderful, especially when seen against the light. An under-planting of selaginella provides a rich green carpet. The two plants are charming together and would grace any conservatory.

Site
Conservatory.

Container
Terracotta pot: 27.5cm (11″) in diameter, 25cm (10″) deep.

Planting Time
Plant the rhizome in early spring and the selaginellas a few weeks later.

At its best
Yellow flowers should appear in May and June; this one did not oblige in its first year but the leaves were so attractive that they more than made up for any lack of flowers.

Ingredients
1 *Zantedeschia elliottiana* sometimes known as the yellow arum lily.
2 *Selaginella apoda* a pale green, mossy, low growing plant often used these days in terrariums but grown as a carpet plant by the Victorians for pot lilies and the like.
12 litres of a peat-based compost or John Innes No 2 soil.
Drainage material such as old crocks or small pieces of polystyrene.

Method
1. Cover the base of the container with 5cm (2″) drainage material and add 10cm (4″) soil.
2. Plant the rhizome of the zantedeschia in the centre of the pot.
3. Cover with soil so that the level is brought to within 2.5cm (1″) of the rim of the pot.
4. Water well after planting and then keep barely moist until growth begins.
5. When the first shoots appear, plant the two selaginellas on either side of the zantedeschia and then increase the water supply.
6. Fill in the gaps with more soil to bring the level to within 2.5cm (1″) of the rim of the container.

7. Increase the water supply as the zantedeschia leaves grow and mature.

Aftercare
Once the zantedeschia is in full growth it is important to water well. Apply a liquid feed at end May.

After flowering, remove the selaginellas, plant each in their own pot and keep moist. Gradually begin to withhold water from the zantedeschia until the leaves have turned yellow. At this stage stop watering altogether and leave dry hidden away somewhere in the conservatory or heated greenhouse until February when it can be repotted, divided and started into growth again. It needs a minimum winter temperature of around 10–12°C (50–54°F). The selaginellas can be divided, kept at similar temperatures and added at a later stage.

80 EXOTIC CANNA LILIES

Statuesque canna lilies are evocative of the tropics. Some have brown or purple leaves and the flowers can be pink, scarlet, yellow or orange. They will bring an exotic flavour to any conservatory or garden which they grace.

Site
Conservatory or a sheltered, sunny site outdoors.

Container
Medium to large terracotta pot: 30cm (12″) in diameter, 27.5cm (11″) deep. Outside it would be better to have a wider-based pot to make it more stable. A wooden half barrel could be used.

Early Preparation
Plant the fleshy rhizomes in February or March barely covered, in a peaty compost. Put them in the greenhouse or conservatory where there is a minimum temperature of 16°C (61°F). In April plant them in their summer containers. They may be kept under glass throughout the summer or put outside at the end of May.

Planting Time
Plant in their summer pot in April; add the French marigolds in May.

At its best
June to September, each flower lasts only a short time but there is a long succession of beautiful blooms.

Ingredients
2 yellow canna lilies *Canna* × *hybrida* 'Picasso'. Many other colours are available.

½ strip of yellow or orange French marigolds *Tagetes patula*; this one is the 'special marigold' sold by Thompson and Morgan Ltd to deter whitefly from tomatoes. It is a colourful plant and useful in a conservatory setting where it can act as a natural insect repellant.

15 litres of a multipurpose peat-based compost or John Innes No 2 soil.

Drainage material such as a few crocks or pieces of polystyrene.

Method
1. In April cover the base of the container with 5cm (2″) of drainage material and add sufficient soil to bring the level two-thirds of the way up the pot.
2. Plant the rhizomes in the centre of the pot so that they sit about 7.5cm (3″) below the rim of the container.
3. Add more soil around the edge of the pot so that the level is just about 2.5cm (1″) below the rim.
4. Water carefully, but not too much until growth really gets going.
5. In May plant the French marigolds so that they form a circle around the cannas.
6. Water well. Firm in the marigolds and add more soil, if necessary, to bring the level to within 2.5cm (1″) of the rim.

Aftercare
Water regularly; be prepared to do it daily in hot weather, always in the evening when the sun is no longer shining on the leaves or else they will get scorched and spoil. Apply a liquid feed every month from mid June. Deadhead the flowers to keep the plants tidy and encourage further flowering. Spray for greenfly if necessary although you might find that they remain free.

At the end of the summer, discard the French marigolds. Keep the cannas in the greenhouse or conservatory and allow the soil to remain only slightly moist. Remove dead top growth. In the spring shake off all the old soil and repot. Begin to water when growth is evident.

81   LILIES AND SCENTED MIGNONETTE

Lilies are excellent container plants for a conservatory. They come in many glorious colours, to suit all tastes. Here they are underplanted with scented mignonette which fills the air with its delicate sweet scent.

Site
Light shade in the conservatory, porch or outdoors.

Container
Medium terracotta pot: 27.5cm (11") in diameter, 25cm (10") deep.

Planting Time
Autumn or late winter depending on availability. Sow the mignonette seeds in early March according to the instructions on the packet. Pinch out the growing tips of the young pot plants to encourage bushiness. Although you only need one or two plants here, there will be plenty of space for the rest elsewhere in the conservatory or the house, or in outdoor containers for the summer.

At its best
July and August, or earlier if brought inside sooner.

Ingredients
3 apricot/orange lilies Lilium 'African Queen'. There are many different ones to choose from including the Mid Century Hybrids which are so good for pots and the short-stemmed lilies such as 'Sunray' or 'Red Carpet'.
1 or more scented mignonette Reseda odorata grown from seed sown in March.
10 litres of John Innes No 2 soil.

Drainage material such as broken crocks or small pieces of polystyrene.

Method
1. Cover the base of the container with 5cm (2") of drainage material and add 5cm (2") of soil.
2. Space the lily bulbs around the pot and cover with soil, bringing the level to within 2.5cm (1") of the rim. The lilies should be planted at least 10cm (4") – if not 15cm (6") – deep. Water well.
3. After potting, keep the lilies in a cool place to promote good root development; they may be plunged outdoors and protected with ashes, soil or peat or they may be kept in a dark, airy shed or cellar.
4. When top growth is evident, gradually bring the plants into full daylight and keep the compost moist. Conditions at this stage should remain cool.
5. Plant one or two mignonette plants at the front of the pot in early May. Growth is rapid and they will soon act as a foil to the bottom of the pot.
6. Only bring into the conservatory or house when flowering is imminent.

Aftercare
Maintain the soil moisture, especially while the pot is in the conservatory. Apply a liquid feed at the end of June.

After flowering, place in a cool, shaded spot outdoors and keep well watered until growth finally dies down. Discard the mignonette. Repeat the process the following year.

82   A STATELY REGAL PELARGONIUM

Just one regal pelargonium in full bloom can create a stunning picture either in the conservatory or house. Here it is seen underplanted with grape ivy which tumbles out of and around the base of the pot.

Site
Sun or light shade, well ventilated.

Container
Plastic pot: 25cm (10″) in diameter, 20cm (8″) deep. This is placed inside a larger, more decorative china pot.

Planting Time
April or May.

At its best
June and July.

Ingredients
1 large *Regal Pelargonium* 'Wellington'. There are many different ones in the catalogues and garden centres; be guided by your own colour preference and the quality of the individual plants available.
2 grape ivies *Rhoicissus rhomboidea*. This is a common houseplant which will suit a variety of conditions.
4 litres of a peat-based compost or John Innes No 2 soil.
Drainage material such as broken crocks or pieces of polystyrene.

Method
1. Cover the base of the container with 2.5cm (1″) of drainage material and add 7.5cm (3″) soil.
2. Plant the regal pelargonium at the centre-back of the pot and the grape ivies together at the front so that they form a frill underneath the regal pelargonium.
3. Fill in the gaps with soil, bringing the level to within 2.5cm (1″) of the rim.
4. Water well. Firm in the plants and add more soil if necessary.
5. You can then stand the smaller pot inside the larger decorative pot but first raise it up on a few small stones so that the soil never becomes waterlogged.

Aftercare
Maintain soil moisture throughout the summer and apply a liquid feed every week while flowering lasts. Spray for greenfly etc as necessary. Deadhead to keep the pot tidy.

In late August/September remove the regal pelargonium, trim back the roots and remove all top growth back to about 7.5cm (3″) of the roots. Repot on its own or with the grape ivies. Both plants require a winter temperature of around 7–10°C (45–50°F) with just a barely moist soil in winter. Alternatively, remove the grape ivies and plant elsewhere in the greenhouse until early the following summer. For example, they could look very attractive in a wicker basket with cineraria for a colourful spring planting.

83   HEAVEN SCENT

This rose-scented geranium is famous for its delightful fragrance. Brush past it in early summer or use in pot-pourri or cooking and its delights will be revealed.

Site
Conservatory; light shade is best for the setcreasea.

Container
Wallpot: 25cm (10″) long, 17.5cm (7″) wide, 27.5cm (11″) deep.

Planting Time
Late spring/early summer.

At its best
The geranium flower is a pretty but insignificant pale lilac. It is grown for its fragrant leaves and should be in a position where you brush past it or are able to reach out and feel it as you pass by. The setcreasea continues to grow and bloom all summer but is at its prettiest in July and August.

Ingredients
1 scented leaf geranium *Pelargonium* 'Attar of Roses'.
1 *Callisia elegans (Setcreasea striata)* 'Bridal Wreath' with dainty white flowers from May to September. It is a spreading plant with a similar habit to a tradescantia.
9 litres of John Innes No 2 soil.
Drainage material such as old crocks or small pieces of polystyrene.

Method
1. Cover the base of the container with 5cm (2″) of drainage material and add sufficient soil to bring the level about three-quarters of the way up the pot.
2. Plant the geranium at the centre-back of the pot with the setcreasea in front so that they sit about 2.5cm (1″) below the rim of the pot. You might

divide the setcreasea to spread it all around the front rim and sides of the pot.
3. Fill in the gaps with soil. Firm in the plants.
4. Water well. Add more soil if necessary to bring the level back to within 2.5cm (1″) of the rim.

Aftercare
Maintain soil moisture throughout the summer months, and feed once every two weeks from end May to August.

A winter temperature of 7°C (45°F) is needed. The soil should be kept barely moist. Repot the geranium in March. Either cut back or, if in a poor state, discard the old setcreasea and replace with basal cuttings taken the previous summer.

84   FRAGRANT PINK AND BABY BLUE

This is a beautiful planting combination for a conservatory. The fragrant pink verbena flowers intermingle with the pale blue plumbago all summer long.

Site
Light shade in a conservatory.

Container
Terracotta pot: 20cm (8″) in diameter, 20cm (8″) deep.

Planting Time
April to May.

At its best
May to October; it can be prolonged if the temperature is kept between 13–16°C (55–61°F) up to December, in which case you must continue to feed.

Ingredients
1 *Plumbago auriculata (capensis)*; a climbing evergreen which needs tying to a support (generally a small plastic-coated arch is supplied with container-grown plants). Wonderful pale blue flowers are produced throughout the summer long and into the autumn.
1 *Verbena* 'Silver Anne' with fragrant pink flowers which fade to a very delicate shade with age. It is an upright plant which intermingles well with the plumbago during the first year, and will form a good base for the plumbago as it grows taller in subsequent years.
5 litres of John Innes No 3 soil.
Drainage material such as a few small crocks or small pieces of polystyrene.

Method
1. Cover the base of the container with 2.5cm (1″) of drainage material and add 10cm (4″) soil.
2. Plant the plumbago at the centre-back of the pot and the verbena at the front so that the top of their rootballs sit about 2.5cm (1″) below the rim of the pot.
3. Fill in the gaps with soil to bring the level to within 2.5cm (1″) of the rim.
4. Water well. Check that the plumbago support is firmly in place.

Aftercare
Maintain soil moisture throughout the summer and apply a liquid feed every week from end May/early June onwards. Beware of greenfly etc and spray immediately if infested. Deadhead regularly to encourage flowering and to keep the pot tidy. After flowering, cut back all the new growth on the plumbago by two-thirds.

Gradually give less water as late autumn approaches and only increase supplies when new growth appears in the spring. A minimum winter temperature of 7°C (45°F) is required. Take cuttings of the verbena in early March and grow on so that they can be planted with the plumbago when repotting takes place annually in April. Increase the pot size very gradually as the plumbago gets larger each year.

The plumbago could be trained to grow up a trellis or, on repotting, use a larger plastic-coated wire frame.

85   SWEET MIMOSA

The delicate pale pink blossoms of the geranium 'Sweet Mimosa' are a joy. The flowers are amongst the prettiest of all the scented leaf geraniums, making it a perfect specimen for a conservatory.

Site
Sunny conservatory, in a position where the scented leaves can be brushed past and enjoyed.

Container
'Cherub' pot: 30cm (12″) in diameter, 25cm (10″) deep. NB: The plant pictured here is four years old so this pot would obviously be too large for a new plant.

Planting Time
End April or May, although the geranium could be purchased at any time. The lobelia will only be available end April/early summer.

At its best
Mid summer, although flowering continues all summer.

Ingredients
1 scented leaf geranium *Pelargonium* 'Sweet Mimosa' with lovely pale pink flowers and deeply-cut lobed leaves.
½ strip of mixed upright lobelia *Lobelia erinus* 'String of Pearls'.
Up to 15 litres of John Innes No 2 soil.
Drainage material such as small pieces of polystyrene or a few broken crocks.

Method
1. Cover the base of the container with 5cm (2″) of drainage material and add 7.5cm (3″) of soil.
2. Plant the geranium in the centre of the pot so that the top of the rootball sits about 2.5cm (1″) below the rim of the container.
3. Add more soil so that it is brought to the same level.
4. Divide the strip of lobelia and plant around the geranium.
5. Water well. Firm down the plants. Add more soil if necessary.

Aftercare
Maintain the soil moisture throughout the summer. The lobelia will soon wilt if the soil becomes too dry. Apply a liquid feed every two weeks from mid June until the end of the flowering season. Deadhead the

geranium regularly. Spray for greenfly etc as necessary, although I have found these plants to be generally trouble-free.

Repot the geranium using fresh soil in late summer or early autumn; trim back the roots and any straggly top growth. Discard the lobelia. New growth will soon be made and watering is still necessary but as winter approaches keep the soil only barely moist. Through the winter it requires a minimum temperature of 7–10°C (45–50°F). Take cuttings in early spring and so bring on plants for other use in the conservatory or eventually to replace this one. Renew the lobelia in May each year.

86   COOL AND GREEN LIKE A WOODLAND SCENE

Boston ferns are an old-fashioned parlour and conservatory plant. This one is particularly attractive under-planted with a creeping helxine which helps to create a picture of luxuriant growth.

Site
Draught-free conservatory or indoors in a light position out of direct sunlight.

Container
Three-legged pan (made by Whichford Pottery): 25cm (10″) wide, 12.5cm (5″) deep. Any small to medium terracotta pot would be suitable.

Planting Time
April ideally.

At its best
Once the helxine has begun to creep over the edge of the pot. Good all year round.

Ingredients
1 Boston fern *Nephrolepis exaltata* 'Bostoniensis' with gracefully drooping foliage.
2 *Helxine (soleirolia) soleirolii* 'Aurea' with golden green foliage and 'Argentea' with silver variegated leaves; also known as Mind Your Own Business or Baby's Tears.
4 litres of a peat-based compost.
Drainage material such as small pieces of polystyrene.

Method
1. Cover the base of the container with 2.5cm (1″) of drainage material and add 5cm (2″) soil.
2. Plant the Boston fern in the centre of the container.
3. Divide the helxines in half so that you plant a gold and silver helxine next to each other, both at the front of the pot and at the back. In time they will intermingle and create a rich tapestry.
4. Fill in the gaps with soil bringing the level to within 2.5cm (1″) of the rim of the container.
5. Water well and firm in the plants. Add more soil if necessary.

Aftercare
Maintain soil moisture throughout the year but particularly in the spring and summer. Apply a weak liquid feed once a month from April to September. A minimum winter temperature of 10°C (50°F) is needed for the fern.

Remove any damaged or brown leaves on the fern and trim back the helxines if any dead patches have occurred. Propagate the helxines in early summer by detaching several rooted stems and potting them up. These will then grow on and replace the old helxines which may be discarded when the fern is repotted the following April. Eventually the fern may be divided by removing the young, active-growing clumps and planting several together surrounded by the helxine. The fern may also be propagated by growing on the plantlets which develop at the ends of runners.

87 A NEST OF FERNS AND FLOWERS

This simple fern basket makes an interesting indoor container. Lined with plastic sheeting, it can be filled with all sorts of low-growing plants and so be transformed into an attractive and rather unusual present.

Site
Bright but out of direct sunlight, in the conservatory or indoors.

Container
Round basket: 25cm (10″) in diameter, 10cm (4″) deep. This one is a light wooden structure with small fern leaves and moss interwoven all around it to create a nest-like appearance, and was bought from a garden centre. To prevent water from damaging the basket walls, I used a plastic sheet to form an inner lining. Any round wicker basket would be equally suitable.

Planting Time

April or May, but it can be planted earlier or later in the year as the nurseries seem able to produce African violets in flower at almost any time.

At its best

African violets flower best from June to October. They can be made to flower, however, almost all year round depending on treatment in the nurseries.

Ingredients

2 polka dot plants *Hypoestes phyllostachya* 'Pink Splash'. Choose ones with lots of pink in the leaves to make an interesting contrast to the velvety heart-shaped leaves of the African violet.

2 African violets *Saintpaulia ionantha*. These two pale pink ones were chosen to complement the foliage colours in the polka dot plants. But there are so many rich purples, lilacs, pinks and whites to choose from that you must be guided by your own taste.

3 litres of peat-based compost or, ideally, a special African violet compost.

Drainage material in the form of 4 large handfuls of horticultural grit.

1 large piece of plastic sheeting, cut from a soil bag or refuse bag, to fit inside the basket.

Method

1. Place the plastic sheeting inside the basket so that it sits snugly all around the bottom and comes right up the sides. Cut six 2.5cm (1") slits in the middle to allow excess water to drain away.

2. Cover the lining with a shallow layer of drainage material and add sufficient soil to bring the level to within 5cm (2") of the rim of the container.

3. Make four holes with a plant pot so that you are able to plant each of the plants without disturbing the soil again. The problem is that if you spill soil on the leaves of the African violets it is difficult to clean off because they are so hairy. The soil level after making these holes should be 2.5cm (1") below the rim of the basket.

4. Plant the two polka dots first on opposite sides of the basket.

5. Plant the two African violets in between.

6. Water very carefully in the centre of the basket, making sure that you do not allow any to fall onto the African violet leaves or flowers as they will spoil.

Aftercare

The basket will enjoy bright light but not direct sunshine. It will thrive in a humid atmosphere and with moisture at its roots but it will hate to be over-watered and would prefer to be left on the dry side. If you are worried about spoiling the African violet leaves when you water, then water the polka dot plants instead. The container is so small that the roots of the African violets are sure to find the moisture. Apply a diluted high potash liquid feed every two weeks from early June to September or buy a special African violet liquid feed and follow the instructions given by the manufacturer.

Keep the polka dot plants pinched back to prevent them growing too straggly, and eventually replace. The African violets only need repotting every two years.

A minimum winter temperature of around 13°C (55°F) is required which is quite high for most conservatories, so it may be better to bring the plants indoors to a warmer room for the winter.

88 CONSERVATORY BELLS

Lapageria is one of the best conservatory plants. It has the most beautiful, elegant wax-like flowers and can be trained to grow up and over a window so that the bells hang down and can be enjoyed both from the conservatory and in this case from the kitchen as well.

Site
Against a conservatory wall where a trellis can be fixed to allow the plant to climb up. If you can train it to come overhead or to frame a window then there will be double the pleasure as it is wonderful to see the bells hanging freely. It will need protection (blinds) from direct sunlight in hot summer weather. It was very much used by the Victorians in their conservatories; 'Rosea' was the first colour to be introduced to this country in 1847 or 1848, so if you have a Victorian-style conservatory one of these plants would be most apt.

Container
Terracotta pot: 32.5cm (13″) in diameter, 30cm (12″) deep. NB: The plant pictured here is four years old so for a new plant use a much smaller 20–25cm (8–10″) pot to begin with.

Planting Time
April or May.

At its best
The main flowering period is July to October, but it can continue to bloom right up to Christmas.

Ingredients
1 *Lapageria rosea* with soft pink flowers (red and white flowering lapagerias can also be found). It is known as the Chilean bell flower. It is evergreen with strong, wiry stems which produce flowers on the end.
1 *Campanula isophylla* with pale blue flowers during mid to late summer to provide interest at container level.

Lime-free soil. Use 3 parts peat-based compost or ericaceous soil and add 1 part coarse sand and 2 parts leaf-mould.

Drainage material such as broken crocks or pieces of polystyrene.
Trellis or wires for support.

Method
1. Cover the base of the container with 5cm (2″) of drainage material and add sufficient soil so the lapageria will sit 2.5cm (1″) below the rim of the container.
2. Plant the lapageria and firm in. Tie in young growths to the trellis or wires. Eventually they will twine themselves around the supports.
3. Plant the campanula at the front of the pot. Fill in the gaps with soil.
4. Water well.

Aftercare
Maintain moisture with lime-free water such as natural rain water but not from the tap. It needs quite a lot during the growing period but less during the winter months. Apply a liquid feed every month during the flowering period. It is important to provide shade during the summer as the leaves will scorch. If this should happen in a disastrous way (as it did once with me while away on holiday) cut all growth back to ground level and wait for new shoots to rise up.

Encourage new growth on the lapageria to go in the direction in which you want it and don't prune unless stems or leaves are damaged. The exception is when you want a few stems to grace your dining table: tumbling out of a silver vase they look exquisite.

A minimum winter temperature of 7°C (45°F) is required. Cut back the campanula each spring when you repot. Gradually increase the size of your container.

89   CHRISTMAS CHEER

This wicker basket looks very cheerful with its red kalanchoes and golden foliage plants: a perfect colour scheme for a Christmas arrangement. But it is easily adapted into a spring or Easter planting using yellow kalanchoes instead.

Site
Conservatory or indoors.

Container
Old wicker basket: 30cm (12″) long, 10cm (4″) deep, lined with black plastic sheeting to prevent the soil from escaping and to prevent the wickerwork making contact with the damp soil.

Planting Time
About one month before you want a special display. It can be planted at almost any time of year so long as the plants are available and the conservatory is warm enough. *Ficus radicans* requires a minimum winter temperature of 13–16°C (55–61°F) which is quite high and it may be that this arrangement would suit your conservatory better in the spring rather than in mid winter.

At its best
Kalanchoes flower for many months; February to May is the usual flowering period but they can be brought into flower by the nurseries at almost any time of year and are particularly used as winter pot plants.

Ingredients
1 *Ficus radicans* 'Variegata'; this is a variegated creeping fig which trails prettily over the edge of the basket and contrasts well with the red kalanchoe.
2 *Kalanchoe blossfeldiana* 'Vulcan'; it has been hybridized to produce yellow, white, pink, orange and red flowers.
2 *Helxine (Soleirolia) soleirolii* 'Aurea' with tiny golden leaves; so small it is often called Baby's Tears.
5 litres of John Innes No 2 soil.
Drainage material such as horticultural grit.
Black plastic lining, cut from a soil bag or refuse sack, to cover the base and sides of the basket.

Method
1. Cover the base of the basket with the black plastic lining so that it fits snugly and comes right up the sides. Cut six 2.5cm (1″) slits in the bottom to allow excess moisture to drain away.

2. Cover the lining with a shallow layer of horticultural grit and add 5cm (2″) of soil.
3. Plant the creeping fig in the centre of the basket so that it will trail over the sides.
4. Plant the two kalanchoes at either end of the basket in opposite corners.
5. Plant the two helxines in the two remaining corners.
6. Fill in the gaps with soil, bringing the level to within 2.5cm (1″) of the rim. Firm in the plants and arrange the trails of the creeping fig so that they extend towards or over the edge of the basket.
7. Water well.

Aftercare

Water regularly during the flowering season and apply a liquid feed every two weeks. The helxines and ficus in particular will thrive in moist conditions. After the kalanchoes have finished flowering they should be discarded. Replant the basket with ones of different colours, or use the foliage plants in a hanging basket display with a Boston fern, for example.

The helxines can tolerate quite a low minimum winter temperature of 4–7°C (39–45°F) but the creeping fig needs rather warmer conditions: 13–16°C (55–61°F).

KITCHEN GARDEN SCHEMES

INTRODUCTION TO THE KITCHEN GARDEN RECIPES

A rich variety of plants may be grown in containers for culinary purposes. The practice of growing herbs in pots and window boxes is well established. Many of the plants, such as rosemary, thyme and marjoram, are used to hot Mediterranean summers and thrive well in warm, sunbaked terracotta containers. Tomatoes, too, are another common homegrown crop. In a greenhouse these are often put in a grow-bag, itself a container. They are very productive in the protected climate and do well. In good summers they will also grow in pots outdoors, especially in a sheltered, sunny corner of the patio, out of the wind, where the walls reflect the heat.

PRODUCTIVE AND ORNAMENTAL
In the recipes which follow you will find ideas to grow herbs and their flowers and different fruit and vegetables in various ways which will make the containers both productive and ornamental. A few of the ideas are commonplace but several are quite unusual. In some cases where basil and French marigolds are grown, the combination of plants is actually thought to assist the food production by deterring aphids. In others, cropping rates are helped by the abundance of bees attracted by the sweet-smelling flowers grown in association with the food crop. Some are planted merely because they create a striking colour scheme. The golden pot marigolds look marvellous against the bronze fennel leaves. The yellow courgette flowers and fruit appear even more exotic against blue lobelia and a red container.

For those without access to garden soil, why not try growing some of your favourite summer vegetables which, though plentiful in the shops, always taste better when picked and eaten the same day? Tomatoes are an obvious choice and do very well in pots and window boxes, but you could try growing runner beans out of wooden barrels. Plant them with nasturtiums or sweet peas and you will have a truly delightful sight which proves both decorative and useful in the kitchen. The best of it is that the more beans you pick, the more productive the barrels seem to become. The same is true of the sweet peas. Cut all the flowers twice a week and they will flourish quite happily. Meanwhile their perfume attracts the bees and the bean flowers are pollinated without any trouble at all.

Try growing some vegetables which are hard to find in the shops. Green courgettes are readily available but yellow ones are rarely seen and if they are available in the shops they are usually much more expensive. They taste very similar to green ones and look most attractive, especially when lightly cooked with aubergines and tomatoes. Have you ever tried stuffing or frying courgette flowers like the Italians? Now is your chance! They are almost impossible to buy, but when you grow your own you can pick them fresh and eat them the same day.

A containerized kitchen garden bearing tomatoes, aubergine, green peppers and beans: colourful and fully productive

I have to admit that my crop of tomatoes and strawberries in a hanging basket was not as great as those growing in window boxes or in the garden soil. Their root space was very restricted and watering was more difficult. However, the results were pleasing and the containers certainly looked and smelt attractive with their various partners. Seeing the vivid red of the tomatoes with the orange of the French marigolds was wonderful, not to mention the whiffs of basil which emerged every time the basket was watered. So, too, with the strawberries: the bright red fruit looked very exotic against the white flowers of the alyssum which, as a bonus, made the basket smell just like honey. The bees loved it and, of course, there was no problem in pollinating the strawberries.

For even more surprising hanging baskets try the combination of mints, lemon balm and variegated ground elder. All of them would be a menace left to their own devices in the garden; once planted they would be hard to get rid of. But lock them up in a hanging basket from which there is no hope of escape and they can be enjoyed for their beauty and aromas. They will all grow quite happily, intermingle at their leisure, and reward you generously every time you want a special snippet for a cool drink in high summer. Ground elder leaves used to be eaten as a vegetable. Here I am growing them purely for their decorative purposes. The variegations are extremely fetching and combine well in the basket with the other coloured leaves. Moreover, the flower is very dainty and adds interest in both its shape and form. It is one of my favourite containers to water. Just like the basil, French marigolds and tomatoes in the basket mentioned above, it gives off a powerful mixture of aromatic and spicy fragrances. If you are looking for something different to grow, then this is certainly worth a try.

EDIBLE FLOWERS
Edible flowers are just beginning to be accepted again after centuries of neglect. Grow them in window boxes, pots and baskets, either on their own or mixed with herbs. Freshly picked primroses, violets, rose-

mary, violas, daisies and cowslip flowers make wonderful additions to spring salads, or to the decoration on top of a dish of pâté. Dusted with egg white and sugar, then left in a warm place to dry thoroughly, they can transform a pavlova, Easter biscuits or the icing on top of a cake. They taste just like they smell. I especially love primroses and violets – all so delicate and pretty, but full of flavour as well. The sugar coating seems to accentuate it. In the summer use fresh flowers of thyme, marjoram, fennel and sage. They can be equally as attractive and again can be very tasty. Yet nothing appears more colourful than nasturtium flowers. Either leave the petals whole or cut them into little pieces and mix them in a salad for a peppery, tangy addition. Pot marigold petals, roses and scented geranium flowers are among the many others which can be used. Try them out and enjoy their exciting faces and flavours.

GROUPINGS

When you plan your kitchen garden in containers, create a picture which will be attractive as well as practical. Match the plants in a window box and hanging basket, as with the tomatoes, basil and French marigolds (see Recipes 90 and 95). With the herb containers, why not try to coordinate the shape or overall design? Try matching the styles of the pots but vary the contents. Plant two 'four-in-one' pots (for the address of Whichford Pottery see the list of specialist suppliers on page 226) and add height with a taller strawberry pot behind. In these three containers you can plant parsley, lemon balm, mint, golden marjoram, lots of different thymes, sages, rosemary and oregano (see Recipes 104, 105 and 106). Place them in a sunny position where you can easily look after them and you will have an abundance of green herbs and edible flowers.

COLOUR THEMES

Alternatively, create a colour theme. Dominate several containers with lots of bright French marigolds, for example. In 1989 I planted just one packet of special seed, supplied by Thompson and Morgan Ltd, described as being a companion plant to tomatoes because it deterred whitefly. Germination was easy and I had an abundance of plants. All my tomatoes, aubergines and green peppers were allotted one or sometimes two plants to each pot.

The result was a colourful mass of bright oranges which were magnificent. They transformed both the greenhouse and the kitchen garden element of the patio. Furthermore, I had hardly any trouble with whitefly or greenfly, particularly in the greenhouse where there was also lots of basil (also said to be a deterrent against whitefly) growing. I highly recommend them.

• • •

There are various recipes tucked away in other sections of the book where edible flowers and herbs are grown. See Recipe 21 for growing tiny white roses and parsley; Recipe 15 for growing pretty pink roses; Recipe 76 for growing early herbs in the conservatory; and Recipes 80 and 83 for growing scented leaf geraniums in the conservatory.

Whatever you choose, it will be fun to watch the plants develop and produce their crop. The exciting – and immensely satisfying – moment comes when you gather the harvest and are able to eat it as fresh as can be. To be able to pick fresh basil and enjoy it with warm, tasty tomatoes is a great pleasure, to decorate a pavlova with your own violas and cowslips is a joy. With just a little imagination you can dress up the most commonplace dishes and transform them into a dinner party piece.

90   A COMPANION PLANTING FOR TOMATOES

Dwarf tomatoes are interplanted with French marigolds and basil as a companion planting scheme to deter whitefly and other aphids. It makes an extremely attractive arrangement which can be cropped for weeks.

Site
Sunny position outdoors or partially shaded in the conservatory or greenhouse.

Container
Large window box: 80cm (32″) long, 20cm (8″) wide, 17.5cm (7″) deep.

Early Preparation
Basil, tomatoes and French marigolds can all be purchased as plants in May but dwarf tomato plants will probably not be on sale. Therefore, try growing them all from seed. Start them off in gentle heat in March according to the instructions on the packet.

Planting Time
End May. Cold nights will damage young tomato plants. Either keep them in the greenhouse or conservatory until the nights warm up or place them in a very sheltered spot outdoors and, if necessary, cover them with a newspaper at night-time. They can remain in the conservatory or greenhouse all summer as long as they are not subjected to too much direct sunlight.

Ingredients
  4 dwarf tomatoes with small fruit *Tomato* 'Pipo' or 'Pixie F1 Hybrid' sold by Thompson and Morgan Ltd (see the list of specialist suppliers on page 225). They are both rapid-growing early bush varieties.

  4 French marigolds *Tagetes patula* 'Special' sold by Thompson and Morgan Ltd as a companion plant for tomatoes.

  6 bush basil plants *Ocimum minimum* with fragrant spicy leaves. There are taller forms as well.

20 litres of a multipurpose peat-based compost or John Innes No 3 soil.

Drainage material such as small pieces of polystyrene.

4 2-foot canes and garden string to support the tomatoes.

Method
1. Cover the base of the container with 2.5cm (1″) of drainage material and add 7.5cm (3″) of soil.
2. Space the four tomatoes along the centre of the window box.
3. Plant the four French marigolds one at each end of the box, one in the middle at centre-front and one at centre-back.
4. Plant the basil either side of the central French marigolds both at the front and the back of the window box. In this way the tomato plants are surrounded by a protective ring of basil and French marigolds.
5. Fill in any remaining gaps with soil, bringing the level to within 2.5cm (1″) of the rim.
6. Water well and add more soil if necessary to regain the level.
7. Stake the tomatoes and tie securely as they grow. Once the fruit starts to swell the trusses become quite heavy.

Aftercare
Water regularly; this is of paramount importance. Be prepared to do it once or twice a day in hot weather, particularly once the tomatoes have formed. A great deal is being asked of a very confined planting space so food and water are essential. Apply a liquid feed once a week after the first flower truss has set. Stake the tomatoes with a strong 2-foot cane and tie securely. You will see that in the group photograph the canes rise above the tomatoes. By the time the window box photograph was taken the tomatoes had grown a little further and the canes had been

151

chopped off at the top to neaten the appearance of the arrangement.

There is no need to remove any side shoots. Spraying for aphids should not be necessary or should be minimal. However, you must act quickly if they are apparent, using a safe insecticide suitable for fruit or vegetables. Good ventilation will help to keep the plants healthy. If indoors, provide shading.

Pick the tomatoes regularly as they ripen. Slice them up and enjoy them with a sprinkling of chopped basil on top. Together they make a wonderful treat in high summer.

You could bring the window box inside the greenhouse at the end of the summer to allow the last tomatoes to ripen. Otherwise use the green ones for chutney or allow them to ripen indoors on a windowsill. Remove all the basil leaves and mix with breadcrumbs for a Provençale mixture. Freeze and enjoy it throughout the winter. Discard the French marigolds but keep some of the seeds for next year.

91 A LATE SPRING WINDOW BOX OF HERBS AND EDIBLE FLOWERS

Cowslips and pink bellis daisies provide a delightful display for several weeks from mid to late spring. Here they are under-planted with variegated mint and golden marjoram.

Site
Outdoors; sunny.

Container
Small window box: 30cm (12″) long, 15cm (6″) wide, 15cm (6″) deep.

Planting Time
February to March.

At its best
April to May.

Ingredients
1 golden marjoram *Origanum vulgare* 'Aureum' with yellow leaves when young and scented pink flowers in July and August.
1 variegated pineapple mint *Mentha rotundifolia* 'Variegata' with pungent leaves and attractive foliage. Excellent culinary uses and as a garnish.
3 pots or just under ½ strip of pink daisies *Bellis perennis* 'Dresden China'. These are a lovely colour and make a beautiful addition to any salad or icing etc.
2 cowslips *Primula veris*. The flower can be used for jam, wine or pickle, tossed in salads or as a garnish on a cake.
7 litres of John Innes No 2 soil.
Drainage material such as broken crocks or pieces of polystyrene.

Method
1. Cover the base of the container with 2.5cm (1″) of drainage material and add 5cm (2″) of soil.
2. Plant the marjoram at one end and the mint at the other end, both at the front edge of the window box.
3. Plant the daisies behind the marjoram and mint and one in the centre of the box.
4. Plant the two cowslips either side of centre.
5. Fill in the gaps with soil, bringing the level to within 2.5cm (1″) of the rim. Water well.

Aftercare
Water regularly so that the soil is kept moist at all times. Apply a liquid feed every week from mid April.

Use the daisy and cowslip flowers when very young. The daisy and cowslip petals may be taken off and scattered on salads or cake icings etc to make attractive garnishes. Use the mint and marjoram leaves for flavourings and also for decorative purposes. Don't be afraid to use the mint continually, keeping it well clipped; it will survive unabated. In fact, it lasts well into late autumn/early winter, unlike many of the other mints, and so is of particular value then. The marjoram will have pretty pink flowers in July and August which are wonderfully aromatic. Cut the marjoram back by two-thirds before the winter sets in but leave the seedheads for the birds.

Treat the arrangement either as a longterm planting or transfer the cowslips after flowering to a spot in the garden and plant parsley or basil instead. Basil will be a temporary summer resident but parsley could stay throughout the autumn and winter.

92   VIOLAS AND PARSLEY

The bright little faces of the 'Johnny Jump-Up' violas peep out amongst the parsley. The viola flowers are edible and, of course, so is the parsley. Simple to plant and easy to look after.

Site
Outdoors, sheltered for the winter; sun or partial shade. It could be grown in a conservatory in March and April.

Container
Small window box: 35cm (14″) long, 17.5cm (7″) wide, 17.5cm (7″) deep.

Planting Time
Autumn or March/April.

At its best
April to June.

Ingredients
3 violas *Viola tricolor* 'Johnny Jump-Up' with little blue and yellow faces. They are easily available as strip bedding or in pots. Try the flowers as a decoration on a meringue.
2 parsley plants *Petroselinum crispum*. Use the parsley leaves on salads, as a garnish and in sauces.
6 litres of John Innes No 2 soil.

Drainage material such as small pieces of polystyrene.

Method
1. Cover the base of the container with 2.5cm (1″) of drainage material and add 5cm (2″) soil.
2. Plant the violas in the centre and one at either end.
3. Plant the parsley in between the violas.
4. Fill in the gaps with soil, bringing the level to within 2.5cm (1″) of the rim.
5. Water well. Firm in the plants and add more soil if necessary.

Aftercare
Maintain moisture throughout the period but take care never to water in frosty weather. Apply a liquid feed once a week from April onwards. Use the flowers as much as you like; cropping will encourage more to form. Once the parsley is well established, cut the leaves, using the outer ones first. The parsley can remain in the box throughout the summer and winter. Cut it down in September and then water well to encourage fresh new growth before the winter. It should survive for two years. Remove the violas when they become too straggly in mid summer, replacing them with basil, dill or nasturtiums instead, and then plant new violas in the autumn.

93   A MIXED GREEN SALAD

'Saladisi' is a mixture of different salad leaves. It is so easy to grow and lasts for the whole of the summer and well into the winter. It is now February and I am still cutting lettuce leaves from the original sowing, not just ordinary green ones but leaves with deep red veining and some almost purplish-black.

Site
Any. I started this window box off in the greenhouse in March for an early crop, then took it outside in May. It could be started outside just as well.

Container
Medium window box: 60cm (24″) long, 12.5cm (5″) wide, 12.5cm (5″) deep. A pot or tub would be equally good. If you plant a succession of containers you will have a prolific crop for many weeks.

Planting Time
March in the greenhouse, or April onwards outdoors.

At its best
8 weeks after sowing you can cut the leaves down to about 2.5cm (1″) growth. When they have grown another 10cm (4″) you can crop again. After that it is best to plant all the contents in the garden and allow them to mature normally. As winter approaches the least hardy will die off, leaving the hardiest ones to survive through to spring. With such a flexible crop, it is hard to say when it is at its best!

Ingredients
1 packet of Thompson and Morgan's 'Saladisi'; a marvellous combination of salad plants which grow together to produce the perfect mixed salad. (For the list of specialist suppliers see page 225.)
10 litres of a multipurpose peat-based compost.

Method
1. Fill the container with the compost so that the level comes within 2.5cm (1″) of the rim.
2. Water gently with a fine hose attached to the watering-can.
3. Carefully sow the seeds over the top of the compost, not too thickly. The excess can be saved for another container or later sowings.
4. Cover with a very fine layer of compost.

Aftercare
Water regularly to maintain a steady growth. Crop the top 7.5cm (3″) of leaves when the plants have grown about 10cm (4″) high. Remove all debris. Watch out for slugs and pick them off if you see any. Apply a liquid vegetable feed once a week after the first cutting and allow to grow up again; the same applies after the second cutting. You can then separate the plants and put them into the vegetable or herb garden or leave them until the autumn and then transplant. Some of the leaves are so colourful it is a shame to cut whole plants at a time, so I just cut a few leaves when I need them and let the plants continue to grow.

94 AN EARLY SPRING WINDOW BOX OF HERBS AND EDIBLE FLOWERS

Sage, rosemary and thyme are amongst our best known culinary herbs. Golden varieties are always valuable for their bright foliage while the prostrate rosemary acts as a colourful and unusual centrepiece. Combine the pale yellow primroses and the pretty blue rosemary flowers and transform a spring salad.

Site
Sheltered outdoors; sun or partial shade.

Container
Medium window box: 40cm (16″) long, 15cm (6″) wide, 15cm (6″) deep.

Planting Time
September to October.

At its best
February to April, although the daisies, sage and thyme will flower until mid summer.

Ingredients
1 golden sage *Salvia officinalis* 'Aurea'. It has tubular violet-blue flowers in June and July which are as tasty as they are fragrant.
1 golden thyme *Thymus × citriodorus* 'Aureus'. The pale lilac flowers should be used in salads and garnishes, the leaves may be used in salads and stuffings.
1 prostrate rosemary *Rosmarinus lavandulaceus* (syn. *R. officinalis prostratus*). Not totally hardy, hence a sheltered site is required. Pale blue flowers from early spring or even late autumn, through to April. Beautiful colour for scattering on salads, use leaves in stuffings etc. Also medicinal.
1 golden feverfew *Tanacetum parthenium* 'Aureum'. Uses are mainly medicinal and for pot-pourri, rather than culinary.
2 wild primroses *Primula vulgaris*; our well-known native. Use the flowers in a salad, as a garnish on a pâté dish or to decorate a pavlova.

½ strip of bellis daisies *Bellis perennis*; mixed or pink, white or red. It will flower on and off throughout the winter in a mild season, but mainly in spring and early summer.

10 litres of John Innes No 2 soil.

Drainage material such as broken crocks or small pieces of polystyrene.

Method

1. Cover the base of the container with 5cm (2″) of drainage material and add 75cm (3″) of soil.
2. Plant the golden sage at one end of the box and the golden thyme at the other.
3. Plant the rosemary in the centre of the box so that it trails over the front.
4. Plant the feverfew behind it and the primroses on either side.
5. Divide the strip of daisies and tuck into any spaces, particularly in the corners.
6. Fill in the gaps with soil to bring the level to within 2.5cm (1″) of the rim. Water well and firm in the plants.

Aftercare

Maintain the soil moisture, but take care never to water in frosty weather. Keep the rosemary on the dry side rather than too wet, particularly during the winter months. Apply a liquid feed every two weeks once the primroses are in flower.

Spray for aphids using a mixture suitable for edible plants, though, from experience, this will probably not be necessary.

Use the flowers of the primroses, daisies, rosemary, thyme and sage for salads and for decorative purposes on pâtés, cakes or pavlovas etc. Use the leaves of thyme, rosemary and sage for stuffings, adding flavour to stews or omelettes etc. Feverfew and daisy flowers may be used for pot-pourri.

Treat the sage, thyme and rosemary as a permanent planting and leave them for two or three years to mature. In the autumn add new daisies and feverfew and divide the primroses. Or you could remove the daisies and primroses, transfer them to the garden in early June and replace with a temporary tender herb such as bush basil.

HANGING BASKETS

See notes on pages 4–6.

95   TOMATOES IN A HANGING BASKET

Here again dwarf tomatoes are interplanted with French marigolds and basil as a companion planting scheme to deter whitefly and other aphids. The tomatoes were not as prolific as those grown in the window box but they were successful and the basket certainly looked most attractive. The two containers made a very bright and cheerful combination.

Site
Sunny position outdoors or partially shaded in the conservatory (if you enjoy the smell of basil) or greenhouse.

Container
Wire hanging basket: 35cm (14″) in diameter with a sturdy 27.5cm (11″) bracket.

Early Preparation
Basil, French marigolds and tomatoes can all be bought as plants in May but dwarf tomato plants will probably not be available. Try growing them all from seed. Start them off in gentle heat in March following the instructions on the packet.

Planting Time
End May. Cold nights will damage young tomato plants so either keep them in the greenhouse or conservatory until the nights warm up or place them in a very sheltered spot outdoors and, if necessary, protect them with a newspaper covering at nighttime. They can remain in the conservatory or greenhouse all summer as long as they have some shade.

Ingredients
13 French marigolds *Tagetes patula* 'Special' sold by Thompson and Morgan Ltd as a companion plant for tomatoes. Otherwise buy 2 strips of a good dwarf variety.
 7 bush basil plants *Ocimum minimum* with fragrant

spicy leaves. Otherwise buy a pot of basil seedlings available in most greengrocers at the end of May and carefully separate.
 3 dwarf tomatoes with small fruit *Tomato* 'Pipo' or 'Pixie F1 Hybrid' sold by Thompson and Morgan Ltd (see the list of specialist suppliers on page 225). They are both a rapid-growing bush variety.
10 litres of a multipurpose peat-based compost or John Innes No 3 soil.
2 handfuls of horticultural grit.
1 basketful of moss, sphagnum preferably, or ordinary wreath moss from a florist.
1 circle of plastic sheeting about the size of a dinner plate, cut from a bin liner or strong plastic bag.
Garden string.

Method

1. Line the basket with a generous thickness of moss, starting at the base and working about one-third of the way up the sides.
2. Cut four 2.5cm (1″) slits in the plastic circle and place over the moss in the base of the basket.
3. Spread two handfuls of grit over it and then add 5cm (2″) of soil.
4. Plant six French marigolds in a circle so that they are lying snugly on top of the moss. Make sure their roots have good contact with the soil and that the plants are not sticking out more than is necessary.
5. Add another layer of moss and more soil. Then plant four basil plants alternating with four marigolds in a circle so that they, too, lie snugly on top of the moss.
6. Now bring the moss right to the top of the basket so that it forms a collar above the rim.
7. Plant the three tomato plants around the edge in the top of the basket with a French marigold and basil plant in between each one.
8. Fill in the gaps with soil so that the level comes just below the rim of the basket.
9. Water gently. Firm in the plants and add more soil and moss to the top of the basket if necessary.

Aftercare

Water regularly; this is of paramount importance. Be prepared to do it once or twice a day in hot weather. The evening is probably best so there is no risk of the sun scorching the wet leaves. A great deal is being demanded of a very small planting space so food and water are essential to the basket's success. Apply a liquid feed once a week when the first flower truss has set. The easiest way to support the tomatoes is to tie some garden string through the basket chains so that it forms a circle around the tomatoes. Spraying for aphids should not be necessary or at least should be minimal. However, you must act quickly if they do become apparent, using a safe spray suitable for fruit or vegetables. There is no need to remove any side shoots of these tomatoes.

Pick the tomatoes regularly as they ripen. Eat them fresh or cooked with basil for a special taste of high summer.

You could bring the basket inside the greenhouse at the end of the summer to allow the last tomatoes to ripen. Otherwise use the green ones for chutney or allow them to ripen indoors on a window-sill. Remove all the basil leaves and mix with breadcrumbs for a Provençale mixture. Freeze and enjoy it throughout the winter. Discard the French marigolds but keep some of the seeds for next year.

96   MAINLY MINT

Here is a surprising and indestructible mixture of variegated ground elder, lemon balm and many different mints. Put them direct in the garden and they would all run wild. But plant them in a container with its confined space and they can do no harm at all. Enjoy the spicy and fragrant aromas of ginger, eau de cologne, spearmint, pineapple mint and lemon balm.

Site
Outdoors; any position.

Container
Wire hanging basket: 35cm (14″) in diameter with a sturdy 27.5cm (11″) bracket.

Planting Time
March to May.

At its best
June to August.

Ingredients
1 ginger mint *Mentha × gentilis* 'Variegata'; a spicy, smooth gold-splashed leaf.
1 eau de cologne mint *Mentha × piperita* 'Citrata' with a purple stem and purple-tinged dark green leaves. Good for its scent and colour.
2 variegated pineapple mint *Mentha rotundifolia* 'Variegata' with very pretty leaf variegations, so good for decorative and culinary purposes.
1 red raripila spearmint *Mentha raripila rubra* with dark green leaves and purple stems. A sweet spearmint flavour.
Don't worry too much if you can't find all these different plants. The variegated pineapple mint is my favourite and I think the single most attractive one, but there are many to choose from and you might find others which you prefer rather than these.
1 ground elder *Aegopodium podagraria* 'Variegata'. The foliage is extremely attractive (these are the larger variegated leaves you can see in the photograph) and the flowers are very dainty and pleasing as they rise up or fall in their own undisciplined way. Use tender new leaves in salads.
2 variegated lemon balm *Melissa officinalis* 'Variegata'. Good for stuffings, or add to drinks, infuse for tea etc. Or try it as a rinse for greasy hair.
10 litres of a multipurpose peat-based compost or John Innes No 2 soil.
2 handfuls of horticultural grit.
1 circle of plastic sheeting the size of a dinner plate, cut from a strong plastic bag.
1 basketful of moss, sphagnum preferably, or ordinary wreath moss from a florist.

Method
1. Cover the base of the basket with a generous thickness of moss and bring the moss like a thick wall almost halfway up the sides of the basket.
2. Cut four 2.5cm (1″) slits in the plastic circle and place in the bottom of the basket.
3. Cover the plastic lining with grit and add 7.5cm (3″) of soil.
4. Remove all the plants from their pots and see if there are any you can divide. It should be possible to multiply them all. The ground elder needs only a small piece of white root to survive and flourish. Both the mints and the balm will divide easily and thrive.

5. Plant a middle ring of mints, ground elder and lemon balm, taking care to plant the ground elder and variegated pineapple mint away from each other so as to make full use of their variegations. Contrast them with the purple-stemmed mints. Plant at least four or five round the middle, preferably six. Make sure their roots have good contact with the soil and that they do not stick out further than necessary.

6. Add more moss so that it fits snugly round the plants and bring it to the top of the basket so that it forms a collar above the rim. Add more soil, bringing the level to within 2.5cm (1″) of the rim.

7. Plant the remaining mints, balm and ground elder in the top of the basket, again making maximum use of their various colourings.

8. Water carefully. If the water finds escape routes out of the sides of the basket or through the moss collar at the rim, add more moss to make secure.

Aftercare

This is one of the easiest baskets to maintain. Water regularly, and in hot weather be prepared to do it at least once a day. It is always a delightful job for as the water touches the leaves all the lovely aromas fill the air. Spraying for aphids should not be necessary but if they are apparent then use a safe insecticide suitable for use with fruit and vegetables. A liquid feed may be given once or twice throughout the summer.

Crop continually to encourage neat growth; otherwise by the end of August the basket will look rather wild with long growths protruding out of the bottom of the basket. If this happens, be ruthless. Cut off all stems to about 1cm (0.5″), water well and allow it to make new growth. You could use the clippings as stem cuttings and root them in water. Pot up and grow on the window-sill for fresh supplies in the winter.

All the plants are perfectly hardy and the basket can be split up and replanted the following spring. By then you will have enough root systems to make several baskets. You could give one away as a present!

97   A STRAWBERRY BASKET

Strawberries make handsome basket plants especially when they are set off by sweet-smelling white alyssum and the bright green foliage of marjoram and parsley.

Site
Outdoors; sunny.

Container
Wire hanging basket: 35cm (14″) in diameter with a sturdy 27.5cm (11″) bracket.

Planting Time
Mid to late April, whenever the alyssum is available.

At its best
End June to end July, possibly later depending on your choice of strawberries.

Ingredients
1 strip of white alyssum *Lobularia maritima* 'Little Dorrit'; its sweet scent attracts the bees which then pollinate the strawberries.

3 strawberry plants *Fragaria* × *ananassa*; 'Cambridge Favourite' is a good mid-season one to try. But if you want to extend the cropping try 'Gento', a perpetual variety which fruits from June to September. The plants shown in the photograph were new ones, purchased in April. You could use alpine varieties instead: 'Baron Solemacher' ripens in summer and autumn.

1 golden marjoram *Origanum vulgare* 'Aureum' with yellow leaves early in the season useful for stuffings etc. Produces aromatic flowers in July and August.

3 parsley plants *Petroselinum crispum*; attractive foliage which is very useful for all sorts of culinary purposes.

10 litres of John Innes No 2 soil.

2 handfuls of horticultural grit.

1 basketful of moss, sphagnum preferably, or ordinary wreath moss from a florist.

1 circle of plastic sheeting about the size of a dinner plate, cut from a bin liner or strong plastic bag.

Method
1. Line the basket with a generous thickness of moss, starting at the base and working almost halfway up the sides.

2. Cut four 2.5cm (1″) slits in the plastic circle and

place over the moss lining in the base of the basket.

3. Spread two handfuls of grit over it and then add 5cm (2″) of soil.

4. Divide the strip of alyssum and plant six of the little plants in a circle in the middle of the basket so that they rest snugly on the moss. Make sure that their roots have good contact with the soil and that the foliage is not sticking out more than necessary.

5. Bring the wall of moss right up to the top of the basket so that it forms a good collar above the rim. Add 5cm (2″) of soil.

6. Plant the three strawberries in the top of the basket quite near the rim. Save the strongest-looking one for the centre-front and plant the other two on either side, leaving space for the parsley in between.

7. Plant the marjoram in the centre of the basket with a parsley behind and the other two on either side of the strawberry plant at the front.

8. Tuck in the two remaining alyssum plants at the rim of the basket beside the two parsley plants at the front.

9. Fill in the gaps with soil, bringing the level 2.5cm (1″) below the rim of the basket.

10. Water carefully. If any water escapes over the sides through the moss, add more moss to make secure.

Aftercare

Water regularly throughout the summer, especially in hot weather when you should be prepared to do it daily. This is vitally important as the plants will stop cropping if the roots dry out. This basket is a treat; not only can you watch the progress of the strawberries developing and ripening but you can enjoy the marvellous scent of the alyssum which smell just like honey.

Apply a liquid feed weekly once the strawberries have begun to flower. Use a safe vegetable spray if greenfly etc appear.

Crop the strawberries as they ripen. You will be able to crop a few each day for several weeks, but make sure you reach them before the birds do. Cotton wound round the basket chains will help prevent them finding a safe landing. Cut and use the parsley at will once it has matured a bit, generally by mid June. The marjoram leaves can be enjoyed throughout the summer. They make a pretty garnish and taste good in salads and in stuffings.

Cut off any strawberry runners which appear although some of the alpine and perpetual varieties will not form them. At the end of the summer, dismantle the basket. Transfer the strawberries to the garden where they will overwinter and may be cropped the following summer. Divide the marjoram into two or three plants and plant in the garden as well. Discard the alyssum.

98   A GREEN PEPPER POT

Green peppers and colourful French marigolds make an attractive pot for a sunny patio, porch, greenhouse or conservatory.

Site
Sunny and sheltered patio or porch, greenhouse or conservatory.

Container
Clay pot: 27.5cm (11″) in diameter, 25cm (10″) deep.

Early Preparation
Both the pepper and the French marigolds may be grown from seed starting them off in March. They can also be bought from garden centres in May. Three plants should provide a good crop for a family of four.

Planting Time
End May/early June.

At its best
Attractive throughout the summer; will crop August to September.

Ingredients
1 green pepper *Capsicum annuum* 'Gypsy F1 Hybrid' from Thompson and Morgan Ltd (see the list of specialist suppliers on page 225), would be a suitable one for the south, while 'Canape F1 Hybrid' would be more suitable for northern areas.
2 French marigolds *Tagetes patula* 'Special', a Thompson and Morgan Ltd companion plant to deter whitefly and other aphids.
12 litres of John Innes No 2 soil.
Drainage material such as broken crocks or pieces of polystyrene.
1 three-foot cane for support.

Method
1. Cover the base of the container with 5cm (2″) of drainage material and add sufficient soil to bring the level up to within 5cm (2″) of the rim of the pot.

2. Plant the pepper at the centre-back of the pot with the French marigolds on either side of the front.
3. Bring the soil level to within 2.5cm (1″) of the rim of the container. Water well.
4. Fix the cane so that it will give support as the pepper plant grows.

Aftercare
Maintain soil moisture throughout the summer. Apply a liquid feed weekly once the peppers have begun to set fruit. Under glass, shade in very hot weather; here red spider may be a problem. Whitefly and greenfly should be kept at bay by the French marigolds, but spray with a safe vegetable insecticide if necessary. Keep cropping the peppers as soon as they are big enough to eat to encourage further production. Deadhead the French marigolds.

At the end of the summer, discard all the plants.

99   SCARLET RUNNERS AND NASTURTIUMS

Here is a simple planting scheme which can provide runner beans for many weeks from mid to late summer as well as a tasty crop of nasturtium leaves and flowers for salads. Together they make a very attractive arrangement.

Site
Outdoors, sheltered; sun or partial shade.

Container
Large, deep pot or half barrel: 45cm (18″) in diameter, 30cm (12″) deep.

Early Preparation
Buy the runner bean and nasturtium seeds and sow at end April/early May indoors, or mid May outdoors. Sow in twos; double the number required and remove the weakest of each pair. Plants of both can easily be purchased in May although the nasturtiums will probably be of mixed colours.

Planting Time
Outdoors in mid May. Frost is a hazard so the young plants will need protection on cold nights.

At its best
August and September.

Ingredients
6 runner beans plants (12 seeds). Those with red flowers make a colourful arrangement *Phaseolus coccineus* ‘Scarlet Emperor’. The Victorians used to grow this plant for ornamental purposes only, often out of the ends of window boxes where they could climb up the side of the window and create a frame. Here it is grown for its fruit and its colour.
3 yellow semi-trailing nasturtium plants (6 seeds) *Tropaeolum majus* ‘Golden Gleam’ with fragrant golden double and semi-double flowers.
50 litres of John Innes No 2 soil.

Drainage material such as broken bricks or clay crocks. Something weighty is needed in the bottom of the pot to prevent it being blown over in the wind, plus finer pieces on top.

6 eight-foot canes plus garden string or wire to draw them into a circle at the top.

Method
1. Cover the base of the container with 7.5cm (3") of heavy drainage material. Then cover with a shallow layer of fine pieces.
2. Add sufficient soil to bring the level to within 2.5cm (1") of the rim of the container.
3. Plant six pairs of runner bean seeds 5cm (2") deep, or six individual plants, in a circle near the edge of the pot.
4. Plant three pairs of nasturtium seeds 2cm (0.5") deep, or three individual plants, in between the beans to form a triangle.
5. Water well.

Aftercare
Remove the weaker seedling of each pair of both nasturtiums and beans. Encourage the beans to climb the canes and when they reach the top, pinch out the growing tips.

Water regularly; be prepared to do it daily in hot weather. The soil needs to remain damp and heavy to prevent the whole pot toppling over in the wind. Apply a weak liquid feed every two weeks after end July.

Blackfly may be a problem on both the nasturtiums and the beans. Spray with a safe vegetable insecticide as necessary.

Harvest the beans frequently once they have begun to set in order to encourage further production. Keep using the nasturtium flowers for salads or table decorations, and deadhead any that are not cut.

At the end of the autumn, discard all the plants.

100   SWEET PEAS AND RUNNER BEANS

Old-fashioned sweet peas make a lovely scented pillar which can be used for cut flowers from June to September. Combine them with runner beans and you have the double advantage of flowers for the house and beans for the table.

Site
Outdoors, sheltered; sun or partial shade.

Container
Large, deep pot or wooden barrel: 45cm (18″) in diameter, 30cm (12″) deep.

Early Preparation
Sweet pea 'Antique Fantasy' is very fragrant but the seed is not always available in the garden centres, though it can be ordered from Thompson and Morgan Ltd (see the list of specialist suppliers on page 225). (Of course, there are other sweetly scented sweet peas available as well but do be careful as not all sweet peas have a strong scent.) In March sow two seeds each to four 7.5cm (3″) pots.

Planting Time
May. Runner beans will be killed by frost so give protection on cold nights.

Ingredients
4 sweet pea plants (8 seeds); remove the weaker of each pair. *Lathyrus odoratus* 'Antique Fantasy' is available from Thompson and Morgan Ltd (see above). There is a lovely range of colours and good long stems for cutting.

4 white-flowering runner bean plants (8 seeds) *Phaseolus coccineus* 'Desiree'; a very productive stringless variety.

50 litres of John Innes No 2 soil.

Drainage material such as broken bricks or clay crocks to add weight to the bottom of the container and so prevent the planting being blown over in the wind. In addition finer drainage material to go on top.

8 eight-foot canes plus garden string or wire to draw them into a circle at the top.

Method
1. Cover the base of the container with 7.5cm (3″) of heavy drainage material. Then cover with a shallow layer of fine pieces.
2. Add sufficient soil to bring the level to within 2.5cm (1″) of the rim of the container.
3. Alternate the four sweet pea plants and the four runner beans around the outside of the container to form a wide circle. The runner beans can be sown direct at this stage (sow four groups of two beans and remove the weakest once they have germinated).
4. Water well. Firm in the plants and place the canes near to each one so that they will all have early support. Tie the wire or string to each one near the top of the canes so that they will give each other support.

Aftercare
Pinch out the growing tips of the sweet pea plants when they are 10cm (4″) high to encourage lateral shoots. Pinch out the growing tips of the runner beans when they have reached the top of the canes.

Keep the container well watered throughout the growing season; be prepared to water daily in hot weather. Turn the pot around regularly to allow the sun to reach all sides. The sweet peas should attract the bees and help pollinate the beans. If attacked by aphids use an insecticide suitable for vegetables and which will not harm bees. Apply a liquid feed every two weeks from end June.

Be careful to remove all seed pods on the sweet peas to encourage further flowering. Better still, cut the flowers and so enjoy their fragrance inside. New buds will soon open and that way you will get an abundant crop. I generally cut all the flowers on a Friday for the weekend and then again early the next week.

Crop the beans as soon as they are long enough. Take them while young and tender to encourage further production.

At the end of the autumn, discard all the plants.

101 DARK SECRETS

Aubergines have attractive lilac flowers and wonderful glossy black fruit which hang down amongst the foliage. The carpet of orange marigolds sets them off beautifully.

Site
Greenhouse or conservatory.

Container
Clay pot: 27.5cm (11″) in diameter, 25cm (10″) deep.

Early Preparation
Both the special French marigolds and the aubergines may be grown from seed, although the aubergines need quite high temperatures to get them started in early February. Follow the instructions on the packet. They can also be bought from garden centres in May. Three plants is enough to supply most family needs throughout the summer.

Planting Time
May.

At its best
July to September.

Ingredients
1 aubergine 'Black Prince F1 Hybrid' commonly known as the egg-plant.
2 French marigolds *Tagetes patula* 'Special'; a Thompson and Morgan Ltd companion plant to deter whitefly and other aphids (see the list of specialist suppliers on page 225).
12 litres of John Innes No 2 soil.
Drainage material such as small pieces of polystyrene.
1 three-foot cane for support.

Method
1. Cover the base of the container with 5cm (2″) of drainage material and add sufficient soil to bring the level to within 5cm (2″) of the rim of the pot.
2. Plant the aubergine at the centre-back of the pot and the two marigolds at the front, one on either side.
3. Add more soil, bringing the level to within 2.5cm (1″) of the rim of the container. Water well.
4. Fix the cane so that it will give support to the aubergine plant as the branches grow and are weighed down by fruit.

Aftercare
You want to encourage two leading shoots to develop, so when the plant is about 15cm (6″) high, pinch out the top of the plant. (NB: This may already have been done if you have purchased one from the garden centre.) Remove any side shoots which appear.

Maintain soil moisture throughout the growing season and apply a liquid feed every two weeks once the aubergines has begun to set fruit. Red spider may be a problem under glass; whitefly and greenfly should be kept at bay by the marigolds, but if necessary spray with an insecticide which is safe for fruit and vegetables. Deadhead the marigolds. Pick fruit regularly to encourage further production.

Discard the plants at the end of the fruiting season.

102   YELLOW COURGETTES

Both the flowers and the fruit of yellow courgettes make an attractive display in a pot. Here they show up well against blue lobelia.

Site
Outdoors, sheltered and sunny.

Container
Red plastic pot: 32.5cm (13″) in diameter, 27.5cm (11″) deep. Any medium to large pot would be appropriate, but red does make a change!

Early Preparation
Sow two seeds under heat in April or early May, one each in a 7.5cm (3″) pot, following the instructions on the packet. You will only need the stronger of the two plants for this scheme. Three or four plants would provide enough courgettes for a family of four.

Planting Time
End May. Courgettes are susceptible to frost so protect them on cold nights.

At its best
July to September.

Ingredients
1 yellow courgette *Cucurbita pepo* 'Gold Rush F1

Hybrid' which has been chosen for its attractively coloured fruit. They make an interesting change from green courgettes and may be used in salads or cooked.
½ strip of lobelia *Lobelia erinus* 'Cambridge Blue'.
16 litres of John Innes No 2 soil.
Drainage material such as small pieces of polystyrene.

Method
1. Cover the base of the container with 5cm (2″) of drainage material and add 20cm (8″) soil.
2. Plant the courgette in the centre of the pot.
3. Divide the lobelia and plant around the edge.
4. Water well. Firm in the plants.

Aftercare
Water regularly; in hot weather be prepared to water daily. Apply a liquid feed every week from the middle of July or whenever the courgettes first begin to flower to set fruit. Aphids should not present a problem but if they do, spray with a safe insecticide suitable for fruit and vegetables.

Harvest the exotic yellow flowers so that they can be stuffed in the Italian style of cooking or cut the fruit when it is between 7.5–20cm (3–8″) long and then bake or fry. Do not attempt to eat the lobelia as it is poisonous.

At the end of the autumn, discard all the plants.

103 HERBS FOR FISH

Bronze fennel is a delightful herb with its graceful feathery foliage, pretty yellow flowers, and distinctive smell and flavour of light aniseed. Underplanted with parsley and bright orange pot marigolds, it makes a fine combination for fish dishes.

Site
Outdoors, sunny and sheltered; conservatory or greenhouse for the winter, if desired.

Container
Large pot: 45cm (18″) in diameter, 40cm (16″) deep.

Early Preparation
You could sow seeds of the parsley and marigold in early spring following the instructions on the packets, but both plants are easily obtainable in garden centres in May.

Planting Time
Spring.

At its best
June to September.

Ingredients
1 bronze fennel *Foeniculum vulgare*. The bronze form which has been used here is particularly attractive in spring and early summer when the new growths show the strongest bronze colourings. However, both the green and bronze form are worth growing so you can plant either. The lacy leaves make a delicate garnish as well as being used to flavour sauces. The flowers make a very pretty addition to a late summer salad.
3 pot marigolds *Calendula officinalis* with bright orange flowers which make such a striking contrast to the bronze fennel. The leaves can be used in stews and salads while the flowers can be cooked with fish, used to make a sauce or tossed in salads.
4 parsley plants *Petroselinum crispum*. Its foliage is popular for many culinary dishes.
55 litres of John Innes No 2 soil.
Drainage material such as broken crocks or small pieces of polystyrene.

Method
1. Cover the base of the container with 7.5cm (3″) of drainage material and add sufficient soil to bring the level to within 2.5cm (1″) of the rim.

2. Plant the bronze fennel in the centre of the pot.
3. Plant the pot marigolds around the front near the edge with the parsley in between and at the back.
4. Water well and firm in the plants.

Aftercare
Maintain soil moisture throughout the growing season; be prepared to water daily in hot weather.

Apply a fortnightly liquid feed from end June onwards.

Deadhead the marigolds to prevent seeds forming and so prolong the flowering period; better still, use them in the kitchen while still young. Some sources suggest pinching off the fennel flower buds as they form but I think the flowers are too good to miss and the seeds can be used in cooking as well. Harvest the parsley (sparingly at first) and fennel leaves from June onwards.

The fennel is a hardy perennial; it can be left outdoors for the winter and will grace the pot the next year. Cut down the stems in the autumn. It should be repotted in the spring when it can then be divided into two or more plants, and new parsley and marigolds added.

The pot could be brought into the protection of a cool greenhouse or conservatory in late autumn where it will produce new greenery for the winter. Cut down the fennel foliage and stems to within a few inches of the soil and then wait for fresh foliage to grow. Cut the parsley right back as well and you will have fresh growth there too. Don't forget to keep watering. The marigolds may be discarded.

104   PLENTIFUL HERBS

Parsley, golden sage, variegated lemon balm and lemon thyme make up the second collection of herbs to be planted in a four-in-one pot. They all have lots of culinary uses as well as being highly decorative.

Site
Outdoors; sunny.

Container
Four-in-one terracotta pot (made by Whichford Pottery). Each of the four pots is 15cm (6″) in diameter, 15cm (6″) deep. The middle one is slightly raised above the others.

Planting Time
March or April.

At its best
May to August.

Ingredients
1 parsley plant *Petroselinum crispum*. Its foliage is popular for stuffings, sauces and garnishing.
1 golden variegated sage *Salvia officinalis* 'Icterina'. A mild but characteristic flavour.
1 variegated lemon balm *Melissa officinalis* 'Variegata'. Finely chop the leaf and use in both savoury and sweet dishes.
1 lemon-scented thyme *Thymus* × *citriodorus* with bright green leaves, particularly in early summer, which are useful for stuffings and salads, and pale lilac flowers in mid summer which are pretty for decorative purposes on pâtés etc.
4 litres of John Innes No 2 soil.
Drainage material such as polystyrene or horticultural grit.

Method
1. Cover the base of each of the four pots with 2.5cm (1″) of drainage material and add the same amount of soil.
2. Plant the parsley in the top pot and the sage, lemon balm and thyme around the bottom.
3. Fill in the gaps with soil, bringing the level to within 2.5cm (1″) of the rim of each pot.
4. Water well. Add more soil if necessary.

Aftercare
Maintain soil moisture throughout the growing season; be prepared to water daily in hot weather. Apply a liquid feed every two weeks from early June onwards. Harvest the herbs regularly although the parsley is best picked sparingly at first until it gets established; wait until June for the first cut. Keep the lemon balm well cut back to prevent it becoming too untidy. Constant shearing will do no harm; on the contrary it will rejuvenate the growth. Cut the thyme flowers back after they have died down, or better still, use them as they open for kitchen purposes.

Keep the pot in a sheltered spot for the winter. If you trim back the parsley in September you should get new fresh growth. Repot the herbs into a larger container next spring. You might like to replace the parsley.

105   A GALAXY OF GREENS

Variegated mint, oregano, sage and rosemary make a delightfully attractive planting scheme. Together with the next recipe they encompass almost all the commonly used culinary herbs.

Site
Outdoors; sunny. Greenhouse or conservatory for winter if desired.

Container
Four-in-one terracotta pot (made by Whichford Pottery). Each of the four pots is 15cm (6″) in diameter, 15cm (6″) deep. The middle one is raised above the others.

Planting Time
March or April.

At its best
May to August.

Ingredients
1 variegated pineapple mint *Mentha rotundifolia* 'Variegata'. Excellent for culinary purposes and lovely as a garnish. Its growth lasts well into the winter.
1 compact oregano *Origanum vulgare* 'Compactum'. Good flavour for stuffings and salads. The aromatic flowers are good for decorative purposes.
1 variegated green and pink sage *Salvia officinalis* 'Tricolor'. It is milder than the common sage but still has the characteristic flavour; pretty but only half hardy.
1 prostrate rosemary *Rosmarinus lavandulaceus* syn. *R. officinalis prostratus*. Early in the spring it has a lovely pale blue flower which can be used as well as the leaves for culinary purposes. You could substitute an upright form, in which case plant it in the top of the pot.
4 litres of John Innes No 2 soil.
Drainage material such as polystyrene or horticultural grit.

Method
1. Cover the base of each of the four pots with 2.5cm (1″) of drainage material and add the same amount of soil.
2. Plant the mint in the top pot and the oregano, sage and rosemary in the bottom pots.
3. Fill in the gaps with soil, bringing the level to within 2.5cm (1″) of the rim of each pot.
4. Water well. Add more soil if necessary.

Aftercare
Maintain soil moisture throughout the growing season; be prepared to water daily in hot weather. Apply a liquid feed every two weeks from early June onwards. Harvest the herbs regularly.

This sage is not hardy; you could replace it with a red or common sage in the autumn and allow to stand outdoors in a protected place. Rosemary is not fully hardy either but should survive in a sheltered spot. The mint will last well into the late autumn and then grow up the next spring when you can repot the herbs into a larger container.

Alternatively, bring the pot into a cool greenhouse or conservatory, cut back the mint and oregano, water well and feed, and you will have fresh new growth throughout the winter. The rosemary will burst into flower and look very pretty.

Create an entire herb garden in pots arranged with a sense of balance and shape

106   HERBS IN A STRAWBERRY POT

Herbs can be both decorative and useful. Here is a glorious rich mixture of colours, shapes and aromas.

Site
Outdoors; sunny.

Container
Terracotta strawberry pot: 30cm (12") in diameter, 40cm (16") deep.

Planting Time
March/April.

At its best
June to September.

Ingredients
  2 oregano *Origanum vulgare* 'Compactum'. If it is a large plant you may be able to divide it, in which case only buy one.
  4 different thymes: *Thymus* 'Anderson's Gold' with pretty pink flowers; *T. pseudolanuginosus* known as the woolly thyme with very hairy grey leaves and pale pink flowers; *T. × citriodorus* 'Silver Queen' with variegated silver splashed leaves; and *T. drucei* 'Albus' with white flowers. Buy any four which you find pleasing and which have a variety of form and colour.
  1 oak-leaved geranium *Pelargonium quercifolium*. It has scented leaves and attractive lilac flowers with deep maroon blotches which can be used for decorative purposes on salads and pâtés etc. It is not hardy so must be given warmth during the winter.
  1 variegated sage *Salvia officinalis* 'Tricolor', again not hardy but if planted at the top it can be removed and given winter protection.
14 litres of John Innes No 2 soil.
Drainage material plus some horticultural grit.

Method
1. Cover the base of the container with 5cm (2") of drainage material and add sufficient soil to reach the bottom layer of holes.
2. Plant one oregano, the woolly thyme and 'Silver Queen' around the bottom tier, carefully passing the roots through the holes. If the plants are too big, divide them.
3. Add two handfuls of grit in the centre of the pot and then add more soil to bring the level up to the second layer of holes.

4. Plant 'Anderson's Gold', 'Albus' and the other oregano around the top tier. Make sure the oregano appears on opposite sides of the pot.
5. Add more grit in the centre and then a little more soil so that all the roots are covered.
6. Plant the oak-leaved geranium towards the centre-front of the pot with the sage behind.
7. Fill in the gaps with soil, bringing the level to within 2.5cm (1") of the rim.
8. Water carefully but well. You do not want to wash the soil out through the holes. In a few weeks the roots will have grown and this will not longer be a problem. Make sure all the plants are firmly in place.

Aftercare
Water regularly especially in hot weather. Apply an occasional liquid feed after early June.

  Crop the herbs as needed. Use the leaves and flowers. Cut back all remaining thyme and oregano flower-heads after flowering. In September, remove and pot up the geranium and sage to overwinter in the greenhouse or conservatory. Replant the following summer or replace with another scented leaf geranium and perhaps a hardy sage. After the second summer the herbs should be divided and fresh soil used to repot.

VICTORIAN AND EDWARDIAN SCHEMES

INTRODUCTION TO THE VICTORIAN AND EDWARDIAN RECIPES

Container gardening was extremely popular in the Victorian period, a fashion which continued right up to the First World War. It paralleled the growing interest in gardening generally, one which was inextricably linked to the discoveries of far-off lands.

Since the sixteenth century, there had been a growing surge of new plants introduced to this country, many from Europe but also from the Southern hemisphere and the Americas. By the early part of the nineteenth century, it had become a veritable flood including all the petunias, verbenas, the sweet-smelling mimulus, many geraniums and fuchsias, feverfew and white lobelia. New hardy imports could be planted permanently in the garden, or used to create temporary displays in winter and spring flowerbeds. But tender ones could not stand our winter cold and damp climate. These had to be kept indoors in the warmth of a greenhouse or conservatory, and only put outside in the early summer.

With the removal of the glass tax in 1845, it became much cheaper to overwinter the plants, grow on the new cuttings and raise tender annuals from seed. As a result, bedding-out plants became much cheaper and far more available. Interest surged. Excitement grew. The summer, and later the winter, bedding-out system became all the rage, colour schemes were debated in great detail and everywhere

there was enormous enthusiasm. A gardening revolution was taking place, one which reached all classes of society from the poor city-dweller to the fashionable squares of inner London and the new villas in suburbia. Even the rural areas were affected, as country house and country cottage gardens were all caught up in the greater movement. What better place to show off the new plants than to put them in containers where they could be well exhibited, easily seen and become focal points in their own right. The Victorians used a great variety of window boxes, wooden tubs, clay pots, stone, artificial stone and lead vases, wire baskets and wire hanging baskets to beautify the garden and the outside of the home.

LARGE SCALE USE OF CONTAINERS

Such was the fashion that great numbers of containers were often used in each garden, far more than would generally be found today. As early as 1837 C. F. Ferris was suggesting ways of improving a garden where the view was limited. He wanted to make 'every object about it, such as differently formed vases, wire or wooden baskets, pots etc – and the variety and shapes in the beds – sufficiently interesting to the eye, without wishing to carry the view any farther'. In one plan alone he drew the plot for sixteen vases and pots. Loudon wrote about villa gardens in 1850, with drawings to demonstrate how seven wire baskets placed on turf could be used to surround a high fountain, and another picture of them grouped more informally, showing at least six different baskets, pots and vases with a statue and trees behind.

In 1879 Mollison described some of the window boxes in the West End of London as 'one of the richest treats of London. Some of the houses have every window full of flowers. There you can study the tasteful arranging of a window box in the highest style of the art. No lover of flowers can pass through such streets without bringing away a serviceable hint stored up for future use.' In the summer of 1900 the Oxford colleges had outstanding displays. At Trinity, the garden quad had sixty three separate arrangements of trailing and upright geraniums, marguerites, lobelia and feverfew. At Christchurch in Peckwater, 'there were a hundred and fifty windows dressed . . .' using geraniums, fuchsias, marguerites, calceolarias, musk, lobelia and nasturtiums. Magdalen, Queen's, University, Exeter, New, Wadham and many more all had great numbers in full array.

THE IDEAS OF JOHN MOLLISON ON WINDOW BOXES, SOIL AND LIQUID MANURE

Old gardening books and journals, paintings and later photographs are all vital sources of information. The most revealing of all is John Mollison's book called *The New Practical Window Gardener* published in 1879. He dealt in detail with all aspects of window gardening, both inside and outside the house, and also with balcony gardening. He described the window box in detail: how 'it should be eight inches wide and ten inches deep, inside measurement, to allow two inches at the bottom for drainage and one inch on the surface for watering. This prevents the soil being washed over the sides of the box and dirtying the paint or tile, which looks bad. There will be seven inches left for soil for the roots to spread about in; quite a sufficient depth, if good rich soil is used. A pinch or two of guano or dissolved bones may be added and incorporated well with the soil.' Drainage consisted of old broken crocks, tiles or oyster shells covered with a little sphagnum moss to prevent the water from being washed down into the crocks.

On the question of soil, he was most insistent that the soil should never be common garden soil. According to the plants to be grown in it, it should consist of one part fibrous turfy loam, cut from good old pasture to the depth of four or five inches and left to rot for six months. Or for peat-loving plants he suggested peat taken from a heathy common added to sharp sand and again left to rot. Either of these two should form the principal part of the compost. To either one might be added an equal amount of leaf mould which has been gathered and turned for at least a year and then sieved to get rid of all old sticks etc. The third part would be mainly silver or river sand and 'dry cow dung, rubbed down fine'. A pinch or two of ground bones might be added for quick growing soft wooded plants. However, it was quite possible to order compost from a nurseryman, or mix it from his supplies. In 1881 the cost of coarse silver sand was 1s 9d per bushel, 26s per ton. Fibrous loam, peat mould and leaf mould was 1s per bushel.

Mollison said that liquid manure should be applied twice a week. A very safe one was made 'with sheep droppings dissolved in water, not too strong, just sufficient to give a dark brown appearance'! He recommended tobacco water, liquid ammonia and very weak glue water as well.

OLD FAVOURITES

One of the reasons for writing about container gardening in this period is to draw attention to some of the many plants which were used then, much more than today. The Victorians loved scented plants and grew a great deal of mimulus, heliotropes and mignonette. They adored vibrant colours and often used yellow calceolarias, so good for showing off scarlets and other colours of the bedding plants. They liked plants with interesting foliage including coleus, perilla and coloured leaf geraniums. They used golden feverfew as an edger both for summer and winter, regularly clipping it so that it retained its golden colourings. Some of these plants are quite out of fashion, or grown much less than they were a century ago. But they are still available in one form or other, as plants or seed. It is certainly worthwhile returning to some of them, particularly the scented ones which can give so much pleasure to the passer-by and often attract butterflies as well.

OLD PLANTING TECHNIQUES

A second reason is so that some of the old planting techniques might be revived. Mollison was very keen on growing annuals up out of the sides of window boxes so that they could be trained to frame a window. He used nasturtiums, sweet peas, canary creeper and scarlet runners (runner beans with red flowers grown for their bright colour, not for their fruit). He described an example of a box he had seen in a small manufacturing town some time before where scarlet and white geraniums, yellow calceolar ias, musk and lobelia were planted with an arch of canary creeper growing over the top. He had an interesting idea for hanging baskets. Green and variegated ivy was to be grown out of them and pegged all round the bottom and sides so as to create a green covering for the moss and wires. It would remain throughout the winter and summer, with other plants being interchanged according to the season.

RECREATE PERIOD SCHEMES

The third reason for my research and writing on this subject is to help people who are interested in garden history. With the help of some of these recipes they can plant their containers to match the original style of the garden and so create a period atmosphere to the outside of the house. To replan an entire garden might seem rather daunting. But to plant a few window boxes or tubs using some of the old combinations would be a simple and pleasurable task. Fortunately there are quite a few references to actual planting schemes for garden vases, tubs, pots, balcony plantings, hanging baskets and, most of all, for window boxes. Mollison kindly wrote down thirteen ideas for them in 1879 – five for the winter months and eight for the summer and early autumn. Such detail allows us a wonderful glimpse into mid-Victorian container gardening.

SOURCE OF CONTAINERS

In order to recreate some of the old schemes you might feel tempted to purchase some original containers from auctions, architectural heritage shops or specialist garden antique shops. On the other hand, cheaper modern containers faithfully following the old designs can be obtained easily from our garden centres or direct from the suppliers: Haddonstone Ltd for reconstituted stone, Whichford Pottery and the Olive Tree Trading Company Ltd for terracotta pots and Renaissance Casting Company Ltd for lead vases and urns. Some of them are delightful. (A list of their addresses is given on page 226.) Furthermore you might consider using old chimney pots or upturned sea-kale pots. Their original use would have been different but if they provide the right feel then that is what is important. I have seen wonderful old lead water cisterns used to contain plants. This was

certainly not their original purpose but no one would question their use in a period garden.

SOURCE OF PLANTS

What about the plants themselves, where do we find those? Recent interest in the subject has led to more nurseries stocking and selling these old plants and they are now far more available than they used to be. However, you will still have to track them down. Some will be much easier than others. Nearly all the old bulbs listed are available through those garden centres which stock O. A. Taylor and Sons Bulbs Ltd. A good many other garden centres will sell some of them as well. Many of the plants are quite common; golden lemon thyme, aucubas, ivies, pansies, violas and violets, to name just a few, are all easy to find. However, you might have to search harder for auriculas, hepaticas and double primroses, although they do seem to be appearing more often at the spring RHS shows and some of the larger garden centres. Some of the old geraniums are quite common even now, but others are rarer. Fibrex Nurseries Ltd hold the National Collection and have the biggest source to my knowledge. Indeed, there will be quite a few plants where only the specialist nursery will be able to help.

Here arises a problem: should we only grow the early varieties or can we substitute modern ones where the old ones are difficult to find? Where possible I have used the old plants. However, where the same species of plant exists today but the cultivar has changed or a new hybrid been developed, then I can see no reason not to substitute. The Victorians were very fashion conscious about their plants, and would happily try out the new hybrids at the expense of the old ones. Just because we can't trace a certain white hepatica, tulip, petunia or geranium does not mean we should not grow another white one which is available today. For the general enthusiast I think it is enough to follow the overall idea, shape and colour scheme of the recipe and not to be too worried by exact copies. Faithful reproductions are wonderful where they can be achieved but are often almost impossible to carry out completely.

To help the reader further with this subject I have written a few notes about all the plants used in this section. If they are not easily available I have listed the suppliers where they might be found. Some will have to be grown from seed; this, too, is made clear.

VICTORIAN AND EDWARDIAN PLANTS USED IN THE WINTER AND SPRING RECIPES: THEIR ORIGINS, USE AND AVAILABILITY

With the exception of tulips, this list of plants refers only to those used in the planting schemes contained in this book. Many others would have been used in containers as well.

ARABIS Arabis caucasica was available from the Caucasus from the end of the eighteenth century. Mollison suggested it as a winter bedder for window boxes in 1879, both in its green and variegated form. It was also suggested for edging garden vases in winter in 1900. It is easily available from most garden centres.

AUBRIETIA Aubrietia deltoidea, our common aubrietia, was introduced from the Levant in 1710. Mollison suggests it for one of the winter window box schemes growing alongside arabis. Easily available at many garden centres.

AUCUBA Aucuba japonica, introduced from Japan in 1783, was seen in many Victorian and Edwardian gardens. It was well liked because it survived the fog and smoke better than many other evergreens. Mollison referred to it as a winter specimen plant for balconies, and as a centrepiece for winter hanging baskets. *Gardening for Beginners* in 1914 suggested it as a good plant for winter window boxes. Other varieties of the species, both male and female, all differing in their leaf colourings, were also in cultivation.

BELLIS Bellis perennis, our common native daisy, has been popular for centuries as a garden plant. By the late sixteenth century red and white forms, both double and single, existed and by the eighteenth century, pink ones had evolved. They were a very fashionable edger to spring flower beds in Victorian times, and Mollison used them in several of his spring window box schemes (he only mentioned red and white). They are easily available today either in the autumn or in early spring. Unfortunately they are often sold in bedding strips of mixed colours which means you are not able to alternate the reds and whites as Mollison suggested. However, with perseverance you should be able to track the single colours down. If you can't, don't worry too much as the pink which will be included is very pretty.

CHEIRANTHUS The wallflower was probably introduced as early as Norman times. Its origins are Southern Europe. It was very popular in the Middle Ages as a plant to be held in the hand at festivals because of its sweet scent. In the early 1600s Parkinson grew six varieties, including three doubles, one of these being a double red. One of the old doubles which still survives is the miniature yellow one, now known as 'Harpur Crewe', which was rescued and propagated at the end of last century by the Rev. Henry Harpur Crewe. The Victorians grew yellow and rusty red colours but among their favourites were white, scarlet and reddish-black. Two of Mollison's five spring window box schemes include dwarf wallflowers, both to be planted with Brompton Stocks surrounded by red and white daisies and pansies. One was to be underplanted with daffodils and the other with lily of the valley. Modern strains of dwarf wallflower plants are easy to buy in the autumn, but to get the more unusual darker reds and browns look for packets of seeds. Thompson and Morgan Ltd do a good range of dwarf doubles and Tom Thumb varieties.

CROCUS Known already in the sixteenth century, the orange *Crocus aureus* came from Greece and is one of the parents of our well-known 'Dutch Yellow'. *Crocus vernus*, the parent of all our bright purple and white Dutch crocuses, was introduced at about the same time. Mollison suggests either mixed or yellow, white and blue crocuses in the window boxes. He also used them in hanging baskets, but waited until early spring to plant them. This would mean that the shoots were already quite long and could be made to face out through the sides of the basket. It seems to work well with no detriment to the flower. All the above named crocuses are easily available today.

EUONYMUS Euonymus fortunei and *E. japonicus* both originate in Japan and were introduced in the nineteenth century. *Gardening Made Easy* written in 1906 and *Gardening for Beginners* in 1914 referred to them as good window box subjects and in 1900 H. T. Martin of Stoneleigh had mentioned them in *The Gardener* magazine as being suitable for garden vases in winter. Mollison did not mention them in 1879, although he made passing reference to many shrubs suitable for winter balcony use. Presumably they gained favour towards the end of the century. Many varieties are available today, all welcome for winter work because of their variegated and cheerful appearance.

HEDERA (ivy: see page 182).

HEPATICA Hepaticas are natives of much of Northern Europe and America. They were much used by the Victorians along with snowdrops and winter aconites for late winter/early spring colour, being commonly available in blue, red and white, both double and single. Mollison used them alongside sweet violets in one of his winter window box schemes, which is slightly surprising as they don't really like being disturbed too much, and although plentiful they were not cheap. In May 1881 they were being advertised for sending through the post, all well-rooted and post-free; double pink and single blue cost 5s per dozen while the white single was 7s 6d per dozen. Compared with geraniums and fuchsias they seem to have been very expensive. They are not easily available today, although they seem to have made a comeback at the RHS shows and there are some nurseries which sell them such as Hopleys Plants, Plants From The Past and Manningford Nurseries; certain garden centres sell them also.

HYACINTHUS The hyacinth was introduced to Britain prior to 1597, and by 1629, apparently, it was plentiful. Even then the white Roman hyacinth was being grown. The hyacinth was much loved by the Victorians for both indoor and outdoor container work. Mollison included them in two of his five winter window box schemes and mentions a whole range of colours including red, blue, lilac and mauve, white and yellow. Few, if any, of the same names are available today. However, their choice was so great that almost any one which we would choose today would have found a similar colour form in Victorian times. Moreover, we do have the very good white 'L'Innocence' which dates from before the First World War, and we still have the white Roman hyacinth.

MUSCARI Commonly known as grape hyacinths, these originated from Europe. They were much used by the Victorians in spring bedding schemes. In 1879 Mollison describes them as 'a charming subject for both pots and boxes'. He wrote that the best were M. botryoides caeruleum 'Album', and pallidum, racemosum and racepalleus. Of these the most easily available today is M. botryoides 'Album', the white muscari also known as the Pearls of Spain. The blue form has been overtaken in popularity by M. armeniacum 'Heavenly Blue' from Asia Minor. This is the most common one for sale in every garden centre.

NARCISSUS The daffodil has its origins around the Mediterranean and in the Iberian peninsula. Commercial hybridizing did not take place until the second half of the nineteenth century so most of the early and mid Victorian daffodils grown would have been species or natural hybrids. Mollison refers to one window box scheme with narcissus, but does not describe it in detail like the other bulbs and plants he uses. His use of the word 'narcissus' probably refers to the white Narcissus poeticus and the bunch-flowered daffodils. I have planted Narcissus poeticus 'Actaea' because it is easily available and one of the old ones grown. Surprisingly few daffodils were grown in containers outdoors, the reason being possibly because the dwarf daffodils we now use so often for this type of gardening were not developed until the twentieth century. Among those that are available today are still the species ones and Narcissus poeticus 'Actaea' and 'Recurvus' which is occasionally called 'Old Pheasant's Eye'.

PRIMULA 1. Double primroses based on our native wild primrose, Primula vulgaris, were developed in the sixteenth century, the first ones being yellow or white. In the 1630s a red primrose, a native of Caucasus, Greece and North Persia, was introduced and so began the development of other colours in the spectrum. By the beginning of Queen Victoria's reign seven or eight doubles were grown, the hardiest of which and probably the most common was the lilac variety known as 'Ladies Delight'. Blue was not introduced again until 1889; earlier forms had been lost. In 1879 Mollison suggests both the double and single varieties for container work, either for balcony or window boxes. The doubles are more difficult to look after than the single primroses and need to be kept very moist. Just a few years ago they were very difficult to obtain, but with new propagation methods the process is more commercially viable and they are now available from quite a number of garden centres and nurseries. Thompson and Morgan Ltd sell both the seeds and plantlets.

2. Polyanthus has developed as a cross between a cowslip and a primrose. Known for centuries, it was much developed in the 1700s and the 1800s. In 1879 Mollison suggests double and single polyanthus for both balcony and window box work. The gold- and silver-laced varieties, with their yellow or white edge to the petals, were extremely popular and certainly very fashionable in the early and middle part of the nineteenth century. Though not particularly effective as a border flower they do look very exciting as a container-grown plant when associated with other yellows or whites. They are not very common in the garden centres although they are now prominent at the RHS shows. Seeds are easily available from Thompson and Morgan Ltd.

3. Garden auriculas were developed from two alpine flowers, *Primula auricula* and *Primula hirsuta* towards the end of the sixteenth century. Their popularity increased over the next 150 years until the early part of the nineteenth century in and around London and, a little later, further north. They were still grown but came to be seen as the poor man's flower, probably more typical of the cottage window box than the London balcony. Towards the end of the 1800s they enjoyed a revival. Both double and single sorts of red, crimson, yellows, purples and buffs were grown throughout the period. Comparable yellow ones are available today, often with a lovely perfume. Many other shades can be found as well, although some plants will stand outside in the garden far better than others. When buying from a specialist grower, check to see which ones are best for outdoor containers. Thompson and Morgan Ltd sell seed for both singles and doubles.

SCILLAS Scillas, also known as Siberian squills, had been introduced from Siberia at the end of the eighteenth century. They were suggested for spring window boxes in *The Garden*, 15 March 1902, and in *Gardening for Beginners* in 1914. No doubt they would have been used in pots and vases as well. They are available as dry bulbs in the autumn at all garden centres.

TANACETUM PARTHENIUM 'AUREUM' (Feverfew: see page 183).

THYMUS Originating in the Mediterranean countries, *Thymus × citriodorus* 'Aureus', golden lemon thyme, was grown here in the early 1600s. I was surprised to see it suggested for a winter bedding scheme, by H. T. Martin in 1900, to be planted in a garden vase, but having tried it out, I am full of enthusiasm. Not only did it look bright throughout the winter, but after rain or whenever it had been watered it gave off a wonderful smell. It is easily available from garden centres.

TULIPA Tulips were introduced from Turkey to central Europe and Holland from the 1550s onwards, and to Britain in 1578. By the early seventeenth century they had become extremely fashionable and in some cases very expensive. Many old paintings reveal them grown in containers, a legacy which continued well into Victorian times. Mollison describes them in 1879 as 'the queen of spring flowers and the grandest of all for balcony display. Nothing can excel the effectiveness of a mass of its magnificent blooms.' He also said they were 'very suitable for pots and window boxes'. He describes the double

tulips as best for this purpose and specifically names the early 'Duc-van-Thol' (red and yellow) tulips as being suitable for window boxes. Constant breeding has taken place and not many of the old ones are readily available today.

However, a few survive, and amongst those available in the bulb catalogues and garden centres are:
'Brilliant Star': single early, red (1906).
'Clara Butt': mid season, tall pink tulip good for tubs (1889).
'Coleur Cardinal': single early, velvet red (1840).
'Diana': white single early, good for tubs, not too tall (1909).
'Electra': double early (1905).
'Fantasy': parrot mid season (1910). Large heads, needs sheltered position. Later grown in hanging baskets.
'Keizerskroon': mid season, red flower edged with yellow, suitable for pots and window boxes if deep (1750 or even earlier). Mixes well with wallflowers.
'Murillo': double early, white flushed with pink (1860).
'Peach Blossom': double early, pink (1890). Excellent for window boxes; mix with feverfew, pansies, bellis daisies.
'Van de Hoef': double early, yellow (1911). Also excellent for window boxes; mix with feverfew, white hyacinths, blue pansies etc.

This list is by no means exhaustive, but in spite of its brevity, don't let this stop you using other tulips in old container schemes. The Victorians had a huge selection to choose from and you can be sure that almost any colour you choose would have had a Victorian equivalent.

VIOLA *Viola odorata* is our native sweet violet. They are mentioned by Mollison in one of his winter window box schemes. They were much loved by the Victorians and are easily available today, particularly in our garden centres in the spring.

Viola × wittrockiana, our common garden pansy, was probably based on *V. tricolor*, our native wild pansy or heartsease, and *V. lutea* var. *sudetica*, a native of central Europe. Between 1835 and 1838 there were 400 named varieties. Mollison suggests blue, white and yellow violas, white pansies for summer work in window boxes, and yellow and blue pansies for one of his winter schemes. The frequent choice of yellow pansies and violas is interesting, as it always shows up so well in winter arrangements and makes a good contrast in summer ones. It is under-used these days. Mollison describes pansies as being indispensable for balcony and window boxes. Violas were advertised for sale in May 1881 at 5s per 100 carriage-free, cash only.

VICTORIAN AND EDWARDIAN PLANTS USED IN THE SUMMER RECIPES: THEIR ORIGINS, USE AND AVAILABILITY

This list of plants refers only to those used in the planting schemes contained in the following recipes. Many other plants would have been used in containers as well.

AGAVE AMERICANA 'MARGINATA' The agave, commonly known as the Century plant, came from tropical America in about 1554. For centuries it has been used as a statuesque container plant. In 1879 Mollison suggests their use for balconies, halls, vestibules and rooms. We know from other sources that they were grown in wooden half barrels with lobelia around the side.

CALCEOLARIA Known commonly as slipperworts or slipper flowers, it first arrived from South America in the late eighteenth century. New species were discovered later and by the 1830s the great commercial production of them had begun in earnest. They were widely favoured amongst Victorian gardeners both for use in bedding schemes and in container displays. Mollison recommends them for balcony and window box usage. Yellow, bronze and scarlet were most common. Today they are available from seed and from most garden centres as bedding plants where they will be almost exclusively yellow.

CAMPANULA ISOPHYLLA 'ALBA' This pretty creeping white campanula was introduced from Italy after 1868. In *The Gardener*, 18 June 1904, it was suggested for planting with ferns in an umbrella hanging basket. In *Gardening for Beginners* in 1914 a photograph was shown of a campanula basket measuring 'five foot three inches from base to summit'. It is available in the houseplant section of most garden centres.

CHRYSANTHEMUM (ARGYRANTHEMUM) FRUTESCENS Known as the white 'Paris Daisy' and also as the marguerite, it was brought from the Canaries to France in the late sixteenth century. Marguerite de Valois grew it around 1600 in her garden near Paris. The plant reached England in 1699. It was not mentioned by Mollison in 1879, but was frequently referred to in gardening journals towards the turn of the century. They were certainly grown in the window boxes of several Oxford colleges as reported in *The Gardener* magazine, 14 July 1900, including Trinity, Worcester and Christ Church. In 1914 it was highly recommended in the book *Gardening for Beginners* for use in garden vases. It is available as seed and is common in garden centres as bedding plants in May.

ECHEVERIA SECUNDA Echeverias are small succulents with attractive grey rosettes which Mollison claimed to be excellent for bedding work in balcony and window boxes. Four of his eight summer window box schemes included them. In the same way they lend themselves to edging garden vases and pots. They were also used in autumn hanging baskets for the conservatory. Often available, but particularly in spring in the garden centres as houseplants or conservatory plants. They are easy to propagate. Once planted, they soon create a mass of little plants which can be successfully overwintered.

FERNS Ferns were a favourite Victorian plant for planting in basement areas. Many of the ones used were our native British ferns. Less hardy ones were used in conservatory baskets. Fibrex Nurseries Ltd are a good source.

FRAGARIA × ANANASSA 'VARIEGATA' Variegated strawberry plants were apparently first mentioned in 1859 when it was recommended to drape the sides of flower baskets and urns and was said to associate well with fuchsias. In 1879 Mollison thought *Fragaria indica*, the Indian Strawberry, *Fragaria vesca*, the common wild strawberry, and *Fragaria alpina*, the Alpine strawberry, all excellent hanging basket plants.

FUCHSIA Fuchsias were mostly introduced from South America and Mexico from the 1820s onwards. Popular in window boxes (though never used as much as geraniums), Mollison suggested them in two of his seven summer boxes in 1879 and they were used at several Oxford colleges in 1900. They were also planted as standards in garden vases. Rooted cuttings in May 1881 cost 2s per dozen, or 3d each, post-free! New fuchsia cultivars were rather more expensive, however, and 'Miss Lizzie Vidler' was offered for sale at 2s 6d, 3s 6d or 5s 6d each, the different prices referring, presumably, to the varying sizes. This was at a time when gardener's wages were being advertised in Dorset at 17s per week, including cottage. Mollison refers mainly to single and double reds and whites. Victorian plants are available from several nurseries, including Jackson's Nurseries. They still stock 'Lye's Unique', a salmon/orange and white upright fuchsia bred by Lye in 1886, an unusual colour for the period, and 'Charming', a hardy rich carmine/rosy red fuchsia with a more lax habit, also bred by Lye in 1895.

HEDERA This includes *Hedera helix*, the common native English ivy, *H. hibernica*, the Irish ivy, and *H. canariensis* from the Canaries. Together, they form the basis of one of the favourite plants in Victorian times for both winter and summer use, inside and outside the house. In 1879 Mollison suggested its use as the green covering to hanging baskets, pegged in round the sides and base to cover the moss and wires. Another adaptation was to allow it to hang 'in graceful festoons from baskets or make trained specimens in pots'. He does not seem to use it in window boxes, except as a climber out of the ends of the box to frame the window. Some of the old varieties are still grown by Fibrex Nurseries Ltd although many of our modern cultivars are probably not very different.

HELIOTROPIUM Heliotrope or cherry pie, another plant from Peru introduced in the mid-eighteenth century, was a favourite plant for containers both outdoors by way of pot, vase or window box, and in the conservatory. It has a wonderful scent and lovely violet, blue or white flowers. In 1879 Mollison strongly recommended it for window boxes, for which purpose it was also mentioned in *Gardening Illustrated*, 13 May 1899, along with trailing geraniums and yellow nasturtiums. It is interesting, however, that there was no mention of its use in the Oxford college window boxes in 1900. *Gardening for Beginners* in 1914 suggested standard heliotropes to be used for large containers. It is available as seed, and from some garden centres in June, but sadly it is not nearly as common today as a century ago.

LOBELIA The first small bedding-type lobelias were pale blue and came from South Africa in the 1750s. White was added in 1847 and by the 1860s and 1870s lobelias existed in all shades of blue, blue-grey and, of course, white. It was used in association with white alyssums for the first time at Kew Gardens in 1862, and then began a very long bedding partnership which has lasted to the present day. However, among Mollison's eight ideas for summer window boxes, six mention lobelia but none name alyssum; he mentions other edgers such as mignonette, violas, pansies, echevarias and musk to be planted along with lobelia. Mollison wrote in 1879 that lobelia was 'the best of all plants for the edges of window or balcony boxes . . . pretty for baskets and brackets'. Lobelia is one of

the easiest plants to grow from seed and also to find growing in bedding strips in the garden centres. The names of the seed packets are all different from Victorian times but the habit and colour range is very similar.

LOTUS *Lotus berthelotii* was introduced from Teneriffe in 1884. Its attractive grey foliage meant that it became a well-used plant for trailing down the front of pots and urns.

MIMULUS *Mimulus moschatus* was collected from western North America in 1826. It had a very strong musk scent and was highly popular both as indoor pot plants, and for use at the front of window boxes and around hanging baskets. Strangely the scent disappeared from all plants around 1914. Despite its lack of scent, mimulus is still a very attractive and colourful plant. It is easily obtainable by seed, and as strips of bedding plants from some garden centres.

PELARGONIUM Geraniums were tender plants from South Africa. During the course of Queen Victoria's reign they grew in prominence to become the single most important container plant for summer schemes.

1. The ivy-leaved trailing geranium was introduced in 1701. In his book in 1879, Mollison mentions four ivy-leaved geraniums (possible more for indoor than outdoor work) two of which can still be obtained today. 'L'Elegante' is a white variegated form which is still one of the most popular trailers today and can be obtained from most garden centres. It is also available from Fibrex Nurseries Ltd and the Vernon Geranium Nursery. The second is 'Duke of Edinburgh' a pink variegated trailer, available from these same two nurseries. These varieties were used for conservatory hanging basket work as early as 1876.

Surprisingly, Mollison seems to suggest the use of upright geraniums for window box work, not these trailers. However, they were used by the end of the century, if not earlier. A report in *Garden Illustrated*, 29 April 1899, said that 'ivy-leaved Pelargoniums, such as the salmon-pink "Madame Crousse" and the cerise "Souvenir de Charles Turner", succeed admirably in window boxes, soon making growth which hangs down in front and covers the front of the box, and blooming profusely until late in the autumn'. Moreover, by 1902 there were claims in *The Garden* that the use of ivy-leaved and zonal pelargoniums, marguerites and lobelia in window boxes had become monotonous. By then doubles were fashionable and their general usage seems to have been much greater. 'Madame Crousse' is a reliable and very beautiful semi-double trailing geranium available today from both Fibrex Nurseries Ltd and the Vernon Geranium Nursery.

2. Zonal pelargoniums were introduced in 1710. Silver and golden variegated sorts, tricoloured and butterfly-marked varieties were all the rage by the 1850s. Many varieties are still available from Fibrex Nurseries Ltd and the Vernon Geranium Nursery. Until 1864 the zonals were all single-flowered. The first double was produced in France in the early 1860s. But the doubles were often controversial and many gardeners disliked them. However, in 1914 *Gardening for Beginners* recommended 'King of Denmark' as an excellent double both for its flower and leaf. Fortunately it is still available from geranium nurseries. The first (very double) rosebud types were introduced from 1880 (all the cultivars available today are modern). The first white-flowered zonal came in 1860.

Only one of Mollison's eight suggestions for summer window boxes in 1879 excludes geraniums! Typical of his generation, scarlet seems to be his favourite colour for this purpose, making a good contrast to the yellow calceolarias of which he was so fond. 'Beauty' is a good rich red still available today from Fibrex Nurseries Ltd. They also stock pink 'Cleopatra' and white 'Immaculata'.

Coloured and variegated leaf varieties were very much in favour. 'Hills of Snow' was a very beautiful upright variegated leaf geranium which has a pink tinge to its leaves and very pretty pink flowers. 'The Czar' has pinky-red flowers and golden leaves with a broad bronze ring. This was an expensive geranium being offered in a collection of bronze varieties at six for 2s 6d. 'Mrs Pollock', a golden tricolour with orange flowers, was very much in favour according to Smee in *My Garden*, 1872, and Mollison in his book in 1879. She was also expensive at two for 1s or 4s 6d per dozen in May 1881. 'Mrs Parker', with silver leaves and rose-pink flowers, and 'Caroline Schmidt', with silver leaves and bright red flowers, are all easily available today from specialist geranium nurseries, such as Fibrex Nurseries Ltd.

3. Scented leaf geraniums are mainly pure species. The majority arrived in Europe in the eighteenth century though some had been known earlier. The oak-leaved geranium *Pelargonium quercifolium*, and the rose-scented ones *Pelargonium graveolens* and *P. radula* were all introduced in 1774. The very pretty variegated leaf 'Lady Plymouth' was a little later arriving in 1802. They were used mainly as indoor or conservatory pot plants, not in a massed display. They are still available today from Fibrex Nurseries Ltd and other specialist geranium nurseries.

PETUNIA White petunias were the first to be discovered in 1823. Eight years later a violet one was discovered in Argentina. They soon became very fashionable and by the 1840s there were many hybrids with lots of doubles and singles and bi-coloured varieties. In 1879 John Mollison recommended them as a splendid class of showy bedding plants ('gorgeous plants for windows and balconies'). In 1914 they were strongly recommended in *Gardening for Beginners* as a good plant for sheltered garden pots and vases. It is interesting to read that despite all the breeding, the best were still regarded as the 'good whites, whether single or double, the purples being nearly all infected with an unpleasant rankness of colouring that makes them unbearable to the critical colour eye'.

RESEDA Reseda odorata, known to the Victorians as mignonette, came from Ancient Egypt where it was used to adorn the tombs. It was not used in England as a garden plant until the middle of the eighteenth century. Its scent was so popular, however, that in 1829 Henry Phillips remarked that it was grown in London window boxes until 'whole streets were almost oppressive with the odour'. In 1879, Mollison named it in four of his eight summer window box schemes, another testimony of its favour even at this later date. But it was not mentioned as part of the Oxford college window box schemes of 1900. By then, perhaps, its heyday was probably over, being overtaken by other more colourful bedding plants. It is easily grown from seed but is seldom available as a bedding or pot plant.

TANACETUM PARTHENIUM 'AUREUM' Commonly known as golden feather or golden feverfew, it was introduced from the Caucasus in 1804. During the height of the Victorian bedding schemes it was much used as a summer edger to be kept repeatedly clipped so that it would constantly regenerate its bright new leaves. In May 1881 it was advertised for sale, along with lobelia plants, at twenty-five for 9d and 100 for 2s; elsewhere in the same journal they were a dozen for 3d! Mollison suggested it as an edger for window boxes, particularly for spring work where it contrasts beautifully with tulips. It is easily raised from seed and is often to be found in the herb section of garden centres. More recently it is appearing in strips for summer bedding purposes.

TROPAEOLUM Tropaeolum majus, our common nasturtium, was introduced in 1684 from Peru. Doubles were introduced before 1769 and were propagated only from cuttings. But the dwarf Tom Thumb forms date only from the nineteenth century. By then yellow, orange, rose and scarlet flowers were all available. Mollison keenly promoted the use of the climbers at the end of a window box where they would be trained up and around the window, often with sweet peas and canary creeper. The dwarf forms were grown in many of the Oxford college window boxes in 1900. The Victorians often ate the leaves and flowers in salads. It is easily available as seed. Choose the climbing or Tom Thumb varieties.

Tropaeolum peregrinum, Canary-bird creeper, known today as canary creeper, was introduced to Britain in 1755 from Peru. Mollison liked to use it in the same manner as nasturtiums for training up the side of the window out of a window box. It is available as seed or sometimes seen as plants, and is easy to grow.

VERBENA Verbena × hybrida is the result of plants brought into this country from South America between 1826 and 1837. The hybrids soon became extremely popular and by the 1850s and 1860s they were fully established as one of the mainstays of the bedding system. Mollison describes them as being of low trailing habit 'first rate for balconies and window boxes'. He never used them, however, in his eight summer schemes, nor were they mentioned as part of the Oxford college window boxes in 1900. Apparently they were less in favour once the geranium had become established as the principal bedding plant. Another clue may be drawn from Smee in his book *My Garden* in 1872, where he suggested it had been difficult to grow in recent years as 'aphids, fungi and unknown causes make it die during the summer'. They are readily available as seed today, however, and can be easily bought as bedding plants in May. Look for the low trailing ones.

In *Gardening Illustrated* in May 1881 (the price of which was 1d), all sorts of bedding plants were offered for sale: rooted cuttings per dozen such as verbenas at 1s 2d; fuchsias 1s 6d; coleus 2s; ageratum 1s 2d; petunias 1s 2d. Lobelia, golden feather, stocks, asters, zinnias, *Phlox drummondii*, perilla and helichrysum were all priced at fifty for 1s post-free. Rooted cuttings of geraniums were 2s per dozen. In the same magazine but from a different nursery, musk was priced at 9d per dozen; violet roots 1s per dozen; pansies 2s per dozen; daisies, double white and double pink, 8d per dozen. Gold-laced polyanthus, splendid strain, were being offered at 1s per dozen; auriculas in flower 2s per dozen; echevarias 1s 6d per dozen.

Of course, the quality, size and strain of each type of plant might vary depending on the nursery, as would the price. It is difficult to make comparisons and these are given only as a guide.

107   EARLY TULIPS FOLLOWED BY HYACINTHS

This combination is adapted from John Mollison's idea published in 1879 where he suggested planting a window box with 'early Duc-van-Thol Tulips, early Hyacinths, Arabis and Aubrietia inside'. There were to be snowdrops and crocuses, too, but these have not been included in this scheme. This is a bright and cheerful window box which lasts for several weeks in flower and, of course, is highly scented once the hyacinths are in bloom.

Site
Sunny.

Container
Small wooden window box: 75cm (30″) long, 20cm (8″) wide, 20cm (8″) deep.

Planting Time
October.

At its best
Early to mid spring.

Ingredients (see notes on pages 178–84)
10   early single red and yellow tulips *Tulipa* 'Stresa'. This is a modern tulip; the 'Duc-van-Thol' tulips are no longer available.
 5   yellow bedding hyacinths *Hyacinth orientalis* 'City of Haarlem'. The Victorians grew yellow ones but the old ones are difficult to trace today.
 1   strip of white arabis *Arabis caucasica* 'Snowflake'.
 1   strip of aubrietia *Aubrietia deltoidea* 'Blue Cascade'. A similar plant to the old ones.
20 litres of John Innes No 2 soil.
Drainage material such as small pieces of polystyrene.

Method
1. Cover the base of the container with 2–3cm (1″) of drainage material and add 5cm (2″) of soil.
2. Plant the tulip bulbs in two rows along the front and back of the box.

3. Plant the hyacinth bulbs spaced out along the centre.
4. Cover the bulbs with soil until just the tips show.
5. Now divide up the strips of arabis and aubrietia and plant them in between the hyacinths in the centre of the box.
6. Fill in the gaps with more soil, bringing the level to within 2.5cm (1″) of the rim of the container.
7. Water well. Firm in the plants. Add more soil if necessary.

Aftercare
Maintain soil moisture throughout the autumn, winter and spring but never water in frosty conditions.

After the bulbs have finished flowering, lift them carefully and transfer them to a sunny spot in the garden. However, make sure they do not dry out until the leaves die down naturally in the early summer. The arabis and aubrietia should also be planted out in a sunny position where they can establish themselves. Cut them well back after flowering to encourage a neat growth for the next season.

108 SWEET VIOLETS, HEPATICAS AND PRIMROSES

The Victorians were fond of using tiles to decorate their window boxes. It is easy to see how a few simple hand-painted tiles can transform an ordinary wooden box into something rather decorative and special. This planting scheme is adapted from another of John Mollison's ideas from 1879, this time using 'late tulips, Hyacinths, Crocuses, double and single Primroses and Polyanthus inside; Sweet Violets and Hepaticas round the outside'. Hepaticas are hardly seen these days but they were a favourite spring plant for the Victorians, along with the violet and double primrose.

Site
Partial shade.

Container
Wooden window box: 90cm (36") long, 20cm (8") wide, 20cm (8") deep, fronted with six hand-painted tiles and beading. Alternatively, traditional Victorian 'fireplace' tiles are now easily available from any good tile shop.

Planting Time
October.

At its best
The violets, hepaticas and primroses will be in flower from early spring onwards, joined by the hyacinths in early to mid April and then the tulips later in the month. This box has a very long flowering period with lots of colour and scent.

Ingredients (see notes on pages 178–84)

10 late tulips *Tulipa* 'Clara Butt' or 'Keizerskroon' both used in Mollison's time and are still easily available. Otherwise use a modern one to suit your colour scheme; it is quite likely that the Victorians had something very similar.

5 yellow hyacinths *Hyacinthus orientalis* 'City of Haarlem'. This is a modern cultivar. The Victorians certainly had yellow but they would be difficult to trace today.

3 white Roman or multiflora hyacinths *Hyacinthus orientalis albulus*. This hyacinth has remained unchanged.

3 hepaticas *Hepatica nobilis* with small single anemone-like flowers in blue, red or white. Difficult to find but worth it.

2 double primroses derived from *Primula vulgaris*; these are becoming more common in the garden centres now that a new propagation technique has been developed. Doubles may also be found in pink, blue, white or pale yellow.

2 *Viola odorata*, the common sweet violet.

30 litres of John Innes No 2 soil.

Drainage material such as small pieces of polystyrene.

Method

1. Cover the base of the container with 2.5cm (1″) of drainage material and add 5cm (2″) soil.
2. Plant the tulips in a row towards the back of the box.
3. Space the hyacinths along the centre of the box, reserving the dainty white ones for the middle.
4. Cover the bulbs with soil until just the tips show.
5. Plant the three hepaticas, towards the front edge of the box one at either end and one in the centre.
6. Plant the two double primroses and violets in between.
7. Add more soil, filling in gaps and bringing the level to within 2.5cm (1″) of the rim of the container.
8. Make sure that all the plants are firmly in place and that the box looks well balanced.
9. Water well. Add more soil if necessary.

Aftercare

This box is full of plants so take care to maintain soil moisture throughout the autumn, winter and particularly in spring, but never water in frosty conditions.

Be ruthless. After the hyacinths have finished flowering, either remove carefully from the box and transplant into the garden (or simply cut off the flower stalks and leaves). Otherwise their straggly appearance will spoil the tulip display.

After the tulips have finished flowering, you may transfer all the contents into the garden. The tulips will like a sunny position although they may not do so well another year. The hepaticas, violets and primroses all enjoy partial shade. Plant them in a spot where you can continue to enjoy your Victorian collection.

109   BRIMMING OVER WITH COLOUR

This is another of Mollison's 1879 schemes for a window box, characteristically crammed with plants: 'Dwarf Wallflower, Brompton stocks, Polyanthus and Narcissus inside; red and white Daisies, blue and yellow Pansies round the outside'. The effect is stunning and the scents from the wallflowers and pansies delicious. The polyanthus and Brompton stocks did not survive as they were crowded out by the wallflowers and daffodils. If you want to include them move the polyanthus to the front of the box and make sure the Brompton stocks are well-established plants.

Site
Sunny and sheltered.

Container
Long wooden window box: 120cm (48″) long, 20cm (8″) wide, 20cm (8″) deep. This is exceptionally long to fit a very large window. Adjust the contents for a smaller box.

Planting Time
September to October. The earlier the box is planted the more time the plants will have to get well established before the winter. Bigger, stronger plants will, of course, give more flowers so it is worth planting this scheme early.

At its best
The box will be in full glory towards the second half of April lasting well into May. During a mild winter, however, the pansies and, to a lesser extent, the daisies will have been in flower throughout, giving a most welcome splash of colour.

Ingredients (see notes on pages 178–84)
20 late daffodils *Narcissus poeticus* 'Actaea'; easily available.
 6 dwarf wallflowers *Cheiranthus cheiri* 'Tom Thumb Mixed'. This is a modern cultivar but of the type that would have been used. Sometimes they are only sold in bunches of ten, so choose the best six and plant the others elsewhere. Look for fresh, strong, sturdy plants that have branched out well. As soon as possible open up the bunch and give them all a good drink before planting.

 4 pansies, including 2 yellow and 2 blue; unless you can track down the old plants use our modern winter-flowering pansies *Viola × wittrockiana* 'Universal'.
 2 strips of daisies, 1 red and 1 white, *Bellis perennis*. They are not always sold in individual colours, in which case you will be forced to buy them mixed. They have hardly changed since Victorian times.
35 litres of John Innes No 2 soil.
Drainage material such as large crocks or pieces of polystyrene.

Method
1. Cover the base of the container with 2.5cm (1″) of drainage material and add 5cm (2″) of soil.
2. Plant the twenty daffodils bulbs in a row towards the back of the box. Cover with soil.
3. Take the six sturdy wallflower plants and space them along the centre of the box. Make sure the roots are well spread out. Add more soil to bring the level to within 2.5cm (1″) of the rim of the box.
4. Plant the yellow and blue pansies along the front of the box.
5. Alternate the red and white daisies in between the pansies and continue round the sides of the box and along the back.
6. Make sure all the plants are firmly in position. Water well and add more soil, if necessary, to regain the former level.

Aftercare
Maintain soil moisture throughout the autumn, winter and spring, but never water in frosty weather. The box is crammed with plants so pay particular attention to their needs with regard to both water and food. Apply a liquid feed regularly throughout the late winter and early spring so that the pansies and daisies develop into good plants and flower well; likewise the wallflowers.

After the daffodils have finished flowering, they may be transferred to the garden where they will happily flower for many years. Take care that they do not dry out before the leaves die down naturally in late June or July. The rest of the plants may be discarded.

110   A COTTAGE WINDOW BOX FOR WINTER AND SPRING

Old-fashioned flowers tumble out of this window box which is full of character and warmth in sympathy with the charming stone cottage which they adorn. Passers-by can enjoy the wonderful scent of the wallflowers and pansies.

Site
Sunny and sheltered.

Container
Long black plastic window box: 100cm (40″) long, 20cm (8″) wide, 20cm (8″) deep, resting in a wrought iron frame.

Planting Time
September to October. The earlier the box is planted the more time the pansies and wallflowers will have to establish themselves and so make strong plants before the onset of winter.

At its best
Mid to late spring sees this box in its full glory.

Ingredients (see notes on pages 178–84)
12 mid or late tulips; *Tulipa* 'Keizerskroon' is the one used here. It is said to date from 1750.

6 wallflower plants *Cheiranthus cheiri* 'Persian Carpet'. This is a modern cultivar with a mixture of lovely gentle colours. Look for strong, well-branched plants. You might have to buy a bunch of ten and plant the rest elsewhere. Open up the bunch as soon as possible and give them a drink of water before planting.

4 yellow pansies. Unless you can track down the old varieties use our modern winter pansies *Viola × wittrockiana* 'Universal'.

20 grape hyacinths; *Muscari botryoides* 'Caeruleum' and its white form 'Album' were both very popular and can still be found today. However, the one most commonly available now is *Muscari armeniacum* 'Heavenly Blue' which is a more modern discovery. It is the one used here. But, if you want to be authentic, hunt for the ones mentioned above.

30 litres of John Innes No 2 soil.

Drainage material such as large crocks or pieces of polystyrene.

Method
1. Cover the base of the container with 2.5cm (1″) of drainage material and add 5cm (2″) of soil.

2. Plant the tulips in a row towards the back of the box. Cover with soil.
3. Take the six wallflower plants and space them along the centre of the box. Make sure the roots are well spread out. Add more soil to bring the level to within 2.5cm (1″) of the rim of the box.
4. Plant the yellow pansies along the front of the box.
5. Plant the grape hyacinths in between the pansies at the front and around the ends of the box. Push them down to a depth of around 5cm (2″).
6. Make sure all the plants are firmly in place. Water well and then top up with more soil, if necessary, to regain the former level.

Aftercare
Maintain soil moisture throughout the autumn, winter and early spring, but never water in frosty weather. Apply a liquid feed regularly from late winter onwards to ensure lots of flowers from the bedding plants.

After the wallflowers have finally finished flowering, remove the contents of the box and transfer the tulips to a sunny site in the garden, being very careful not to disturb their roots more than is absolutely necessary. The grape hyacinths are much tougher and should establish themselves well in any sunny spot. Discard the pansies and wallflowers.

HANGING BASKETS FOR WINTER AND SPRING

111   A COTTAGE HANGING BASKET FOR WINTER AND SPRING

This was planted deliberately to match the cottage window boxes and so contains the same type of tulip, grape hyacinths, wallflowers and pansies. The main difference is the ivy, one of the most popular Victorian plants often used in basketwork to create a green covering around the bottom and sides. The idea was to peg the ivy trails closely around the moss to encourage them to root so that they formed a neat ball around the basket, thus hiding the wires and the moss. It is a most effective treatment. Not only does it look very neat and attractive, but it also avoids wind damage to the ends of the ivy that would otherwise be blown endlessly during the winter months.

Site
Eye level, sheltered and sunny.

Container
Wire hanging basket: 35cm (14″) in diameter with a sturdy 27.5cm (11″) bracket.

Planting Time
September to October; the earlier the better, then the bedding plants can get established before the winter.

At its best
Depending on the severity of the winter, the pansies should be in flower from the time of planting onwards until early summer. Protect it from very frosty weather by bringing it into a shed or greenhouse (it needs light but little or no water at this stage). All the plants are hardy and should survive, but the basket will fare better in mild conditions. It will be at its best from mid to late spring.

Ingredients (see notes on pages 178–84)
1 mature ivy, or possibly 2 depending on size. The variegated ones add extra interest; this one is a modern cultivar *Hedera helix* 'Goldchild'.

5 red and yellow tulips *Tulipa* 'Keizerskroon'. It is said to date from 1750 or even earlier, so is

particularly apt for use here, and it is still widely available.

2 yellow pansies. Old varieties can be found in specialist nurseries but but our modern winter-flowering ones, *Viola × wittrockiana* 'Universal', are excellent for container work.

3 wallflowers *Cheiranthus cheiri* 'Persian Carpet'. This is a modern but very good cultivar. Choose strong plants.

12 grape hyacinths *Muscari armeniacum* 'Heavenly Blue'. This is modern, the sort most easily available. *Muscari botryoides* 'Coeruleum' and the white form 'Album' would be authentic.

10 litres of John Innes No 2 soil.

1 basketful of sphagnum moss or ordinary wreath moss from a florist.

Approximately 150cm plastic-coated green wire to form the pegs.

Method

1. Line the basket with a generous thickness of moss; start at the base and bring it right up the sides so that it forms a good collar just above the rim.
2. Cover the base of the basket with 5cm (2″) of soil.
3. Plant the ivy towards the centre-front of the basket. If the root system is already very well established and is taking up more than one-third of the space, then don't be afraid to trim the roots, especially those towards the centre of the basket. This will encourage new growth while allowing more room for the other plants.
4. Plant the tulips in a group around the centre of the basket, then cover with soil.
5. Plant the two pansies on either side of the ivy.
6. Plant two wallflowers next to the pansies and the third one at the centre-back of the basket.
7. Add more soil to bring the level to the rim of the

Old-fashioned tulips, scented wallflowers and pansies create a vibrant display in keeping with the cottage style

basket. Space the grape hyacinths around the edge and in the centre, pushing them down to a depth of 5cm (2″) if possible.

8. Firm down all the plants, water well and add more soil or moss if necessary.

9. Lastly peg in the ivy trails around the sides and (if long enough) around the bottom of the basket, concentrating on the centre-front and sides. Use plastic-coated green wire, bend it over into short 5m (2″) lengths and push them firmly into the basket so that the stems are touching the moss. In time the ivy will take root. You may need twenty or thirty of these pegs according to the length and number of the trails.

Aftercare

Maintain soil moisture throughout the autumn, winter and spring, but never water in freezing conditions. Don't despair if, after a sharp night's frost, the wallflowers and pansies look droopy or even dead. They will soon revive when the temperature rises. However, in prolonged severe conditions it is best to bring the basket into the shelter of a shed, greenhouse or porch.

When the weather turns milder towards the end of winter or in early spring give the basket a liquid feed and continue every fortnight. After the basket has finished flowering, plant the grape hyacinths into a sunny spot in the garden. The pansies and wallflowers should be discarded. The tulips will be difficult to remove with roots intact and are probably best thrown away. Leave the ivy in place so that it can be used as the base for a summer cottage basket. Continue to peg it in as it grows and by the autumn it will be fully established around the sides and bottom. Then you will have a splendid base for another planting scheme.

112   A VICTORIAN HANGING BASKET

This is a simple basket for late winter using ivy, aucuba and crocus, three of the most common plants used by the Victorians. Following the same principle applied in the cottage basket, the ivy is again pegged around the bottom and sides of the basket to create a ball effect. This produces a neat and attractive treatment which protects the ivy trails from wind damage and also helps to hide the basket itself, an otherwise difficult task with winter plantings.

Site
Eye level, sheltered and sunny.

Container
Wire hanging basket: 40cm (16″) in diameter with a sturdy 27.5cm (11″) bracket. Mollison wrote in 1879: 'Small baskets are nearly useless, drying up too

quickly and never at all satisfactory.' He suggested the use of a basket two feet across! This size is almost impossible to obtain these days, but it is certainly true that the bigger the basket the more scope there is for the plants to develop.

Planting Time
September to November.

At its best
The foliage of the ivy and aucuba will provide interest from the time of planting, but it will be at its best from mid February through to early spring, first with the yellow and white crocuses, and then with the purple crocuses towards the end of March.

Ingredients (see notes on pages 178–84)
1 *Aucuba japonica* 'Maculata'. This is the common female variegated form with yellow spotted leaves. Choose a mature plant with low branches which will be appropriate for the basket.
30 mixed crocuses; 10 yellow *Crocus* 'Dutch Yellow', 10 white *Crocus vernus* 'Jeanne D'Arc' and 10 purple *Crocus vernus* 'Purpureus Grandiflorus'. Some of the old species are still available.
1 mature ivy, or possibly 2 depending on size. Choose one with long trails. Variegated ones add extra interest; this is a modern cultivar *Hedera helix* 'Goldchild'.
10 litres of John Innes No 2 soil.
1 basketful of sphagnum moss or ordinary wreath moss from a florist.
Approximately 150cm green plastic-coated wire to form the pegs.

Method
1. Line the basket with a generous thickness of moss; start at the base and bring it right up the sides so that it forms a good collar just above the rim of the basket.
2. Cover the base of the basket with 5cm (2″) of soil.
3. Plant the aucuba towards the centre-back of the basket.
4. Now plant ten of the crocuses around the lower middle-front of the basket, nestling them close to the moss with their shoots pointing outwards so that they will grow through the moss and out of the sides. (The purple ones were all used here but they hardly show because they were the last to flower. You can mix the colours if you prefer.)
5. Cover with soil and plant another ten at a slightly higher level around the front, again pointing the shoots outwards so that they grow out through the ivy and moss. White ones were used in this band but mix them if you prefer.
6. Now plant the ivy in the centre-front of the basket. Add more soil to fill in the gaps, bringing the level to within 2.5cm (1″) of the rim.
7. Plant the remaining ten crocuses in the centre of the basket and around the edges. Push the corms well down into the soil. Yellow ones were used for this purpose but, as before, mix them if you prefer.
8. Firm in the plants and water well. Add more soil and moss if necessary.
9. Lastly peg in the ivy trails around the top, sides and (if long enough) bottom of the basket, concentrating on the centre-front and sides. Use plastic-coated green wire, bend it over into short 5cm (2″) lengths and push them firmly into the basket so that the ivy stems are touching the moss. It is here that new roots will form. You may use twenty or thirty of these pegs depending on the maturity of the ivy.

Aftercare
Maintain soil moisture throughout the autumn and winter but never water in frosty conditions. In very severe weather, bring the basket into the shelter of a porch, shed or greenhouse.

After the crocuses have finished flowering, decide whether you want to leave the basket intact and enjoy the same display next year. If so, continue to water when the soil gets dry and regularly check the ivy trails. As they make growth during the summer they will need pegging in. Also give an occasional feed. If, however, you want to use the basket for a Victorian summer display, leave the ivy in place but in May transfer the crocuses and aucuba to the garden.

113   THE WARWICK VASE

This planting scheme is based on a suggestion made by H. T. Martin of Stoneleigh in *The Gardener* magazine in November 1900. He wrote that when vases were 'placed and filled with good taste they add a charm to the garden which can hardly be obtained otherwise'. He liked to use aucuba, golden privet or euonymus with silver and golden thyme and an edging of hardy echeveria, *Arabis caucasica (albida)* 'Variegata' or mixed crocus. White tulips or hyacinths would then be planted among the shrubs.

Site
Sun or partial shade.

Container
This lead container is styled after the famous Warwick vase and is made by Renaissance Casting Company Ltd. It makes a wonderful setting for plants and a perfect focal point in a garden. The diameter is 35cm (14″) and the inside planting depth is 22.5cm (9″).

Planting Time
September to October.

At its best
The crocuses and then the hyacinths will be in bloom from early to mid March through to the second half of April. However, the combination of the golden colourings of the thymes and euonymus ensures that the container is delightful to look at throughout the entire season. The thymes smell wonderful after rain or when they have just been watered.

Ingredients (see notes on pages 178–84)
1 *Euonymus fortunei* 'Emerald 'n Gold'; low growing with gold, pink and green leaves. Many attractive variegated euonymus were introduced in the 1800s.
5 white bedding hyacinths *Hyacinthus orientalis* 'L'Innocence'; one of the older hyacinths still available.
1 *Arabis caucasica* (syn. *A. albida*) 'Variegata'; readily available.
3 golden thyme *Thymus* × *citriodorus* 'Aureus'. This is lemon-scented and has been in cultivation for centuries.
15 yellow and white crocuses: *Crocus* 'Dutch Yellow' and *Crocus vernus* 'Jeanne D'Arc' mixed. The same as or similar to Victorian crocuses.
20 litres of John Innes No 2 soil.
Drainage material such as broken crocks or pieces of polystyrene.

Method
1. Cover the base of the container with 5cm (2″) of drainage material and add 5cm (2″) of soil.
2. Plant the euonymus towards the centre-back of the vase and place the five hyacinth bulbs around it, one on either side at the back, three across the front.
3. Cover the bulbs with soil.
4. Plant the arabis close to the rim at the centre-front of the pot.
5. Plant a thyme on either side of the arabis, and plant the third one behind the euonymus.
6. Fill in the gaps with soil, bringing the level to within 2.5cm (1″) of the rim of the container.
7. Space the crocus corms in between the plants. Push them well down so that they are covered by at least 2.5cm (1″) of soil.
8. Water well. Make sure all the plants are firmly in place and that the arrangement looks well balanced. Add more soil if necessary. H. T. Martin made a useful suggestion in this respect: 'A point to keep in view when vases are planted for a winter display is to well fill them with soil, raising the centre so as to throw off some amount of water, this being most desirable in order to avoid the bursting of the vases in exceptionally severe weather.' This applies more to old terracotta containers than the more frost-resistant new varieties or indeed this lead one. However, it is a useful point to bear in mind.

Aftercare
Maintain the soil moisture throughout the autumn, winter and spring but never water in frosty conditions.

After the crocuses have finished flowering, carefully remove them from the container as the leaves will grow very long and spoil the tidiness of the arrangement when the hyacinths are in bloom. They should come out quite easily and can be planted elsewhere in the garden.

Once the hyacinths have finished flowering they, too, can be transferred to the garden. Cut the arabis back hard after it has flowered to encourage neat growth for the following year. Plant it out along with the thymes and euonymus. The thymes in particular will enjoy a sunny open position.

114 DESIGN WITH COLOUR

This refreshing colour scheme is partly based on H. T. Martin's suggestion for winter vases, published in 1900, where he describes 'white tulips protruding out of green-hued shrubs' (see previous recipe for source). It also draws on Mollison's ideas of 1879 for winter window boxes where he uses feverfew as a winter foliage plant. It provides a welcome vivid green carpet throughout the winter months, the perfect setting to show off the white tulips as they emerge in mid spring.

Site
Sun or partial shade.

Container
Large Haddonstone basket pot: 37.5cm (15″) in diameter, 32.5cm (13″) deep. The basketweave design was very popular in Victorian times.

Planting Time
September to November.

At its best
Mid spring, although the fresh green foliage of the feverfew and the euonymus is attractive throughout the planting season.

Ingredients (see notes on pages 178–84)
  1 *Euonymus japonicus* 'Aureopictus'; use a mature specimen which will be in proportion to the pot and higher than the tulips. Many attractive variegated euonymus were introduced in the 1800s.
  12 mid-season white tulips *Tulipa* 'White Virgin'. A modern white tulip; I don't know of a Victorian equivalent which is still available.
  4 golden feverfew *Tanacetum parthenium* 'Aureum'. To the Victorians this plant was known as golden feather and was one of their favourite bedding plants. Once you have it in the garden and allow it to set seed, you will have no difficulty in finding suitable bedding material for containers, in summer or winter!
25 litres of John Innes No 2 soil.
Drainage material such as large crocks or pieces of polystyrene.

Method
1. Cover the base of the container with 10cm (4″) of drainage material and add 10cm (4″) of soil.
2. Plant the euonymus at the centre-back of the pot, adjusting the soil level beneath the rootball so that the top of it sits just beneath the rim of the pot.
3. Plant the tulips around in front of the euonymus.
4. Cover the bulbs with soil and then plant the feverfew in a circle around the front and sides of the pot.
5. Fill in the gaps with soil, bringing the level to within 2.5cm (1″) of the rim of the container. Water well, firm down the plants and add more soil if necessary.

Aftercare
Maintain soil moisture throughout the autumn, winter and spring but never water in frosty weather.

After the tulips have finished flowering, remove them from the container, carefully keeping the roots intact, and plant in a sunny position in the garden. Do not allow the leaves to dry out until they die down naturally in June. But leave them in place if you want to use the euonymus and feverfew as the basis of a Victorian summer planting and when they have died down just add three bright salmon-pink geraniums 'King of Denmark'. To keep the feverfew looking such a vivid green, cut back the leaves continually throughout the spring and summer so that it is not allowed to flower. On the other hand, if you want some little seedlings for the autumn work then you should let at least one plant set seed.

115 EDWARDIAN SPRING

This early double yellow tulip called 'Van de Hoef' was first available commercially in 1911, just before the First World War. It makes a vibrant combination with the old-fashioned gold-laced polyanthus.

Site
Sun or partial shade.

Container
Small oval Haddonstone pot: 40cm (16″) long, 17.5cm (7″) wide, 17.5cm (7″) deep, based on the traditional basketweave design.

Planting Time
September to November.

At its best
Early to mid spring.

Ingredients (see notes on pages 178–84)
10 early double yellow tulips *Tulipa* 'Van de Hoef'.
 2 gold-laced polyanthus *Primula × polyantha* 'Gold Laced'; available from garden centres or as seeds from Thompson and Morgan Ltd.
 2 garden auriculas *Primula auricula*. Unlike the Show auriculas, these did not have farina on their foliage and so were far more suitable for outdoor containers. There remains a wide choice of colours available and some old names are still produced commercially. The one used here is an unnamed specimen from a cottage garden. A better colour combination would have been achieved by planting the bright yellow one used in the recipe overleaf.
12 litres of John Innes No 2 soil.
Drainage material such as broken clay pots or pieces of polystyrene.

Method
1. Cover the base of the container with 2.5cm (1″) of drainage material and add 5cm (2″) of soil.
2. Plant the tulips close together in the centre of the pot.
3. Plant the two gold-laced polyanthus in the centre-front and centre-black of the pot near the rim of the container.
4. Plant the auriculas at either end of the pot.
5. Fill in the gaps with soil and bring the level to within 2.5cm (1″) of the rim.
6. Water well and firm down the plants. Add more soil, if necessary, to regain the former level.

Aftercare

Maintain soil moisture throughout the autumn, winter and spring but never water in frosty weather.

After the tulips have finished flowering, discard them. Transfer the polyanthus to a shady, moist part of the garden. The auriculas prefer an open position with a well-drained soil.

116 OLD-FASHIONED FAVOURITES

This is a wonderful combination to plant at eye and nose level so that you can enjoy the rich mixture of colour and the heady fragrance of the hyacinths. Hyacinths were firm favourites of the Victorians, as were the auriculas, feverfew and bright little scillas.

Site
Sun or partial shade. Raise the pot up if possible so you can enjoy the colours and fragrance to the full.

Container
Square moss-encrusted Haddonstone pot: 40cm (16″) square, 17.5cm (7″) deep.

Planting Time
September to October.

At its best
Early to mid spring.

Ingredients (see notes on pages 178–84)
  6 bedding hyacinths of any colour combination. Here are three *Hyacinthus orientalis* 'L'Innocence' which is an old white one and three modern lilac ones called 'Amethyst'.
  4 yellow or other coloured garden auriculas *Primula auricula*.
  2 golden feverfew or golden feather *Tanacetum parthenium* 'Aureum'.
  20 squills or scillas *Scilla siberica*; a very bright sky-blue flower which is always a welcome sight in early spring.
  30 litres of John Innes No 2 soil.
  Drainage material such as several old crocks or small pieces of polystyrene.

Method
1. Cover the base of the container with 2.5cm (1″) of drainage material and add 5cm (2″) of soil.

2. Plant the hyacinth bulbs well spaced out in the centre of the pot and cover with soil so that just the tips show.
3. Plant the auriculas and feverfew around the sides of the pot with the scillas planted in between in small groups.
4. Fill in the gaps with soil and bring the level to within 2.5cm (1″) of the rim.
5. Water well. Firm in the plants and add more soil, if necessary, to regain the former level.

Aftercare
Maintain the soil moisture throughout the autumn, winter and spring, but never water in frosty weather.

After flowering, transplant the bulb contents carefully to the garden where they should continue to flower another year. The feverfew may be planted out as well. If it is allowed to seed, it will produce new plants by the autumn. Otherwise keep it well clipped so that you can continue to enjoy fresh foliage.

117 MULLION WINDOWS IN SUMMER RAIMENT

We know from John Mollison's book published in 1879 that it was fashionable to grow window box plants up around the side of the window to create a frame on either side. This house was built by the Duke of Bedford in 1876 so it seemed appropriate to use the same treatment. Canary creeper and, in late summer, nasturtiums festooned the sides of the window. A glorious mass of old-fashioned favourites such as Paris daisies, heliotropes (or cherry pie), lobelia, lovely musk, calceolarias and, of course, pink fuchsias and geraniums completed the scene. The window box was eleven feet long. Every inch was vibrant with colour which lasted for nearly six months, changing in outline and intensity as the plants matured and the focus altered. It hummed to the sound of insects. Butterflies danced all summer long. The scent from the heliotropes was exquisite.

Site
Sunny and sheltered.

Container
This O'Connor window box was specially designed to extend beyond the window so that the plants could grow up the wooden framework above. Because of the unusual length of the window two boxes were made to sit snugly together, each 165cm (5ft 6") long, 25cm (10") wide, 25cm (10") deep as an inside measurement. They are supported on six sturdy wrought iron brackets fixed to the wall beneath the box.

Early Preparation
Plant the nasturtium and canary creeper seeds in early April, according to the instructions on the packet, so that they form good plants to add to the box in May. Alternatively, if making up the box early in the greenhouse, then plant direct (see below).

Planting Time
Mid to late May onwards (unless you have a green-house, in which case plant from mid April onwards and keep it indoors until the end of May). Leave spaces for the heliotropes which should not be added until mid June.

At its best
All summer long, although different plants will dominate at different times. The Paris daisies are an early flowerer. By September they will be over. Then the nasturtium will be at its peak.

Ingredients (see notes on pages 178–84)
8 salmon upright geraniums *Pelargonium* 'King of Denmark'; a lovely semi-double flower with strongly marked leaves. Another old favourite, although probably late Victorian rather than mid.

6 tall white Paris daisies *Chrysanthemum (Argyranthemum) frutescens*, now more commonly known as marguerites.

6 upright bush fuchsias *Fuchsia* 'Lye's Unique' with a white corona and a salmon-orange sepal. Dates back to the 1880s.

4 purple heliotropes or cherry pie *Heliotropium × hybridum*. It is highly scented and an old favourite. Butterflies are very attracted to them.

4 yellow calceolarias or slipper flowers *Calceolaria integrifolia*. Much loved by the Victorians for the good colour contrast they provide.

4 pink trailing geraniums *Pelargonium* 'Madame Crousse'. A Victorian favourite which is still available.

4 dwarf nasturtiums *Tropaeolum majus* 'Tom Thumb Mixed'. They are easily grown from seed. Plant eight and use the strongest four.

1 strip of trailing blue lobelia *Lobelia erinus* 'Mrs Clibran'.

1 strip of white lobelia *Lobelia erinus* 'White Lady'.

1 strip of mimulus. *Mimulus* 'Calypso' F1 hybrids provide a wonderful range of colours.

2 climbing nasturtiums *Tropaeolum majus* 'Climbing Mixed'. This is the common nasturtium which is easily grown from seed. Plant four and use the strongest two.

2 canary creeper *Tropaeolum peregrinum*. It is a pretty yellow fast-growing climber, easily grown from seed. Plant four and use the strongest two. Unfortunately these days, in some rural areas, it attracts the rape beetle and there appears to be no easy solution.

140 litres of John Innes No 2 soil.

Large quantity of drainage material such as pieces of polystyrene.

Method

1. Cover the base of the containers with 5cm (2″) of drainage material and add 15cm (6″) of soil.
2. At the back: begin with the eight upright geraniums, spacing them four to a box towards the back of the containers. Plant the Paris daisies in between the geraniums.
3. In the centre: space the fuchsias well out along the centre of each box. On either side of the two central fuchsias in each box leave space for the heliotropes in mid June (they spread around 40cm (16″) during the course of the summer) and then plant the calceolarias.

4. At the front: plant the trailing pink geraniums and the trailing nasturtiums spaced along the front of the boxes. Divide the strips of blue and white lobelia and mimulus. Plant them alternately along the front of the boxes and around the ends.

5. At the ends: near either end of the (joined) box plant the climbing nasturtiums and canary creepers so that they can be trained up the wall.

6. Fill in the gaps with more soil, bringing the level to within 2.5cm (1″) of the top of containers.

7. Water well, firm in all the plants. It is quite likely that the soil level will drop after watering. Top up with more soil if necessary. The boxes have been closely planted and the amount of soil should not be skimped.

Aftercare
Water generously. In hot weather you may have to do it daily; choose a regular time in the evening or early morning. Do not water in hot sun.

Use string or a wooden framework to train the climbing nasturtiums and canary creeper up the wall on either side of the window.

Once a week give a liquid feed. Spray for greenfly, blackfly (particularly on the nasturtiums) etc. I must add that this planting attracted so many insects, including ladybirds, that pest control was not a major problem apart from the rape beetle on the canary creeper and caterpillars on the nasturtiums. Dead-head fading flowers to prevent seed pods forming and to keep the box tidy. Remove any unsightly damaged leaves. Don't forget to use the nasturtium flowers and young leaves in salads. The Victorians certainly enjoyed them. They look wonderful and have an interesting peppery taste.

At the end of the summer, remove and pot up the fuchsias, geraniums, marguerites and heliotropes (see page 175–76) in order to keep them through the winter for use next year. Discard all the other plants.

118   UNRULY BUT COLOURFUL

Victorians were very fond of vibrant colours and used lots of scarlet geraniums, calceolarias and lobelia. Adapted from a box Mollison describes as having seen in a small manufacturing town in the 1870s.

Site
Sun or partial shade.

Container
Window box which looks like lead but is actually fibreglass (which means that it is light and infinitely cheaper): 90cm (36″) long, 17.5cm (7″) wide, 17.5cm (7″) deep.

Planting Time
Mid to late May.

At its best
June to September.

Ingredients (see notes on pages 178–84)
  5 upright geraniums. These are all of Victorian stock. I intended to plant three red *Pelargonium* 'Beauty' and two white *Pelargonium* 'Immaculata', but one of the whites turned out to be pink *Pelargonium* 'Cleopatra'. It was so beautiful I could not resist leaving it in place.
  3 yellow calceolarias or slipper flowers *Calceolaria integrifolia.*

  1 strip of trailing *Lobelia erinus* 'Blue Cascade'.
  1 single pot of white *Lobelia erinus* 'White Lady'.
25 litres of John Innes No 2 soil.
Drainage material such as old crocks or pieces of polystyrene.

Method
1. Cover the base of the box with 2.5cm (1″) of drainage material and add 10cm (4″) of soil.
2. Plant the geraniums at the back of the box alternating the red and white (and pink if used).
3. Space the calceolarias widely and plant them along the middle of the box.
4. Carefully divide the lobelia and plant individual groups of plants along the front of the box.
5. Water well. Firm in all the plants and add more soil if necessary to bring the level to within 2.5cm (1″) of the rim.

Aftercare
Water regularly throughout the summer, although on a sunny day water only in the early morning or evening when the sun is not on the leaves.

Deadhead fading flowers and spray for greenfly etc as necessary, particularly on the calceolarias, and from end June apply a liquid feed at monthly intervals.

Before the first frosts, remove and pot up the geraniums in order to keep them through the winter. See page 86. Discard the other plants.

119   FERNS FOR SHADY PLACES

This window box is based on an article dated 29 April 1899 in *Gardening Illustrated* which stated that 'the boxes in shady windows may be filled with hardy ferns mixed with Musk now'. The combination is so simple and effective, it is well worth a try. Twenty years earlier John Mollison had also recognized musk as an excellent edger for boxes and baskets, so it had been grown in outdoor containers for many years.

Site
Shade or partial shade; ideal for a basement, whatever the container.

Container
Small terracotta window box: 40cm (16″) long, 15cm (6″) wide, 15cm (6″) deep.

Planting Time
End April to May.

At its best
June to September.

Ingredients (see notes on pages 178–84)
2 hardy ferns. The Victorians were extremely fond of ferns, being attracted by their feathery growth, graceful habit and easy cultivation. There were numerous hardy ferns available to choose from including the common Polypody and the Hart's tongue fern and their many varieties. Any small to medium hardy fern would be appropriate here.

1 strip of musk. *Mimulus moschatus* was the fragrant musk plant of Victorian cottage windows. By 1880 it was said that the scent was disappearing and by 1914 it had gone even from plants in the wild. Although it would be lovely to have a scented window box, the pretty, delicate flowers are so pleasing in their own right that this scheme can still be successful with our modern varieties. *Mimulus* 'Calypso' F1 Hybrid Mixed provides a wonderful range of colours.

10 litres of John Innes No 2 soil.

Drainage material such as crocks or small pieces of polystyrene.

Method
1. Cover the base of the container with 2.5cm (1″) of drainage material and add 5cm (2″) of soil.
2. Plant the two ferns side by side in the window box and fill in the gaps with soil.
3. Carefully divide the strip of mimulus and plant all around the edge of the pot. If the colours are already showing, try and mix them up.
4. Water well. Firm in all the plants. Add more soil if necessary but leave at least 2.5cm (1″) at the top of the container to allow for easy watering. These plants enjoy plenty of moisture and if the window box is too full the water will simply run off.

Aftercare
Regular watering is essential for this window box to flourish. Check daily, especially in hot weather. Deadhead the mimulus flowers and apply a monthly liquid feed from end June. There will be little need to worry about greenfly etc.

These ferns are hardy and so may be planted in a moist, shaded area of the garden. You could leave them in the window box but if they are not evergreen they will not look very attractive until growth restarts the following spring. Discard the mimulus.

120   A COTTAGE WINDOW BOX FOR SUMMER

Pretty as a picture. Here is the cottage window box in all its summer glory. It combines most of the old favourites to create a sumptuous display of rich pinks and purples. Less showy but very distinctive as it tumbles over the corners of the box is the mignonette, a general favourite of the Victorian era known for its exquisite scent. So, too, the purple heliotrope with its heady fragrance loved by butterflies and passers-by alike!

Site
Prefers a sunny position although it would still flourish in light shade for part of the day.

Container
Long black plastic window box: 100cm (40″) long, 20cm (8″) wide, 20cm (8″) deep, resting in a wrought iron frame.

Early Preparation
Sow the mignonette seeds at the end of March or early April, in order to get good plants for use in mid May. The seeds are still readily available but, as yet, the plants are not generally on sale in the garden centres.

Planting Time
Mid to late May (unless you have a greenhouse, in which case plant from mid April onwards and keep it indoors until the end of May). Leave spaces for the heliotropes which should not be added until mid June.

At its best
July and August although it will be much appreciated and enjoyed all summer long.

Ingredients (see notes on pages 178–84)

4 tall white Paris daisies *Chrysanthemum (Argyranthemum) frutescens*, also known as marguerites.

2 old-fashioned fuchsias *Fuchsia* 'Charming' rosy-red and carmine. Many others can still be found if you go to a specialist grower.

1 upright variegated geranium *Pelargonium* 'Hills of Snow'. A beautiful Victorian geranium well worth tracking down. Its grey-green leaves are edged with ivory which combine beautifully with the white daisies and its pretty pink flower is excellent with the heliotropes. A good centre plant.

2 purple heliotropes or cherry pie *Heliotropium* × *hybridum*. Even the modern hybrids are not easy to find these days, but good garden centres should stock them in June.

2 purple verbenas, low trailing habit, *Verbena* × *hybrida*. Trailers are still available.

2 trailing ivy-leaved geraniums *Pelargonium* 'Helena'. This is a modern variety; 'Madame Crousse' is an old one, but a more delicate pink.

2 mignonette plants grown from seed; try *Reseda odorata* 'Fragrant Beauty' with lime-coloured flowers.

1 strip of pale blue lobelia *Lobelia erinus* 'Cambridge Blue'.

1 strip of white lobelia *Lobelia erinus* 'Snowball'.

40 litres of John Innes No 2 soil.

Drainage material such as small pieces of polystyrene or broken crocks.

Old-fashioned cottage flowers including scented mignonette and heliotropes combined with geraniums and 'Paris' daisies

Method

1. Cover the base of the container with 5cm (2″) of drainage material and add 10cm (4″) of soil.
2. At the back of the box, plant the four white Paris daisies.
3. Along the centre plant the two fuchsias at either end, the upright variegated geranium 'Hills of Snow' in the centre, with the two heliotropes on either side (to be planted in mid June).
4. In the front of the box plant the verbena in the centre, the two trailing pink geraniums on either side, and the two mignonettes at either end. Divide the strips of blue and white lobelias and plant alternately as edgers along the sides and front.
5. Water well, firm in all the plants. Add more soil if necessary to bring the level to within 2.5cm (1″) of the rim.

Aftercare

Water regularly; this window box is packed full with plants and will need careful watering and feeding if it is to reach its full potential. Avoid watering when the sun is shining on it; choose a regular time in the early morning or evening. Apply a liquid feed once a week. Deadhead as necessary to encourage more flowers and to maintain a neat appearance. To keep greenfly etc at bay, spray when necessary. It was only rarely needed here, mainly on the fuchsias, perhaps because there were so many predatory insects buzzing and hovering around.

Before the first frosts, remove the fuchsias and geraniums from the window box. Pot up and bring them indoors for the winter (see page 86). If you want to keep the Paris daisies for cuttings in the spring, pot them up too and bring indoors (see page 85 for details). Discard the other plants.

121   A COTTAGE HANGING BASKET FOR SUMMER

To create a harmonious picture with the cottage window boxes, a similar combination of plants has been used. The main difference is the inclusion of the ivy, so loved by the Victorians generally, but in these circumstances it is pegged down around the sides and base of the basket to provide a green covering for the basket and moss.

Site
Eye level, sun or light shade.

Container
Wire hanging basket: 35cm (14″) in diameter with a sturdy 27.5cm (11″) bracket.

Planting Time
Mid to end May, leaving spaces for the heliotropes which should be added in mid June (unless you have a greenhouse or conservatory, in which case plant in mid April and keep it inside until the end of May).

At its best
July and August although it will look lovely all summer long.

Ingredients (see notes on pages 178–84)
1 mature ivy, or possibly 2 depending on size. Variegated ones add extra interest; this is *Hedera helix* 'Goldchild'. Victorian varieties are available from specialist suppliers such as Fibrex Nurseries Ltd (see the list of specialist suppliers on page 225). Once used in this type of hanging basket, the ivy may be left for several seasons.
1 pink upright Victorian geranium *Pelargonium* 'Hills of Snow'. Makes a good centrepiece with its variegated leaves. Well worth tracking down as it is a strong attractive grower.
1 purple verbena *Verbena* × *hybrida*. Find a trailing one to tumble out of the front of the basket.
2 purple heliotropes or cherry pie *Heliotropium* × *hybridum*. This is a modern cultivar. Not as easy

to find as it should be, but good garden centres should stock it in June.
2 pink trailing ivy-leaved geraniums *Pelargonium* 'Helena' to match the window boxes. This is a modern variety; *Pelargonium* 'Madame Crousse' is an old one which could be used here, but it is paler pink.
½ strip of pale blue lobelia *Lobelia erinus* 'Cambridge Blue'.
½ strip of white lobelia *Lobelia erinus* 'Snowball'.
10 litres or less of John Innes No 2 soil, depending on the extent of the ivy roots.
1 basketful of sphagnum or ordinary wreath moss from a florist.
Approximately 150cm plastic-coated green wire to form the pegs.

Method

1. Line the basket with a generous thickness of moss. Start at the base and bring it right up the sides so that it forms a good collar just above the rim.
2. Cover the base of the basket with 10cm (4") of soil.
3. Plant the ivy towards the centre-front of the basket. If the root system is already very well established and is taking up more than one-third of the planting space, trim back the roots, especially those towards the centre of the basket. (NB: If you have already an established pegged ivy basket from a winter planting, you might still need to trim the roots to allow more space for the new summer occupants.)
4. Plant the upright geranium towards the centre-back of the basket with the verbena in the middle.
5. Plant two empty pots on either side for the heliotropes to be placed later in mid June.
6. Plant the two trailing ivy-leaved geraniums at either side of the basket as close to the front as the ivy will allow.
7. Carefully divide the blue and white lobelia and plant all round the rim of the basket.
8. Fill in any gaps with soil, bringing the level just below the rim of the basket. Water well. Firm in the plants and make sure the basket looks well balanced. Adjustments are easy at this stage. Add more soil and moss if necessary.
9. Cut the wire into 5cm (2") lengths and bend them over like a grip. Peg the ivy trails around the sides of the basket and if long enough round the bottom too, concentrating on the centre-front and sides. Push the pegs in firmly so that the ivy stems are touching the moss. In time the ivy will take root. You may need twenty or thirty pegs according to the length of the wires.
10. In mid June, remove the empty pots and plant the heliotropes.

Aftercare

Water daily throughout the summer, being careful to choose a time when the sun is not shining on the basket. Early morning or late evening is the best time. Be generous and let the water soak well into the basket. Deadhead regularly, apply a liquid feed weekly, and spray if necessary against greenfly etc.

Continue to peg in the ivy as it grows during the summer. By the autumn it should be covering the basket well round the sides and under the base.

Before the first frosts, remove the geraniums. Pot up and bring indoors for the winter (see page 86). Discard the bedding plants but leave the ivy in place and replant. (For a winter idea see Recipe 30.)

122 A BALL OF WHITE

Twining ivy forms the frame to this wonderful basket of white campanula and trailing Victorian geranium 'L'Elegante'. This campanula was not introduced from Italy until the last quarter of the nineteenth century so the planting scheme should be considered as late Victorian or Edwardian. Both these plants are common today. The recipe is easy to plant and look after.

Site
Sunny. This could also be treated as an indoor conservatory basket.

Container
Wire hanging basket: 35cm (14") in diameter.

Planting Time
Mid May to June.

At its best
Late July through August and September.

Ingredients (see notes on pages 178–84)
3 white trailing campanulas, or one large specimen, *Campanula isophylla* 'Alba'; very showy.
3 white trailing ivy-leaved geraniums *Pelargonium* 'L'Elegante'. This was mentioned by John Mollison in 1879 and often mentioned in the gardening journals of the late Victorian period. Its popularity has continued to this day.
10 litres of John Innes No 2 soil.
1 basketful of sphagnum or ordinary wreath moss from a garden centre or florist.

Method
1. Line the basket with a generous thickness of moss: start at the base and bring it right up the sides so that it forms a good collar just above the rim.
2. Cover the base of the basket with 10cm (4") of soil.
3. Plant one large specimen of campanula in the centre of the basket with the three geraniums around the rim. Or, if using three campanulas, alternate the campanulas and the ivy-leaved geraniums around the rim of the basket. There will be less breakages to the plants if you avoid planting the geraniums over that part of the basket where the chains join the rim. The campanulas are less brittle and will not damage so easily.
4. Fill in the gaps with soil and bring the level to within 2.5cm (1") of the rim of the basket.
5. Water well. Firm in the plants and add more soil or moss if necessary.

Aftercare
Water daily throughout the summer. Deadhead regularly to encourage the production of more flowers and feed weekly after the middle of July. There should be little or no problem with greenfly etc but keep a watchful eye and if necessary take action.

Before the first frosts, extend the life of the basket by bringing it into a conservatory or greenhouse where it can remain throughout the winter until coaxed into life again the following spring. Alternatively, pot up the plants individually and keep in a heated greenhouse or indoors throughout the winter.

123   PINK FRILLS

This pretty pink basket is based on an idea for a conservatory basket appearing in *The Floral World*, a Victorian gardening journal written in the 1870s. Its success lies in its mass of flowers carpeted by alternating green and variegated 'ivy-type' leaves typical of trailing geraniums. It is a simple basket to plant and the Victorian geraniums which I have used are amongst the easiest to find.

Site
The sunnier the better. By omitting the lobelia this could easily be transformed into a conservatory basket.

Container
Wire hanging basket: 35cm (14″) in diameter with a sturdy 27.5cm (11″) bracket.

Planting Time
Mid to end May, or earlier if you have a greenhouse or conservatory.

At its best
July and August although it will look lovely all summer long.

Ingredients (see notes on pages 178–84)
2 pink trailing Victorian ivy-leaved geraniums *Pelargonium* 'Madame Crousse'.
2 pink trailing Victorian variegated ivy-leaved geraniums *Pelargonium* 'Duke of Edinburgh'.
1 pink upright Victorian geranium *Pelargonium* 'Mrs Parker' with silver leaves and pale pink flowers. This is an optional extra if you want more height at the top of the basket. The colours would be perfect.
2 Victorian *Pelargonium* 'L'Elegante' with fine variegated leaves and white flowers.
1 strip of pale blue lobelia *Lobelia erinus* 'Cambridge Blue'.
10 litres of John Innes No 2 soil.
2 handfuls of grit.
1 basketful of sphagnum or ordinary wreath moss from a florist.
1 circle of plastic sheeting cut from a strong plastic bag, about the size of a dinner plate.

Method
1. Line the basket with a generous thickness of moss: start at the base and bring it right up the sides so that it forms a good collar just above the rim.
2. Cut four 2.5cm (1") slits in the plastic circle and place over the moss lining in the bottom of the basket.
3. Spread two handfuls of grit over the plastic circle, then add 10 cm (4") of soil.
4. Plant the pink trailing geraniums around the rim of the basket alternating the plain green and variegated leaf varieties. Avoid planting any of them right over that part of the basket where the chain meets the rim. The stems are brittle and can easily be broken.
5. Plant the upright geranium 'Mrs Parker' (if you want to) in the centre of the basket with 'L'Elegante' on either side.
6. Carefully divide the lobelia and plant around the edge of the basket.
7. Fill in the gaps with soil and bring the level to within 2.5cm (1") of the rim.
8. Water well. Firm in the plants and add more soil or moss as necessary.

Aftercare
This basket is one of the easiest to look after. Its needs are not nearly so demanding as most other containers. It will thrive in hot conditions, should not be infested with greenfly, and will not require as much feeding as others might do. However, to get the best results do keep a close check on it and be prepared to water daily, particularly in hot weather. The lobelia will soon tell you if it is thirsty! Apply a liquid feed once a month after end June. Deadhead the geraniums to keep the basket looking tidy and to encourage further flowering.

The basket needs to be brought inside towards the end of September. If you have a conservatory it will continue to thrive there for several more weeks. Otherwise it is time to discard the lobelia and pot up the geraniums so that they may be kept over the winter and brought into new growth in the spring (see page 86).

124 THE AGAVE

The agave has been used as a principal subject for containers over the last two or three hundred years. With the subtropical bedding of the Victorian period, there was a greater choice of companion plants. Lobelia was a favourite. Atkinson Grimshaw painted his garden at Knostrop Hall, Leeds, in 1875. His picture shows three tubs each planted with agaves and lobelia.

Site
Sun or partial shade.

Container
Wooden half barrel: 60cm (24") in diameter, 40cm (16") deep, painted green with black hoops, a typical Victorian treatment. The barrel would have been charred inside to preserve it. This one has an inner plastic container (with drainage holes) dropped inside and raised on small supports. A smaller container would be more appropriate for a young plant.

Planting Time
End May.

At its best
June to September.

Ingredients (see notes on pages 178–84)
1 stately agave known as the century plant *Agave americana* 'Marginata'. Unchanged since Victorian times. The larger ones are expensive, but with the help of a greenhouse they can be kept over the winter period.
1 strip of pale blue lobelia *Lobelia erinus* 'Cambridge Blue'.
100 litres of John Innes No 2 soil.
Drainage material such as old crocks or pieces of polystyrene.

Method
1. Cover the base of the container with 10cm (4") of drainage material and add sufficient soil to enable the top of the agave to rest just below the rim of the container – easiest to test out while the agave is still in the pot.
2. Plant the agave in the centre, fill in the gaps with soil, bringing the level to within 2.5cm (1") of the top of the barrel.
3. Carefully divide the strip of lobelia and plant around the edge of the container.
4. Water well, firm in the plants and add more soil if necessary.

Aftercare
Although the agave can stand very hot, dry conditions, the lobelia will soon die if it is allowed to get too dry. Water regularly. There is no need to spray for insects nor to deadhead, and no extra feed will be required, at least until the middle of August when a single application might be made.

The container should be brought indoors towards the end of September. If you have a conservatory it will flourish and the lobelia will continue flowering for many weeks, indeed possibly throughout the whole winter. To overwinter the agave, see page 85.

125 THE TULIP URN

The combination of trailing variegated strawberry plants and the grey ferny foliage of the lotus have a softening effect on the container. These were frequently used as edgers to garden vases in Victorian times.

Site
Sun or partial shade.

Container
Large Haddonstone Tulip vase: the diameter is 35cm (14″) and the planting depth of the bowl is 45cm (18″). It tapers sharply as seen in the photograph.

Planting Time
Mid to end May.

At its best
Mid June to end August.

Ingredients (see notes on pages 178–84)
3 upright variegated geraniums *Pelargonium* 'Caroline Schmidt'. Another Victorian favourite with silver leaves and bright red flowers.
1 fuchsia *Fuchsia* 'Charming'. This is a hardy Victorian one which makes a good colour combination with the geraniums.
2 white Paris daisies *Chrysanthemum* (*Argyranthemum*) *frutescens*, known more commonly today as marguerites.
1 lotus *Lotus elotii* with its soft grey fern-like foliage.
2 variegated strawberry plants *Fragaria × ananassa* 'Variegata' which sends out runners on long trails.
½ strip of lobelia *Lobelia erinus* 'Blue Cascade'.
30 litres of John Innes No 2 soil.
Drainage material such as old crocks or pieces of polystyrene.

Method
1. Cover the base of the container with 10cm (4″) of drainage material and bring the soil level to within 5cm (2″) of the rim.
2. Plant the three geraniums in a triangular shape with the apex towards the back.
3. Plant the fuchsia in the centre of the vase with the two Paris daisies on either side.
4. Plant the lotus so that it trails down the front.
5. Plant the variegated strawberries on either side of the vase so that the runners will trail over the edge.

6. Divide the half strip of lobelia and plant in groups around the edge.
7. Fill in the gaps with soil and then water well. Make sure all the plants are firmed in and that the arrangement is balanced. Add more soil if necessary.

Aftercare
Water regularly throughout the summer. Be prepared to do it daily in hot weather. Deadhead the marguerites, fuchsia and geraniums to encourage flowering and to keep the container tidy. Spray for greenfly etc as necessary and apply a liquid feed weekly.

In the middle of September, or earlier if frost threatens, pot up the lotus, marguerites and geraniums and bring indoors (see pages 85–6). This particular fuchsia and the variegated strawberry are quite hardy and can be planted outside in the garden. Peg the strawberry runners down and you will find they propagate quite easily even at this late stage. Discard the lobelia.

126 THE CZAR

The Victorians were extremely aware of the strong markings on geranium leaves and among their favourites was 'The Czar'. One of the edgers which they used to accentuate leaf colourings was golden feverfew.

Site
Sun or partial shade.

Container
Lead Warwick vase (made by Renaissance Casting Company Ltd): the diameter is 35cm (14″) and the inside planting depth is 22.5cm (9″).

Planting Time
Mid to end May.

At its best
End June to September.

Ingredients (see notes on pages 178–84)
3 strongly marked geraniums *Pelargonium* 'The Czar'. Pinky-red flowers and golden leaves with a broad ring of bronze.
3 golden feverfew *Tanacetum parthenium* 'Aureum'. It must be kept well clipped throughout the summer in order to retain its bright colouring and its role as an edger. It must not be allowed to flower.
1 strip of lobelia *Lobelia erinus* 'Cambridge Blue'.

20 litres of John Innes No 2 soil.
Drainage material such as old crocks or pieces of polystyrene.

Method
1. Cover the base of the container with 5cm (2″) of drainage material and add 10cm (4″) of soil.
2. Plant the three geraniums in a triangle towards the centre of the vase with the three feverfew plants in between.
3. Carefully divide the strip of lobelia and plant around the edge of the container.
4. Fill in the gaps with soil. Water well. Firm in the plants and add more soil if necessary to bring the level to within 2.5cm (1″) of the rim.

Aftercare
Water regularly throughout the summer. Be prepared to do it daily in hot weather. Keep the feverfew constantly clipped to within just a few inches of its roots. It grows very quickly and will soon send up fresh growth. Deadhead the geraniums as needed to maintain a neat appearance. Apply a monthly liquid feed from July onwards. Spray as necessary for greenfly etc although this should hardly be necessary.

Before the first frosts, pot up the geraniums and bring them indoors to overwinter them (see page 86). Divide the feverfew and plant elsewhere in containers or in the garden, or discard along with the lobelia.

127   MRS POLLOCK

This is another simple combination using old geraniums and unusual edgers. The golden tricolour geranium 'Mrs Pollock' with her orange-red flowers is surrounded by a circle of echeverias. These were often used in Victorian bedding schemes.

Site
Sunny.

Container
Small Haddonstone urn: 30cm (12″) in diameter, 12.5cm (5″) deep, resting on a low pedestal.

Planting Time
Mid to end May.

At its best
End June to September.

Ingredients (see notes on pages 178–84)
  3 golden tricolour geraniums *Pelargonium* 'Mrs Pollock'. This was one of the most popular of its type, particularly mentioned in 1879 when Mollison was suggesting geraniums for containers. Fortunately it is still available today.
10 echeverias *Echeveria secunda* with tight grey rosettes (often sold in late spring as houseplants). If these are too expensive then buy just two or three this season. They will produce offsets and by next summer you will have a dozen or more to use which would allow you to try this scheme without any lobelia.
  1 strip of lobelia *Lobelia erinus* 'Cambridge Blue'. This could be omitted if you have enough echeverias to complete the circle.
10 litres of John Innes No 2 soil.
Drainage material such as old crocks or pieces of polystyrene.

Method
1. Cover the base of the container with 2.5cm (1″) of drainage material and add 7.5cm (3″) of soil.
2. Plant the three geraniums to form a triangle towards the centre of the urn.
3. Plant the echeverias in a circle around the geraniums, or if you have just a few plant them towards the front of the urn in between the geraniums.
4. Carefully divide the strip of lobelia and plant around the edge.
5. Fill in the gaps with soil. Water well. Firm in the

plants and add more soil if necessary to bring the level to within 2.5cm (1″) of the rim.

Aftercare
This planting scheme is easy to look after. The geraniums and echeverias both like hot, dry conditions although the addition of the lobelia will mean that a regular check will have to be made. Daily watering may be necessary in hot weather. There should be no problem with greenfly etc. Deadhead the geraniums and – towards the end of the summer – the echeverias in order to keep the urn tidy. Apply a monthly liquid feed from July onwards.

Before the first frosts, pot up the geraniums and echeverias (see pages 85–6). Discard the lobelia.

128 PINK AND WHITE DELIGHTS

In 1914 the book *Gardening for Beginners* recommended a number of plants for garden vases. Geraniums were regarded as far and away the best, particularly the salmon-coloured double 'King of Denmark'. Petunias, too, were highly rated, but only the whites! High on the list was the Paris daisy, or the marguerite as we know it more commonly today. These three favourites combine rather well, particularly in this large stone pot.

Site
Sunny and sheltered.

Container
Large Haddonstone pot: 37.5cm (15″) in diameter, 32.5cm (13″) deep as an inside measurement. The basketweave design was much loved by the Victorians.

Planting Time
Mid to end May.

At its best
End June until the first frosts.

Ingredients (see notes on pages 178–84)
 2 white Paris daisies or marguerites *Chrysanthemum (Argyranthemum) frutescens*.
 3 salmon-coloured geraniums *Pelargonium* 'King of Denmark'. This was highly recommended for its flower and its handsome and well-marked leaf.
 3 single white petunias *Petunia × hybrida*. Both singles and doubles were popular.
 1 strip of lobelia *Lobelia erinus* 'Sapphire'.
20 litres of John Innes No 2 soil.
Drainage material such as old crocks or pieces of polystyrene.

Method
1. Cover the base of the container with 7.5cm (3″) of drainage material and add 20cm (8″) of soil.

2. Plant the two marguerites near the centre of the pot with the three geraniums spaced around them.
3. Plant the three petunias around the edge of the pot in between the geraniums.
4. Carefully divide the strip of lobelia and plant around the rim.
5. Fill in the gaps with soil. Check to see that the arrangement looks well balanced; if not, make any adjustments now.
6. Water well. Firm down the plants and add more soil if necessary to bring the level to within 2.5cm (1″) of the top of the container.

Aftercare
Water regularly throughout the summer; be prepared to do it daily in hot weather. The petunias tend to attract greenfly, so keep a watchful eye and spray as and when necessary. Deadhead the geraniums, petunias and marguerites often to keep the pot tidy and to encourage further flowering. Apply a liquid feed every week from the end of June.

Before the first frosts, remove and pot up the marguerites and geraniums in order to overwinter them (see pages 85–6). Discard the lobelia and petunias.

STRUCTURED GROUPS
OF CONTAINERS

Below A spring grouping using eye-level wallpots and a raised display in a chimney pot. The three schemes are deliberately planted so that they will be in flower for several weeks (see Recipes 29, 30 and 31).

Opposite Arrange a spring hanging basket and chimney pot display so that they form a column of colour. Use the same pink tulips in both containers to give a common thread of colour (see Recipes 32 and 33).

Above A collection of autumn containers which are full of colour and interest long after the main summer ones are over. Stunning nerines take centre stage with colour chrysanthemums and coleus (see Recipes 20 and 72; 4, 23, 25, 60, 122).

Opposite Summer pots (see Recipes 66 and 70), window box and hanging basket (see Recipes 56 and 59), are here all dominated by salmon pink geraniums and matching busy lizzies. Together they frame the window to create a strong summer grouping.

Overleaf A white planting scheme can look wonderful at any time. Seen here are white anemones surrounded by a frill of white alyssum planted specially for an early June wedding (see Recipe 58).

SPECIALIST SUPPLIERS OF PLANTS

This list is by no means exhaustive. For further names and addresses, look among the advertisements in the gardening magazines and in the Sunday newspapers. Many of the suppliers listed below provide a very good mail order service.

Bulbs: Walter Blom and Son Ltd, Coombelands Nurseries, Leavesden, Watford, Hertfordshire, WD2 7BH. Telephone: 09273 72071

Broadleigh Gardens, Bishops Hull, Taunton, Somerset, TA4 1AE. Telephone: 0823 86231

Foxgrove Plants, Enbourne, Newbury, Berkshire RG14 6RE. Telephone: 0635 40554

Fuchsias: Jackson's Nurseries, Clifton Campville, Nr Tamworth, Staffordshire, B79 0AP. Telephone: 0827 86307.

Geraniums, Ferns and Ivies (including old-fashioned varieties): Fibrex Nurseries Ltd, Honeybourne Road, Pebworth, Nr Stratford-on-Avon, CV37 8XT. Telephone: 0789 720788

The Vernon Geranium Nursery, Cuddington Way, Cheam, Sutton, Surrey, SM2 7JB.

Herbaceous, Alpine and Conifers: Bressingham Gardens, Diss, Norfolk, 1P22 2AB. Telephone: 037988 464

W. E. Ingwersen Ltd, Birch Farm Nursery, Gravetye, East Grinstead, West Sussex, RH19 4LE. Telephone: 0342 810236

Old-fashioned plants: Helen Ballard, Old Country, Mathon, Malvern, Hereford, WR13 5PS. Telephone: 088684 215

Herterton House Garden Nursery, Hartington, Cambo, Morpeth, Northumberland, NE61 4BN. Telephone: 0670 74278

Hopleys Plants, Much Hadham, Hertfordshire, SG10 6BU. Telephone: 027 984 2509

Peter Jones, Manningford Nurseries, Mannington Abbots, Pewsey, Wiltshire. Telephone: 0672 62232

Margery Fish Plant Nursery, Lambrook Manor, South Petherton, Somerset, TA13 5HL. Telephone: 0460 40328

Plants From The Past, 1 North Street, Belhaven, Dunbar, East Lothian, EH42 1NU. Telephone: 0368 63223

Rushfields of Ledbury, Ross Road, Ledbury, Herefordshire, HR8 2LP. Telephone: 0531 2004

Southview Nurseries, Eversley Cross, Basingstoke, Hampshire, RG27 0NT. Telephone: 0734 732206

Roses: R. Harkness and Company Ltd, The Rose Gardens, Hitchin, Hertfordshire, SG4 0JT. Telephone: 0462 34027

John Mattock, Nuneham Courtney, Oxford, OX9 9PY. Telephone: 086 738 265

Seeds: Thompson and Morgan Ltd, London Road, Ipswich, Suffolk, 1P2 0BA. Telephone: 0473 688588

Sempervivens, Sedums, Alpines and Rock Plants: Alan C. Smith, 127 Leaves Green Road, Keston, Kent, BR2 6DG. Telephone: 0959 72531

SPECIALIST SUPPLIERS OF CONTAINERS

Garden centres often have a very good display of containers made by many different companies, including some imports from abroad such as those supplied by Olive Tree Trading. All of the companies named below have full catalogues which show the beautiful range which they produce. Many of the items appear in the Historical section of the book. Some products are available at certain garden centres, others are not. They all exhibit at the Chelsea Flower Show.

Lead: Renaissance Casting Company Ltd, Manor Farm Offchurch, Nr Leamington Spa, Worcestershire. Postal address: 19 Cranford Road, Chapelfield, Coventry, CU5 8JF. Telephone: 0926 885567.

Reconstituted Stone: Haddonstone Ltd, The Forge House, Church Lane, East Haddon, Northampton, NN6 8DB. Telephone: 0604 770711

Terracotta: Whichford Pottery, Whichford, Shipston-on-Stour, Warwickshire. Telephone: 0608 84416

folios refer to *page* numbers

Arican violets, watering, 7
agapanthus, soil for, 10
agaves, 85, 181
anemones, in hanging baskets, 52
aphids, control of, 7–8, 83–4, 147
arabis, 52, 178
aubrietia, 52, 178
aucubas, Victorian, 178
auriculas, 49, 180

basil, in pest control, 8, 84, 120, 147
bedding plants: autumn, 83
    in strips, 85
    summer, 83
    Victorian, 175, 177, 178–84
    winter, 49
begonias: care of, 85
    as dry tubers, 83
    tuberous, watering, 7
bellis daisies, Victorian, 178
blackfly, 7–8
budgeting, 85
bulbs: buying, 50
    end of season care, 52
    in hanging baskets, 51–2
    two-tier displays, 49

calceolarias, Victorian, 181
campanulas, 85, 181
canary creeper, 8, 184
century plant, 181
cheiranthus, 178
cherry pie, 182
chrysanthemums, 85, 181
climate, 8
climbing plants for shade, 119
colour themes, 84–5
companion planting, 12
    in pest control, 8
conservatories, 2
    arrangement of flowers, 120–1
    hanging baskets in, 121
    pest control, 120
    shading, 119
    ventilation, 119, 120
    Victorian, 121
    watering, 7, 120
containers, 3–4
    suppliers, 3, 177
    Victorian, 177
continuity of flowering, 12
crocus, Victorian, 178

daffodils: dwarf, choosing, 50
    Victorian, 179
dicentra: dividing, 10
    pink, forcing, 12
    soil, 10
    white, and frost, 12
dividing plants, 9, 10
drainage material, 6

echeverias, 85, 181
edible crops, 2–3, 148
Edwardian schemes, 3, 178–84
euonymus, Victorian, 178
feeding, 6, 7, 10, 85
ferns, Victorian, 181
Ferris, C. F., 175
feverfew, 49–50, 183

as edger, 176
end of season care, 52
flowering, continuity of, 12
flowers, edible, 2–3, 148
fragarias, Victorian, 181
French marigolds, in pest control, 8, 85,
    120, 147
fuchsias: care of, 86
    choosing, 83, 181–2
    pest control, 8, 84

Gardening for Beginners (1914), 178, 181,
    182, 183
Gardening Illustrated (1881), 184
Gardening Made Easy (1906), 178
geraniums: care of, 86
    Victorian, 182–3
    watering, 7
grape hyacinths, Victorian, 179
greenfly, 7–8
    plants attractive to, 83–4

hanging baskets, 4–6
    bulbs in, 51–2
    in conservatories, 121
    upside-down, 51–2
    winter, 51–2
hedera, Victorian, 182
helichrysums, care of, 86
heliotrope, Victorian, 182
hepatica, Victorian, 178–9
herbaceous plants, dividing, 9
herbs, 2, 3, 147
    in conservatories, 120–1
hostas, 9, 12
    dividing, 10
    and slugs, 12
    soil for, 9
hyacinths, Victorian, 179

insecticides, 84
insects, in pest control, 120
instant spring displays, 51
ivies, 49–50, 182
    end of season care, 52
    in hanging baskets, 51

kitchen garden schemes, 147–9

lilies, care of, 86
lily of the valley, 9, 10
lobelias: poisonous, 2
    Victorian, 182
longterm schemes, 2, 7, 9–12
lotus, Victorian, 182

marguerites: Victorian, 181
    white, pest control, 84
Martin, H. T., 178
mignonette, Victorian, 183
mimulus, Victorian, 182
Mollison, John, 3, 176–7, 178–84
muscari, Victorian, 179
My Garden (Smee), 183, 184

narcissus, Victorian, 179
nasturtiums, 8, 184
nerines, soil for, 10
New Practical Window Gardener, The
    (Mollison), 3, 176–7, 178–84
nicotiana, pest control, 84

pansies: pest control, 8
    Victorian, 180
    in winter, 49
Paris daisies, Victorian, 181
Pelargoniums, 86, 182–3
periwinkle, end of season care, 52
pest control, 7–8, 84
    in conservatories, 120
petunias: pest control, 8, 83–4
    Victorian, 183
    watering, 7
Phillips, Henry, 183
planting techniques, Victorian, 176–7
plectranthus, care of, 86
polyanthus, Victorian, 179–80
primroses, double, 49
    end of season care, 52
    gold-laced, 52
    single, 52
    Victorian, 179–80
primula denticulata, 52

rape beetle, 8
runner beans, 147

scented plants, 11, 120–1, 148, 176
scillas, Victorian, 180
seasonal schemes, 2
sedum, end of season care, 10, 52, 86
sempervivums, 9
shade, tolerating, 84, 119
Siberian squills (*scilla*), 180
slugs, 12
smilacina, soil for, 10
soil, 6–7, 176
spraying, *see* pest control
strawberries, 148–181
sun, tolerating, 84
sweet peas, 147

thyme, 52, 180
timing of display, 50
tobacco plants, pest control, 8
tomatoes, 147, 148
tropaeolum, Victorian, 184
tulips: double early, 50
    dwarf single, 50
    pest control, 8
    Victorian, 180

vegetable schemes, 2–3, 147–9
verbena, Victorian, 184
Victorian schemes, 3, 175–7
    liquid manure, 176
    planting techniques, 176–7
    plants, 177–84
    soil, 176
    window boxes, 176
    winter, 49
violas, 149, 180

wallflowers, Victorian, 178
watering, 7, 85
    conservatories, 120
    hanging baskets, 5–6
    winter and spring, 51
whitefly, 7–8, 83–4
wind, problem of, 8
window boxes, Victorian, 176

PLANT INDEX

folios refer to *recipe* numbers

Acer palmatum 'Dissectum', 14
Achillea argentea, 5
Aegopodium podagraria 'Variegata', 96
African violets, *see Saintpaulia*
Agapanthus 'Bressingham White', 17
    A. *campanulatus* 'Albus', 17
Agave americana 'Marginata', 64, 124
Ajuga reptans 'Purpurea', 19
Alchemilla mollis, 12, 15
Allium ostrowskianum, 2
    A. *schoenoprasum*, 76
Amaryllis, *see Hippeastrum*
Anemone 'De Caen', 58
    A. 'St Brigid', 58
    A. *blanda*, 7, 36, 43, 46
        'White Splendour', 13, 43, 37
Antirrhinum 'White Wonder', 59, 66
Arabis albida 'Variegata', 113
    A. *caucasica* 'Snowflake', 107
        'Variegata', 113
    A. *ferdinandi-coburgii* 'Old Gold', 18
Argyranthemum frutescens, 61, 65, 117, 120,
        125, 128
        'Jamaica Primrose', 65
Armeria maritima 'Dusseldorf Pride', 18
Arum lily, *see Zantedeschia elliotiana*
Asparagus sprengeri, 78
Asplenium scolopendrium, 13
Athyrium filix-femina, 13
Aubergine 'Black Prince F1 Hybrid', 101
Aubrietia deltoidea, 39
        Aurea', 31
        'Blue Cascade', 107
Aucuba japonica, 'Maculata', 112

Baby's Tears, *See Helxine (Soleirolia)
        soleirolii*
Balm, *see Melissa officinalis*
Basil, bush, *see Ocimum minimum*
Begonia semperflorens, 22, 54
    B. × *tuberhybrida*, 51, 57, 61, 65, 67
        'Marginata Crispa', 67
Bellis perennis, 109
        'Dresden China', 33, 77, 91
        'Lilliput', 45
Bergenia cordifolia 'Purpurea', 4
Boston fern, *see Nephrolepsis exaltata*
        'Bostoniensis'
Busy lizzies, *see Impatiens*

Calceolaria integrifolia, 117, 118
Calendula officinalis, 103
Callisia elegans 'Bridal Wreath', 83
Campanula carpatica 'Bressingham White', 18
        'Wheatley Violet', 18
    C. *cochlearifolia* 'Cambridge Blue', 19
    C. *isophylla*, 60, 88
        'Alba', 122
Canna × *hybrida* 'Picasso', 80
Capsicum annuum 'Canape F1 Hybrid', 98
        'Gypsy F1 Hybrid', 98
Chaemaecyparis lawsoniana 'Ellwoodii', 6
Chamaedorea bella, 75
Cheiranthus cheiri 'Orange Bedder', 49
        'Persian carpet', 47, 110, 111
        'Tom Thumb Mixed', 109
Chilean bell flower, *see Lapageria rosea*
Chives, *see Allium Schoenoprasum*
Chlorophytum comosum 'Mandaianum', 78
Chrysanthemum 'The 1000 Flowers', 60, 72

C. *frutescens*, 61, 65, 117, 120, 125, 128
        'Jamaica Primrose', 65
Coleus blumei, 53, 61, 72
Convallaria majalis, 11
Courgette, Yellow, *see Cucurbita pepo*
Cowslips, *see Primula veris*
Creeping jenny, *see Lysimachia nummularia*
Crocus aureus 'Dutch Yellow', 34, 112, 113
    C. *chrysanthus* 'Blue Pearl', 1, 3, 7
        'E. A. Bowles', 34
        'Lady Killer', 5
        'Prins Claus', 5
        'White Purple', 5
    C. *vernus*, 'Jeanne D'Arc', 3, 112
        'Purpureus Grandiflorus', 2, 29, 112
Cucurbita pepo 'Gold Rush F1 hybrid', 102

Daffodils, *see Narcissus*
Dahlia 'Little William', 71
Dianthus × *allwoodii* 'Diane', 5
    D. *deltoides* 'Albus', 19
Dicentra spectabilis 'Alba', 10
Digitalis purpurea, 13
Dryopteris erythrosora, 23

Echeveria secunda, 64, 127
Egg-plant, *see Aubergine*
Erica arborea 'Estrella Gold', 7
    E. *carnea* 'Springwood White', 7
Euonymus fortunei 'Emerald'n'Gold', 113
    E. *japonicus* 'Aureopictus', 23, 114

Fennel, *see Foeniculum vulgare*
Ferns, 119
Feverfew, *see Tanacetum parthenium*
Ficus radicans 'Variegata', 89
Foeniculum vulgare, 103
Fragaria × *ananassa* 'Baron Solemacher', 97
        'Cambridge Favourite', 97
        'Gento', 97
        'Variegata', 125
French marigolds, *see Tagetes*
Fritillaria meleagris, 19
    F. *michailovskyi*, 19
Fuchsia 'Aintree', 69
        'Cascade', 22
        'Charming', 120, 125
        'Golden Marinka', 22
        'Lye's Unique', 117
        'Snowcap', 22, 52
        'Swingtime', 22
        'Thalia', 70

Galanthus nivalis, 5
        'Magnet', 19
Gaultheria procumbens, 2, 23
Geranium, *see Pelargonium*
Golden balm, *see Melissa officinalis*
Grape hyacinths, *see Muscari*
Grape ivy, *see Rhoicissus rhomboidea*
Ground elder, *see Aegopodium podagraria*

Heather, *see Erica*
Hebe 'La Seduisante', 60
    H. × *andersonii* 'Variegata', 60
Hedera helix 'Chester', 32
        'Cristata', 25
        'Eva', 71
        'Glacier', 16
        'Goldchild', 111, 112, 121

'Heise', 2
'Kolibri', 23
'Parsley', 25
'Price Lep', 25
'Rokoko', 25
'Sagittifolia Variegata', 23
Helichrysum microphyllum, 56
    H. *petiolare* 'Limelight', 52, 68
Heliotropium × *hybridum*, 117, 120, 121
Helleborus orientalis, 4
Helxine soleirolii, 75
        'Argentea', 75, 86
        'Aurea', 75, 86, 89
Hepatica nobilis, 108
Hippeastrum, 74
Holly, *see Ilex*
Hosta crispula, 11
    H. *fortunei*, 13
    H. 'Thomas Hogg', 11
Houseleek, *see Sempervivum*
Hyacinthoides non-scripta, 20
Hyacinthus orientalis 'Amethyst', 116
        'City of Haarlem', 35, 107, 108
        'Gypsy Queen', 35
        'L'Innocence', 35, 113, 116
    H. *orientalis alba* 'Snow White', 28
    H. *orientalis albulus*, 108
Hypoestes phyllostachya 'Pink Splash', 87

Iberis sempervirens 'Snowflake', 6
Ilex aquifolium 'Aureo-marginata', 2
Impatiens F1 Hybrids, 52, 55, 56, 57, 66, 69
Iris bucharica, 9
    I. *danfordiae*, 7
Jerusalem cowslip, *see Pulmonaria officinalis*

Kalanchoe blossfeldiana 'Vulcan', 89

Lady's mantle, *see Alchemilla mollis*
Lapageria rosea, 88
Lathyrus odoratus 'Antique Fantasy', 100
Lavandula angustifolia 'Hidcote', 16
Lavatera thuringiaca 'Barnsley', 16
Lemon balm, *see Melissa officinalis*
Lenten rose, *see Helleborus orientalis*
Leucojum vernum, 2
Lilium 'African Queen', 81
        'Liberation', 1
        'Red Carpet', 81
        'Sunray', 1, 81
    L. *regale*, 1
Lily of the valley, *see Convallaria*
Lobelia erinus 'Blue Cascade', 22, 125
        'Cambridge Blue', 54, 59, 61, 66, 102,
            120, 121, 123, 124, 126, 127
        'Cascade Mixed', 55
        'Crystal Palace', 54, 59, 66, 67
        'Mrs Clibran', 59, 66, 70, 117
        'Sapphire', 52, 57, 65, 128
        'Snowball', 51, 59, 61, 66, 70, 120, 121
        'String of Pearls', 8, 69, 85
        'White Cascade', 22, 52
        'White Lady', 21, 56, 71, 117
Lobularia maritima, 58, 62
        'Little Dorrit', 97
Lotus elotii, 125
Lysimachia nummularia, 51
        'Aurea', 51

Mahonia japonica, 3
Marjoram, *see Origanum vulgare*

Melissa officinalis 'Variegata', 76, 96, 104
Mentha × gentilis 'Variegata', 96
    M. × piperita 'Citrata', 96
    M. raripila rubra, 96
    M. rotundifolia 'Variegata', 76, 91, 96, 105
Mignonette, see Reseda odorata
Mimulus 'Calypso', 117, 119
Mind Your Own Business, see Helxine
    Soleirolia) soleirolii
Mint, see Mentha
Muscari armeniacum 'Heavenly Blue', 36, 38,
    42, 48, 50, 110, 111
    M. botryoides 'Album', 9, 38, 110, 111
    'Caeruleum', 110, 111

Narcissus 'Binkie', 25, 50
    'Delibes', 49
    'February Gold', 2
    'Orangery', 49
    'Professor Einstein', 49
    'Spellbinder', 50
    N. cyclamineus 'February Gold', 2, 27, 29
    'Hawera', 73
    'Peeping Tom', 26
    'Tete-a-tete', 30, 73
    N. jonquilla 'Double Campernelle', 7
    N. poeticus 'Actaea', 6, 109
    N. tazetta 'Minnow', 7, 31, 38
    N. triandrus, 'Thalia', 48
Neanthe bella, 75
Nephrolepis exaltata 'Bostoniensis', 86
Nerine bowdenii 'Fenwick's Variety', 20
Nicotiana 'Domino F1 Mixed', 68
    'Sensation', 68

Ocimum minimum, 90, 95
Origanum vulgare 'Aureum', 76, 91, 97
    'Compactum', 105, 106
Oxalis adenophylla, 39

Palms, see Chamaedorea bella
Paris daisy, see Chrysanthemum frutescens
Parlour palm, see Chamaedorea bella
Parsley, see Petroselinum crispum
Parthenocissus henryana, 25
Partridge berry, see Gaultheria procumbens
Pelargonium 'Attar of Roses', 83
    'Beauty', 118
    'Brenda Kitson', 55
    'Bruni', 8, 52
    'Burgenland Girl', 55
    'Caroline Schmidt', 125
    'Cleopatra', 118
    'Czar, The', 126
    'Deacon Suntan', 70
    'Duke of Edinburgh', 123
    'Golden Orf', 63
    'Helena', 55, 120, 121
    'Hills of Snow', 120, 121
    'Immaculata', 56, 118
    'King of Denmark', 59, 117, 128
    'Lady Plymouth', 61
    'L'Elegante', 61, 62, 122, 123
    'Madame Crousse', 55, 117, 120, 121,
        123
    'Mary Wilkes', 69
    'Mrs Parker', 123
    'Mrs Pollock', 127
    'Olympia', 69
    'Rouletta', 52
    'Sweet Mimosa', 85
    P. quercifolium, 106

Penstemon procerus, 19
Perilla frutescens, 61, 70
Periwinkles, see Vinca
Petroselinum crispum, 21, 92, 97, 103, 104
Petunia × hybrida, 128
    Grandiflora type, 52, 55
Phaseolus coccineus 'Desirée', 100
    'Scarlet Emperor', 99
Phlox adsurgens 'Wagon Wheel', 19
Phyllitis scolopendrium, 13
    'Christatum', 13
Pinks, see Dianthus
Plectranthus hirtus 'Variegatus', 52
Plumbago auriculata, 84
    P. capensis, 84
Polka dot plants, see Hypoestes phyllostachya
Polyanthus, mixed, 44
Polypodium vulgare 'Cornubiense', 20
Pot marigolds, see Calendula officinalis
Primroses, see Primula
Primula auricula, 115
    P. denticulata, 31, 35
    P × polyanthus 'Gold Laced', 30, 115
    P. veris, 91
    P. vulgaris, 3, 34, 35, 73, 94, 108
    P. 'Wanda', 30
Pulmonaria officinalis, 1
    P. rubra 'Bowles Red', 2
    P. saccharata 'Argentea', 1

Regal Pelargonium 'Wellington', 82
Reseda odorata, 81
    'Fragrant Beauty', 120
Rhoicissus rhomboidea, 82
Rosa 'Fairyland', 21
    'Pink Bells', 15
    'Snow Carpet', 21
    'Suma', 21
Rosilaria sedoides, 14
Rosmarinus lavandulaceus, 94, 105
    R. officinalis prostatus, 94, 105

Sagina glabra 'Aurea', 14, 19
Saintpaulia ionantha, 87
    'Saladisi', 93
Salvia officinalis 'Aurea', 94
    'Icterina', 104
    'Tricolor', 105, 106
Scilla nutans, 20
    S. siberica, 116
Sedum acre 'Aureum', 14, 29, 31, 63
    S. aizoon, 19
    S. 'Lidakense', 18
    S. reflexum, 2, 19
    S. sieboldii 'Medio-variegatum', 56, 60
    S. spathulifolium 'Cape Blanco', 24
    S. spectabile 'Autumn Joy', 10
Selaginella apoda, 74, 75, 79
    S. martensii, 75
Sempervivum arachnoideum, 24
    S. 'Corsair', 24
    S. 'Proud Zelda', 18
    S. tectorum, 14, 24
Setcreasea striata 'Bridal Wreath', 83
Sisyrinchium brachypus, 19
Smilacina racemosa, 12
Snapdragon, see Antirrhinum
Snowdrop, see Galanthus nivalis
Soleirolia soleirolii 'Argentea', 75, 86
    'Aurea', 75, 86, 89
Spider plant, see Chlorophytum comosum
Spotted dog, see Pulmonaria officinalis

Tagetes patula, 80
    'Fireflame', 57
    'Leopard', 57
    'Spanish Brocade', 53
    'Special', 90, 95, 98, 101
Tanacetum parthenium 'Aureum', 27, 41, 94,
    114, 116, 126
Thymus 'Anderson's Gold', 106
    T. × citriodorus 'Aureus', 30, 94, 113
    'Silver Queen', 5, 16, 106
    T. drucei 'Albus', 106
    T. pseudolanuginosis, 106
    T. serpyllum, 1
    'Albus', 18
Tomato 'Pipo', 90, 95
    'Pixie F1 Hybrid', 90, 95
Trillium grandiflorum, 13
Tropaeolum 'Dwarf Cherry Rose', 67
    T. majus 'Climbing Mixed', 117
    'Double Gleam Mixed', 65
    'Golden Gleam', 99
    'Tom Thumb Mixed', 117
    T. 'Peach Melba', 67
    T. peregrinum, 117
Tulipa 'Abu Hassan', 44
    'Angelique', 46
    'Apeldoorn', 45, 47
    'Apricot Beauty', 40
    'Beauty of Apeldoorn', 47
    'Clara Butt', 108
    'Douglas Bader', 40
    'Fidelio', 8
    T. fosteriana 'Orange Emperor', 42
    'Red Emperor', 42
    'White Emperor', 42
    'Yellow Emperor', 42
    T. 'Golden Apeldoorn', 45, 47
    T. greigi 'Red Riding Hood', 37
    T. kaufmanniana 'Stresa', 27
    T. 'Keizerskroon', 108, 110, 111
    'Olaf', 44
    'Peach Blossom', 32, 33, 36, 46
    T. praestans 'Fusilier', 41
    'Unicum', 41
    T. 'Salmon Parrot', 43
    'Stresa', 107
    'Toronto', 28
    'Van de Hoef', 115
    'White Virgin', 114

Verbena × hybrida, 56, 70, 120, 121
    V. 'Silver Anne', 84
    V. spicata, 'Blue Fox', 15
Viburnum tinus, 32
Vinca minor 'Alba', 7, 8
    'Aureo-variegata', 2, 6, 7
Viola cornuta 'Alba', 19
    'Prince John', 33
    V. odorata, 108
    V. tricolor 'Johnny Jump-Up', 27, 39, 92
    'Prince Henry', 6, 39
    V. × wittrockiana, 77
    'Universal', 26, 28, 40, 109, 110, 111
Virginia creeper, see Parthenocissus

Wallflowers, see Cheiranthus cheiri
Woolly thyme, see Thymus pseudolanuginosis

Yellow courgette, see Cucurbita pepo

Zantedeschia elliottiana, 79